Architecture in the
Twentieth Century

Peter Gössel
Gabriele Leuthäuser

Architecture
in the Twentieth Century

Benedikt Taschen

This book was printed on 100 % chlorine-free bleached paper
in accordance with the TCF-standard.

© 1991 Benedikt Taschen Verlag GmbH
Hohenzollernring 53, D-50672 Köln
© 1990 VG Bild-Kunst, Bonn: Peter Behrens, Le Corbusier,
Bernhard Hoetger, Adolf Loos, Auguste Perret,
Gerrit Th. Rietveld
© 1990 Bauhaus Archiv, Berlin: Walter Gropius
© 1990 Frank Lloyd Wright Foundation,
Scottsdale, Arizona

Selection of illustrations, design, production: Peter Gössel,
Gabriele Leuthäuser, Nuremberg
Biographies: Eva Schickler, Nuremberg
Editor: Dr. Angelika Muthesius, Cologne
English translation: Judith Vachon/Mark Atherton (Biographies)

Printed in Germany
ISBN 3-8228-0550-5
GB

Contents

Acknowledgements

Akademie der Künste, Sammlung Baukunst,
  Achim Wendschuh, Berlin
Albertina, Adolf-Loos-Archiv, Vienna
Arcaid, Vivienne Porter, London
The Architects Collaborative, Katherine Gormley,
  Cambridge, MA
Architektursammlung der TU München
The Art Institute of Chicago, The Libraries, Mary
  K. Woolever, Chicago
Arup Associates, Brian Carter, London
Alberto Campo Baeza, Madrid
Maurice Babey, Basle
Gabriele Basilico, Milan
Bauhaus-Archiv, Sabine Hartmann, Berlin
Behnisch & Partner, Christian Kandzia, Stuttgart
Bibliothek der Landesgewerbeanstalt Nürnberg,
  Erna Mißbach, Heidrun Teumer
Bibliothèque Nationale, Paris
Bildarchiv Foto Marburg, Brigitte Walbe
Bildarchiv Preußischer Kulturbesitz, Heidrun Klein,
  Berlin
Maria Ida Biggi, Venice
Mario Botta, Lugano
Busch-Reisinger Museum, Harvard University,
  Elizabeth Gombosi, Cambridge, MA
Santiago Calatrava, Zurich
Centrum Industriekultur Nürnberg, Helga Jubitz
Christoph Bürkle, Zurich
Coop Himmelblau, Angela Althaler, Vienna
Deutsches Architekturmuseum, Vittorio Magnago
  Lampugnani, Frankfurt am Main
Domino's Farms Activities, Thomas P. Nanzig,
  Ann Arbor, MI
Dyckerhoff & Widmann AG, Munich
Ecole nationale supérieure des Beaux-Arts,
  Françoise Portelance, Paris
Peter Eisenman, New York
Arthur Erickson, Vancouver
Esto Photographics, Erica Stoller,
  Mamaroneck, NY
Johanna Fiegl, Vienna
Fondation Le Corbusier, Paris
Foster Associates, Polly Napper, London
Klaus Frahm, Hamburg
Frank O. Gehry, Los Angeles
Giovanni Gherardi, Rome

Glasgow Museums & Art Galleries, Vivien
   Hamilton
The Glasgow School of Art, Peter Trowles
Myron Goldfinger, New York
Michael Graves, Princeton, NY
Vittorio Gregotti, Milan
Charles Gwathmey, New York
Hedrich-Blessing, Michael O. Houlahan,
   Chicago
Keld Helmer-Petersen, Copenhagen
John Hejduk, Riverdale, NY
Hentrich-Petschnigg & Partner, Düsseldorf
Historisches Museum, Frankfurt am Main
Hans Hollein, Vienna
Institut für Allgemeine Bauingenieurmethoden,
   TU Berlin, Jan Pahl, Wilhelm Cattes
Institut für Baugeschichte, Universität Karlsruhe,
   Immo Boyken
Institut für leichte Flächentragwerke, Universität
   Stuttgart, Gabriela Heim
Arata Isozaki, Tokyo
Philip Johnson, New York
Albert Kahn Associates, Joe Bedway, Detroit, MI
Konservatoramt Saarbrücken
Stefan Koppelkamm, Berlin
Rob Krier, Vienna
Kunstbibliothek SMPK, Theodor Böll, Bernd
   Meier, Berlin
Kunsthistorisches Institut der FU Berlin, Kathrin
   Höltge
Landesbildstelle Berlin
Landesbildstelle Württemberg, Stuttgart
Charles Lee, Beverly Hills, CA
Christopher Little, New York
M.A.N. AG, Historisches Archiv, Augsburg
Antonio Martinelli, Paris
Norman McGrath, Georgia Griffin, New York
Richard Meier, New York
Mercedes-Benz AG, Stuttgart
Meritor Financial Group, Shawn Weldon,
   Philadelphia
MERO-Raumstruktur GmbH & Co., Würzburg
Michael Moran, New York
Musée des Arts Décoratifs, Sonia Edard, Paris
Museum für Gestaltung, Zurich

Museum Moderner Kunst, Susanne Neuburger,
   Vienna
Nederlands Architectuur Instituut, Miriam Hejs,
   Amsterdam
The New York Historical Society, New York
A. Oud-Dinaux, Wassenaar
Frank den Oudsten, Amsterdam
Gustav Peichl, Vienna
Cesar Pelli, New Haven, CT
David Phillips, Chicago
Renzo Piano, Paris
Plansammlung der TU Berlin, Dieter Radicke,
   Peter Benkert
Bodo Rasch, Stuttgart
Retoria, Naoko Tanabe, Tokyo
Rhein. Bildarchiv, Ruth Sonnenberg, Cologne
Kevin Roche, Hamden, CT
Roger-Viollet, Paris
Paolo Rosselli, Milan
Royal Commission on the Historical Monuments
   of England, London
Sächsische Landesbibliothek, Deutsche Fotothek,
   Elke Kilian, Dresden
Simon Scott, Vancouver
Klaus-Jürgen Sembach, Munich
Julius Shulman, Los Angeles
SITE, Melode Ferguson, New York
Margarete Steiff GmbH, Giengen/Brenz
Robert A.M. Stern, New York
James Stirling, Michael Wilford and Associates,
   Andrew Pryke, London
Tim Street-Porter, Los Angeles
Studio Chevojon, Paris
Suomen Rakennustaiteen Museo, Laura
   Tuominen, Helsinki
Bernard Tschumi, Paris
University of California, Research Library, Anne
   Caiger, Jeffrey Rankin, Los Angeles
Venturi, Scott Brown & Associates, Stephen
   Estock, Philadelphia
Victoria & Albert Museum, Picture Library, London
Wayss & Freytag AG, Frankfurt am Main
Tod Williams, New York
The Frank Lloyd Wright Foundation, Bruce
   Brooks Pfeiffer, Scottsdale, AR

1784–1916

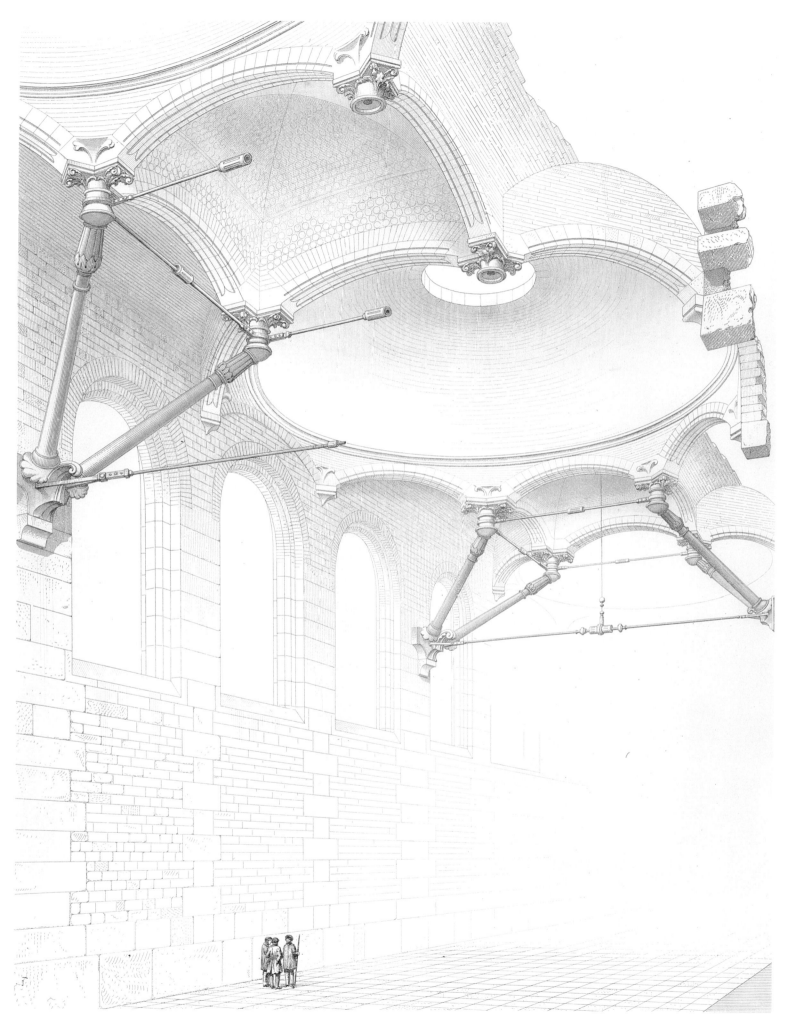

10

Prologue

New aesthetic potential was released at the end of the eighteenth century in the wake of the Enlightenment. The natural sciences were declared a recognized means of explaining the world, and geometric axioms competed with anatomic rules of proportion. The definition of units of measurement based on natural constants was one of the products of the French Revolution; the metre became a valid unit of measurement when the standard metre, one forty-millionth of the earth's circumference, was stored in the Musée des Arts et Métiers in Paris on 22 June 1799. Etienne-Louis Boullée, architect and member of the Academy, also paid homage to the primacy of geometry in his design work. He prized the sphere highest among the "regular bodies" because, in its all-round symmetry and visual uniformity as well as the "tender and flowing" grace of its contours, it contained all the advantages of a volumetric form. He thereby fell within the tradition of Andrea Palladio, the Renaissance architect who praised the sphere in a similar way: "It is suitable to the highest degree for illustrating the unity, the infinite essence, the constancy and justice of God". The earth goddess Vesta was already associated with the round temple in the ancient world. In his Cenotaph for the English physicist, mathematician and astronomer Isaac Newton, Boullée employed the analogy in a symbol of the globe; the sphere alone seemed an appropriate means of expressing the All in architectural terms. The sphere also had specific contemporary relevance for Boullée. The Montgolfier brothers made their first flight in a hot air balloon in 1784; limits believed impossible to overcome had thus been exceeded, gravity surmounted. The Cenotaph also attemped to communicate weightlessness. The tiered sequence of hoops within which the large rotunda was set was interrupted at the entrance. Unlike previously seen dome structures, the sphere was thereby exposed below as well as above the meridian and seemed to rest only lightly on the ground. The wish to control nature is also evident in the starry firmament inside. Boullée wanted to "paint with nature" by including her in his work. A relationship with the world, put into concrete terms through "working with the light", takes the place of subjection, of being at the world's mercy.

Boullée and his contemporary Claude-Nicolas Ledoux appear progressive solely in their love of geometry; in their built works, however, they fall neatly in line with the classicism of the years around 1800. The old concepts of support and load, the wish for monumentality and reverence were in no sense overcome, even when Ledoux formally reduced the basic building blocks to "circle and square; these are the letters of the alphabet". The basic problem of modernism was evident even here: although new goals could be named in abstract terms, and the rejection of outdated style forms agreed upon, no coherent new system appeared to replace the classic canon of aesthetics.

With the advent of industrialization, the academic architect found new competition in the person of the engineer — a title commonly used for officers of the arts of

Eugène-Emmanuel Viollet-le-Duc
"Maçonnerie", 1864
Drawing from the Atlas "Entretiens sur l'Architecture"
Bibliothek der Landesgewerbeanstalt Nuremberg

fortification and siege in post-Revolution France. "And at the same time, in the same country, the contrast between 'construction' and 'architecture' began to express itself both consciously and in distinctly personal terms", concluded art historian Alfred Gotthold Meyer. The Ecole Polytechnique now assumed the role of technical training institute in contrast to the very traditional Ecole des Beaux-Arts, where architecture was considered one of the fine arts. This, according to Sigfried Giedion, was a fatal categorization: "This unity was complete and obvious in the Baroque era, but became contradictory and false over the course of the nineteenth century." Architecture had in some respects grown away from the concept of art and needed redefinition for an industrial age. But architecture's social and societal tasks continue even today to be subsumed under artistic expectations in an essentially intolerable manner.

Boullée's student Jean-Nicclas-Louis Durand published from 1802 on the "Précis des leçons d'architecture" parallel to his lectures at the Ecole Polytechnique. He suggested that architecture be developed from the sensible arrangement of single elements, "which have the same meaning for architecture as words have for language and notes for music". It was subsequently attempted to compile an "architectural language", which was the effective equivalent of a departure from obligatory solutions and which made design criteria to a large extent dispensable. Durand also argued

Night version
Bibliothèque Nationale, Paris
The Newton Cenotaph, an empty tomb,
paid homage to the English physicist,
mathematician and astronomer Isaac Newton (1643–1727), whom Voltaire had, as
early as 1752, termed the "greatest of
men", because "he never constructed systems, never made assumptions and never
preached truths which were not based on
the most sublime geometry and irrefutable
experiments."

Day version of the Newton Cenotaph
Bibliothèque Nationale, Paris
In its first draft, the sphere with the sarco-
phagus was lit by a luminous armillary
sphere which effectively embodied the
Copernican heliocentric system. Boullée
only arrived at the idea of the starry sky in
a subsequent revision. The "stars" are thin
channels cut into the shell, through which
daylight falls. The measured cosmos, con-
densed with a pair of dividers into geometric form, symbolizes the universality of
Newtonian axioms.

Louis-Sylvestre Gasse
Elysium, 1799
Bibliothèque de L'Ecole nationale supérieure
des Beaux-Arts, Paris

This design was awarded first prize by the Ecole des Beaux-Arts in a competition for assembly rooms, a library and a greenhouse. Nénot later built the Sorbonne in Paris, and in as late as 1927 defeated Le Corbusier with his design for the Palace of the League of Nations in Geneva.

the cost factor: only economical building, in conjunction with symmetry and regularity, could produce beauty. The result was a theory of composition which allowed any building complex desired to be created from classically-derived components.

Many a nineteenth-century building, with the benefit of our hindsight looking surprisingly modern, owes its appearance largely to pre-set framework conditions Karl Friedrich Schinkel's Academy of Architecture in Berlin is an example of this – a fully harmonious, self-contained construction based on a pragmatic design. Teaching and administrative rooms were brought under the same roof as shops, which contributed to the building's financing. Schinkel used a flexible inner organization which allowed for different layouts within the same floor. Since the triangular building site did not require an obvious main façade, he could use central symmetry. The basic cubic form is divided into eight axes; its "false symmetry" did not allow for a central entrance and thus prohibited any grandiosity. The layout's 64 single fields were combined to form rooms according to need. The impression of supporting pillars deceives; the closed wall areas actually serve as bearing structures Through his use of fine ribbons in the brickwork and terracotta reliefs on the window breasts and arches, Schinkel distanced himself from industrial construction, which was then not considered architecture.

In the 1870's, Eugène-Emmanuel Viollet-le-Duc emerged in France as one of the

harshest critics of prevailing theories. He studied both Gothic cathedrals and Egyptian and Greek temples and came to the conclusion that proportions with a pleasing effect could be described in certain triangular relationships – in the "Egyptian" isosceles triangle and in a right-angled triangle with sides in the ratio of three to four to five. He interpreteted the Gothic style as a functional architectural form appropriate to its materials in which each part had a deliberate purpose. As form follows construction in the Gothic, so must architecture follow methods of machine construction in a new age. Indeed, industrialization created the bases for a new architecture at the "moment of transformation from the manual to the industrial production process". But this transformation was in no way immediate and conscious. Rather, it has taken many detours which have led to a modernism which today can still be considered to be "work in progress".

Schinkel, as director of the Building Deputation, and his friend Peter Beuth, as head of the School of Architecture, wanted to create a model piece of architecture in this new building for both institutions. Solid ceilings guaranteed it fireproof, while planar, serial façades emphasized objectivity. The only decorative elements were ornaments of Biedermeier-type severity.

Of Iron Giants and Glass Virgins

The nineteenth century was the age of great engineering feats and technical inventions. Art historian Alfred Gotthold Meyer, in his book "Eisenbauten", came to the conclusion in 1907 that iron architecture had brought with it a new quality of building. The aesthetic development was still in "the process of fermentation", a metaphor which Meyer elaborated on further: "Enzymes are causative agents in the fermentation process which bring about, or accelerate, the decomposition of relatively large quantities of other organic substances. The enzymes responsible for the status of the nineteenth century in the history of style are the achievements of modern technology. They come to the fore. Their most important contributions can be grouped within three main material spheres: firstly iron, secondly machinery and thirdly light and fire. These are the mightiest powers having stylistic influence over the present and which, as far as we can see today, must also be reckoned with in the future. Those other organic substances upon which enzymes exert their powers of decomposition are stylistic forms handed down by history." While architects spoke of the search for a new style appropriate to the machine age, civil engineering works attained a previously unknown clarity. These works, however, such as the large exhibition halls frequently intended for only temporary use, were assigned no artistic value. Their overwhelming impact was dismissed as fleeting fascination. Thus the roots of modern architecture are indeed hidden, since the nineteenth century was only good, as Sigfried Giedion once wrote, when "it felt unnoticed".

Numerous fire disasters in English spinning mills led in the 1890's to the construction of factory buildings of cast iron pillars. Iron had previously only been used as a construction material for small auxiliary components, tension rods and connections between ashlars in lintels and cornices. It emerged as an autonomous material with the construction of the first iron bridge in 1777–1779 near Coalbrookdale. On the European continent, iron production and, with it, industrial development lagged behind their English counterparts. This was compensated by a myriad of new ideas, especially in France. In 1837 Polonçeau introduced a new light-weight truss, soon to be named after him. The engineer Joly introduced an I-beam of riveted angle iron. Finally, civil engineering adopted a discovery from the world of the railway – the rolled steel sections of railway tracks. The glass industry boomed at the same time as the iron industry, and glass panes overtook cheap oil paper in the first quarter of the nineteenth century.

Greenhouse construction had reached technical maturity in as early as the seventeenth and eighteenth centuries. The use of iron long remained a matter of controversy, since it is a good conductor of heat and hence brings with it the problem of dripping condensation. Construction with iron only became popular around 1830 due to its light weight and the narrow struts it made possible. The easier methods of wood processing led Joseph Paxton to employ a new type of arched truss made of glued laminated wood. Successful solutions were applied to other areas, such as the glass

Gustave Eiffel with Emile Nouguier and Maurice Koechlin (eng.), Stephen Sauvestre (arch.)
Eiffel Tower in Paris, 1889
Gustave Eiffel (left) with his son-in-law and colleague Adolphe Salles on the spiral staircase connecting the uppermost platform with the tip of the tower
Bibliothek der Landesgewerbeanstalt Nuremberg

Decimus Burton and Richard Turner
Palm House in the Royal Botanical
Gardens in Kew, Surrey, 1844–1848
View from the south-west
Photo Stefan Koppelkamm

The exotic plants of the Royal Botanical Gardens were housed within a miracle of iron and glass 110 metres in length. Twelve boilers supplied warm water for the heating pipes and guaranteed an indoor temperature of 27 degrees even in winter. Rain water was channelled to an underground reservoir via hollow cast-iron pillars and collecting pipes in the stone base. A spoil car for transporting coal, the smoke outlet and the feed pipes for the sprinkler system were housed in a tunnel, which surfaced into a smokestack and campanile-style water tower at a visually acceptable remove.

roofing of shopping malls. The gap to be spanned in such arcades was usually small, posing little challenge to the engineer.

The development of large-area covered halls was furthered in England in the Royal Navy dockyards. Since a warship took up to 13 years to build, it was necessary to protect the unfinished hull from the weather and – as the Venetians had long been doing – to build a hall to house the ship during construction. Wooden versions of such covered berths were built in Portsmouth in 1814 and in Chatham in 1817. The first corrugated-plated iron constructions were introduced in 1845.

Exhibition halls had other specifications and design criteria. Emphasis lay not so much on large spans and robust durability, but on rapid construction and low costs. Joseph Paxton used vast numbers of serially-combined single components to create his now famous Crystal Palace for the Great Exhibition held in London's Hyde Park in 1851. The grid principle, using a 24 x 24 foot module, allowed rational prefabrication and easy assembly. Construction technology was for the most part mechanized; Paxton's transom machine produced building components using industrial methods. Seemingly endless rows of identical parts lent the building an unusual character, in particular since Owen Jones had directed them to be painted so that similar parts had the same colour. The pillars were yellow, the joists blue and the roof trusses

red, while the primary colours red, yellow and blue were deployed in a ratio of five to three to eight as suggested in 1825 by G. Field in his "Chromatography".

The construction was not particularly safe; despite modifications introduced during its reconstruction in Sydenham, a wing later caved in. Neither were the connections between individual components rendered sufficiently non-positive, nor was there effective crossbracing. Questions relating to the statics of the actual frame remained entirely unresolved at the time. The engineer Robert Mallet offered some unsettling observations: "We ourselves had the opportunity, one early afternoon on one of the hottest days of the summer of 1851, to examine the effects on the skeleton of the building of thermal expansion. We can attest to the fact that, at the furthermost west end and in the front parts of the galleries in the nave – in other words, at those points where the columns are tallest and were most heated –, they deviated by approximately two inches from the vertical even at the level of the first floor. Without the help of measuring instruments we were unable to observe whether any change had taken place in the twin columns in the corners of nave and transept. Thanks to their rigidity, and probably to other factors, too, they appeared to have withstood the entire pressure and transferred it to the outermost corners of the frame. As we looked up to the west galleries, full of people, and across the whole width of the

Interior view
Photo Stefan Koppelkamm
This photograph was taken before the start of restoration in 1985, while the Palm House was entirely empty.

The Duke of Devonshire's greenhouse comprised a half-barrel on cast-iron pillars with side naves totalling 85 metres in length, 38 metres in width and 20 metres in height. With the exception of the pillars and a peripheral gallery, the building employed a wooden framework with large, laminated trusses. The profiles of the countless slender transoms were milled with the aid of a steam-driven machine which Paxton had specially built for the purpose. The glazed surfaces of the greenhouse all employed the ridge-and-furrow principle of small gable roofs. Paxton chose this solution, which he subsequently also used in his Crystal Palace in London, for its lighting advantages: it captured the sunlight more easily in the mornings and evenings and partly refracted it at midday. As later in Kew, coal trucks reached the heating plant via a tunnel.

nave, equally densely populated, and reflected upon the immense lateral forces which were at that very moment invisibly burdening the brittle frame of the cast-iron structure, we were very aware that 'ignorance is bliss'."

Free from such concerns, Lothar Bucher was fascinated by the breadth of the longitudinal transept, his gaze magically drawn to the heights: "We cannot tell if this web floats a hundred or a thousand feet above us, whether the ceiling is flat or made up of a host of small parallel roofs, for there is no play of shadows to help our soul understand the impressions of our optic nerve. If we lower our gaze slowly downwards we encounter open-work, blue-painted girders, first at spacious intervals, then ever closer, now overlapping, now interrupted by a dazzling strip of light, finally merging into a distant background where all materiality, even line, dissolves and only colour remains. We can orient ourselves only along the side walls, by isolating a single free column – a column so slim it might be there not to carry load but simply to satisfy the eye's need for an anchor – from amongst the riot of rugs, weavings, animal skins, mirrors and a thousand other draperies, by measuring its height against a passer-by and by looking beyond it for a second and then a third."

The London Crystal Palace served as a model for the industrial exhibition in Munich in 1854. Here, too, an exhibition hall was to be built in a very short period of time,

Joseph Paxton
The London Crystal Palace after its reconstruction in Sydenham, 1854
Interior view
Bildarchiv Foto Marburg

Roof built on the ridge-and-furrow principle

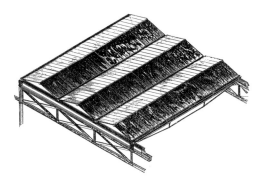

Although the competition for the building for London's Great Exhibition of 1851 had been won by Frenchman Hector Horeau, the exhibition committee ultimately wanted a building which could be dismantled and which employed small, reusable components, and therefore invited tenders from a number of construction firms. Joseph Paxton, interested in the project, join forces with the Fox & Henderson Company and was awarded the contract. The famous Crystal Palace for the "Great Exhibition of the Works of Industry of All Nations" in Hyae Park in London was subsequently built with the extensive use of prefabricated parts, serially manufactured and assembled at the building site. The central cross-aisle was given a wooden barrel vault in order to accommodate a number of large elms. Numerous modifications were introduced during the reconstruction in Sydenham in 1854, and the nave was also given a barrel vault.

Charles Rohault de Fleury
Conservatories in the Jardin des Plantes,
Paris, 1833–1836
Roger-Viollet, Paris
In Rohault's plans, the complex was divided
by a ramp into two symmetrical wings; these
were not to be fully realized, however. In the
centre lie the Australian and Mexican greenhouses, their backs leaning against a wall.
The roofs were modified during repair work
in 1874.

Opposite page:
August Voit (arch.), Ludwig Werder (eng.)
Industrial Exhibition Building in Munich,
1853–1854
View from the south-east
Photo Carl Teufel/Bildarchiv Foto Marburg
Munich's Glass Palace featured an iron
skeleton with cast-iron supports and truss girders with wrought iron on its tensile stressed
members. The square grid was based on an
edge length of almost six metres. The roofing
followed the ridge-and-furrow system of the
London Crystal Palace. Wire netting was laid
over the glass panes as a protection against
hail. The building proved to be extraordinarily durable and was only destroyed in 1931
as the result of arson.

Views, sections and details
Plansammlung der Technischen Universität
München

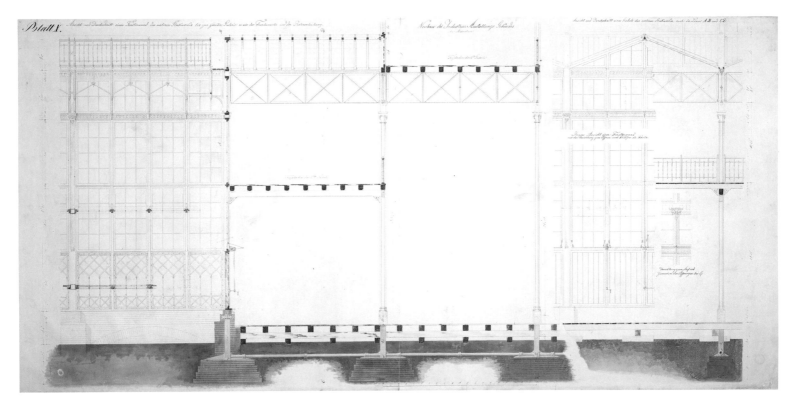

Friedrich Hitzig
Covered Market in Berlin, 1865–1868
Perspective drawing
Plansammlung der Technischen Universität
Berlin

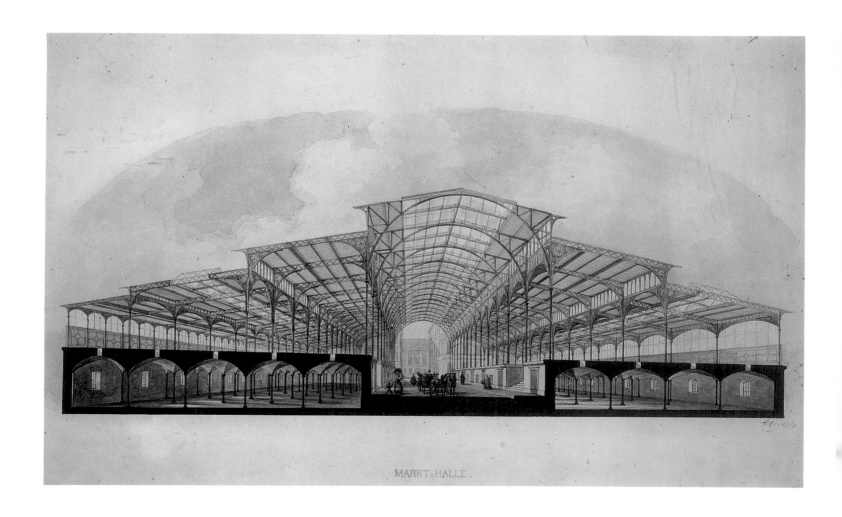

MARKT=HALLE.

Cast-iron columns support this six-aisled building with its total surface area of 5300 square
metres. From the point of view of hygiene, this
market hall represented a substantial step forward: it had running water for the fish vendors'
tanks, toilets and gas lighting. Economically,
however, the private project was unsuccessful.
After the early bankruptcy of its operators, the
hall stood empty until being converted into a
circus in 1874; Hans Poelzig finally turned the
building into Max Reinhardt's Großes Schauspielhaus in 1919. The exterior was faced with
wire-lattice plaster, producing a relatively
monumental effect, while the auditorium was
given an opulently expressive stalactite forest.
This was ripped out in 1938 by workers from
the Deutsche Arbeitsfront, who installed a
"Führer's box". As the "Friedrichstadtpalast", it
continued to serve as a showpiece for the German Democratic Republic until 1980.

Opposite page:
Victor Baltard and Félix Callet
Central Market Halls in Paris,
1854–1857, extended 1860–1866
Interior view
Studio Chevojon, Paris
A hall begun in 1851, an unhappy combination of stone and iron, was abandoned
in mid-construction, probably on the instruc-
tions of Napoleon III. The new City Prefect
Georges-Eugène Haussmann now also announced that he wanted Parisian covered
markets to be made of glass and iron. Baltard, after Hittorf Haussmann's most important architectural colleague, therefore proposed a new design which was subsequently executed.

View and section
The individual pavilions are linked via
covered streets.

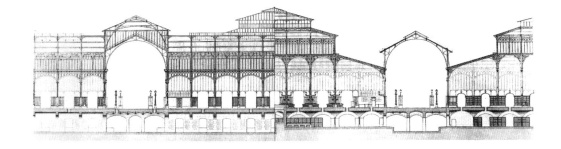

Johann Wilhelm Schwedler
Imperial-Continental-Gas-Association Retort
House in Berlin, 1863
Interior view during construction
Photo F. Albert Schwartz / Plansammlung der
Technischen Universität Berlin
The furnace house, 59 metres long and 33 metres wide, had a roof of twelve arched trusses
which were built as three-hinged arches in the
form of a pointed gable. The cast and wrought-
iron construction did not rest directly on its own
foundations, but on supports in the lateral wall
bond. The two truss halves were hinged
together while still lying on the floor. By bracing
their feet with a chain hoist, the "summit of the
roof" could be raised. The photograph shows
construction at an advanced stage, with
erected arches, extensive corrugated-iron
covering and the – already bricked – retort
ovens in the longitudinal axis of the room.

albeit characterized by "simplicity and smaller scales". Unlike the London Palace,
however, it was to be left in place after the exhibition and used for further events.
The Munich hall was distinguished by its numerous constructional improvements,
with its braced girders non-positively connected to the columns, for example. Its
façades were also more convincing. Its grid system was not confused by interspersed
columns whose load-bearing appearance was purely cosmetic; rather, the overall
construction was clearly comprehensible. The slender lightness of the building was
impressive as in London, and M. E. Schleich asked: "What is boring old stone and
beam . . . compared to the magical growth of these slim columns? The God that
let iron grow wanted industrial exhibitions, not servants!"

But even in the great exhibition halls, supporting structures were buried under a
mass of decoration, superimposed stone façades and monumental portals. The use
of iron in civil engineering, unconcealed and developed logically from arguments
of compositional legitimacy, was restricted to the fields of bridges, lighthouses and
other technical works. This schism was particularly evident in railway station architecture. Although technical and organizational requirements made specific building
planning essential, station exteriors reproduced in only slightly modified form the
historicizing dazzle typical of grandiose urban architecture. The interface between

the grand façade and the undisguised civil engineering of the functional platform hall thus became the meeting-point of two fundamentally different structures – a problem usually carefully disguised with a variety of visual aids.

Buildings became lighter and statically easier to calculate with the replacement of brittle cast iron by rolled steel and sheet profiles and the use of rivet connections. The finished principle girders of the Munich Glass Palace were tested individually under load before installation. Consistent quality of materials made such tests unnecessary. Construction sites became pure assembly lines using prefabricated perfectly measured parts which at most required some finishing work on the site itself.

Iron architecture reached its triumphal climax at the Paris Exposition Universelle of 1889. In addition to the Great Hall, a Hall of Machines for industrial exhibits was built whose 115-metre span set new standards. Opposite lay the Eiffel Tower, at that time the highest construction in the world. The Hall of Machines was a pure three-hinged arch such as Johann Wilhelm Schwedler had effectively realized in 1863 with his Berlin furnace house for the Imperial-Continental-Gas-Association. Two arches meet at the crown joint, their feet resting in foundation basins: ceiling and walls are one. In spite of its gigantic proportions, the Paris Hall of Machines

William Lossow and Max Kühne
Main Railway Station in Leipzig, 1908–1916
Platform hall under construction
Deutsches Museum, Munich

Opposite page:
Charles Dutert (arch.), Contamin, Pierron and Charton (eng.)
Hall of Machines at the Exposition Universelle in Paris, 1887–1889
Sächsische Landesbibliothek, Deutsche Fotothek, Dresden
A large, U-shaped exhibition hall was built on the Champ de Mars for the Exposition Universelle of 1889. The arts were housed in the side wings, while the general exhibition of industry was found in the Great Hall at the top end. Immediately behind it was the Hall of Machines; the Eiffel Tower was built in front of the open courtyard at the opposite end. Next to the Tower, the Hall of Machines was the most spectacular building of the exhibition. With a length of 420 metres, a ridge height of 43.5 metres and a width span of 115 metres, it covered a surface area of 46,000 square metres without supports; to this were added side-aisles 20 metres in width. The huge roof construction was composed of three-hinged arches; its trussed box profile was approximately 3.5 by 0.75 metres in size. In contrast to London's Crystal Palace, it may be described as a mature piece of engineering in which only steel was employed. Components were no longer plugged and wedged, but non-positively connected with hot rivets. Statics were calculated with scientifically-developed formulae. The Hall probably had the technical nature of its exhibits to thank for the fact that it was spared the decoration lavished on the other buildings. Only the white panes of glazing were in part embellished with blue ornamentation.

was not disquieting. Architects nevertheless clearly felt that old notions of heavy load-bearing supports had been thrown overboard. In the press, the Hall of Machines was naturally overshadowed by the Eiffel Tower. Gustave Eiffel, a commercial engineer, personally assumed all the construction risks in order to dissipate reservations about safety; he even added unnecessary elements to the frame's static essentials simply to increase trust in its stability. Therefore the arch reaching up to the first platform is only tacked on to the supporting structure and makes no contribution to stability. The tower's basic form arose from the desire to contain within the square of its cross section the force resulting from vertical and wind loads. Construction was perfectly organized; there were apparently no fatal accidents during building. All the individual components were prefabricated with the utmost precision; only riveting had to be performed on site: "There was no chisel, carving a form out of stone, to be heard on this building site; here thought prevailed over muscle-power, assigning the latter to secure scaffolding and cranes."

Johann Wilhelm Schwedler
Imperial-Continental-Gas-Association
Gasometer in Berlin, 1888–1893
View and section
Engineer Schwedler constructed a new dome system for his gasometers in which the usual tension rods were no longer required, since all the load-bearing parts were laid in the spheroidal roof plane. From 1863 onwards all Berlin gasometers were built with the Schwedler dome. Their methods of assembly were particularly ingenious. In the first roof of this type, in the Holzmarktstrasse, the construction was riveted up to the outer ring at ground level, then raised and connected to the supports with the attachment of the last ring. A still more practical method was then developed which was applied to four gasometers between 1888 and 1893: The roof, assembled entirely on the ground, was jacked up over the foundation ring with the aid of hydraulic presses, and the brickworkers' scaffolding hung on the edge of the dome. As soon as sufficient height had been bricked in, the jacks were moved and the dome raised a further 80 centimetres. Like a circular centipede moving its legs, the roof thus gradually crept upwards on the rising walls until reaching the not inconsiderable average height of 30 metres.

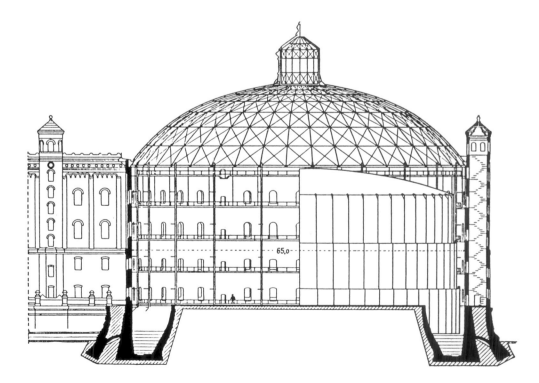

Vladimir G. Schuchov
Adziogol Lighthouse near Chersson,
Ukraine, 1911
Archives of the USSR Academy of
Sciences, Moscow
Schuchov had already built a water tower with
a slim hyperboloid supporting structure of thin
iron bars for the 16th All-Russian Trade and Industry Exhibition of 1896. The tower had more
than just one function; it was also an advertisement for the Bari Company for whom Schuchov was then working. He went on to design
a whole series of further water towers for the
company, as well as the lighthouse illustrated
here, which, with its height of 68 metres,
reached impressive dimensions. The design
was revised and an additional iron pipe was installed in the vertical axis, to which the lattice
framework was attached by beam ties. Such
mesh contructions of thin girders permit stability
at minimum possible weight. Furthermore, since
the surface of a hyperboloid is made of
straight lines despite its curved form, conventional metal rods can be used. The majority of
power-plant cooling towers today have a similar form, although – for functional reasons –
they use thin concrete shells instead of a fine
mesh network.

The Chicago School

In 1785 the American Congress ruled to divide the area which then comprised the United States into uniform grid squares. Many of the rapidly-growing centres adopted this organizational format into their urban planning, including New York, which in 1811 laid out its streets in a stereotypical grid form. The chief arguments behind this move were efficiency and economy: uniform areas could be developed more rationally and economically than those with irregular shapes and varying sizes. In Chicago, where expansion was particularly uninhibited, the first large construction site was staked out in 1830 at the mouth of the Chicago River. By 1900 it was already home to 1.7 million people.

Building proceeded simply and quickly, preferably using the balloon-frame method of construction introduced in 1832, whereby wooden laths were placed at close intervals on a foundation and reinforced with diagonal studs. The parts were not mortised, but were simply joined with steel nails. Over the course of time houses were built closer and closer together, grew taller, and began to require solid masonry. In 1851 Gottfried Semper cited a technician familiar with the American construction industry of the day: "If a Yankee wants a building plan, he goes to an architect in the morning, tells him what he wants, the size of the plot and the amount of money he can spend. He comes back that evening to see the drawings. If he likes them, the foreman is allotted a round sum, building is begun on the third day and he moves in during the sixth week." The side walls and the rear façade were made of brick, and the windows installed immediately. Wooden beams, whose length corresponded to the – always identical – plot width, made up the false ceilings, and only the depth of the houses varied. "Depending on the client's budget, the stonecutter sticks . . . slabs of sandstone, marble or granite on the front façade and hangs this cladding with iron clips to the back masonry and the carpenter's mullion-wings. . . Then the plasterer comes and transforms the whole edifice with some truly excellent stucco into the most solid house in all the world."

After 1855, cast-iron façade parts from Daniel Badger's New York factory were also delivered to Chicago, but the majority of houses were still made of wood. The risks this involved became evident in the great fire of 1871, which destroyed most of Chicago. A second highly destructive fire in 1874 reinforced efforts to develop fireproof building. Since iron constructions had proved very vulnerable to fire, tried-and-tested brick construction was preferred and experimentation provisionally relegated to the background.

Unlike New York, where single, tower-like buildings rose from a sea of buildings to create a typical urban skyline, Chicago's houses grew uniformly and in blocks. Speculative exploitation of desirable downtown development sites forced architecture upwards; there were many multi-storey buildings in Chicago in the 90's which – even if they only had eight or nine floors – were proudly called "skyscrapers". As buildings grew taller, so did the advantages of iron construction. It burdened foun-

Daniel H. Burnham & Co.
"Flatiron", Fuller Building in New York, 1902
Photo Robert Bracklow / The New York
Historical Society

William LeBaron Jenney
Fair Store in Chicago, Illinois, 1890–1891
Fireproof construction method
The iron supports were encased in cement and the cavity brick-filled joist bond was given a concrete floor. The gas pipes were also sealed in concrete.

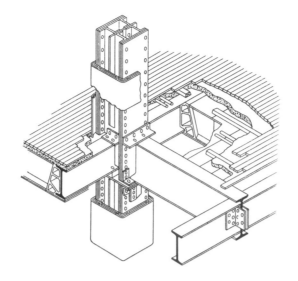

William LeBaron Jenney
Leiter Building in Chicago, Illinois, 1879
Photo Taylor / The Art Institute of Chicago
In Jenney's Leiter Store, iron pillars behind the brick columns supported the wooden ceiling joists for each floor. The narrow frames between the windows were made of wrought iron and rested on stone parapets. Since the construction featured almost no tension-resistant joints, it cannot be said to possess a true framework. Notable is its extensive rejection of façade decoration. In 1888 two storeys were added to the building; when this photograph was taken they had already been completed. The tracks of the "Elevated", the suburban railway which ran in a loop around the city centre, can be seen in the foreground. It gave its name to the "Loop", Chicago's centre of commerce.

William Holabird and Martin Roche
Tacoma Building in Chicago, Illinois,
1887–1889
View from the south-east
David Phillips Collection, Chicago
Technological progress and aesthetics did
not always coincide. Technically-innovative
buildings frequently appeared conservative
in their exteriors, while façades which
seemed to express new concepts merely
concealed conventional stone constructions.
The Tacoma Building ultimately looked like
the skeleton construction it was.

dations with less weight, and made it possible to avoid the thick ground-floor walls
which had stood in the way of generous shop windows and thus the lucrative rental
of ground-floor store space. One by one the preconditions for high-rise building
were all met: the invention of a fireproof steel frame, the technology for sufficiently
load-bearing foundations and, above all, the passenger elevator which Elisha Otis
first introduced in New York in 1857. Access became available to even higher levels,
and the formerly cheaper upper floors now became the more valuable.

In using brick columns on the façades and large, serially-ordered windows, James
McLaughlin put a face on the iron frame construction of a Cincinnati department
store in 1877 which soon became typical for large commercial buildings throughout
America. William LeBaron Jenney followed this trend with his Leiter Store in Chicago.
Extensive glazing and the rejection of ornamentation and any crowning of the façade
made a factual, functional impression. Others building alongside Jenney in Chicago's
Loop included Daniel H. Burnham, John Wellborn Root, John Holabird, Martin
Roche, Henry Hobson Richardson, Dankmar Adler and Louis Sullivan. Richardson

Louis H. Sullivan
Schlesinger & Mayer Department Store in
Chicago, Illinois, 1899–1904
The Art Institute of Chicago
Rich, artfully-crafted ornaments, designed by
Sullivan and George Elmslie, decorate the
base of this consumer's paradise. The sales levels were joined – as was common practice in
the large Chicago department stores of the
time – by an art gallery, café, restaurant and
exquisitely-furnished lounge. Further storeys
were added by Burnham & Co. in as early as
1906, and the original roof, shown in the present photograph, thereby altered.

Plan

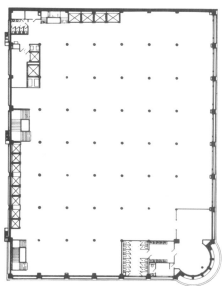

and Sullivan tried determinedly to find an artistic form for commercial building
projects. While Richardson accented his powerful, even stone façades with care-
fully-placed windows and rounded arches, Sullivan took on the challenge at a more
fundamental level. He summarized his thoughts on office building design in the essay
"The tall office building artistically considered". Sullivan structures the building in
terms of three functions. The ground floor is thus for shops and for access to the
upper floors. It is followed by a middle section containing any number of similar
floors of offices; its façade is hence structured by a uniform grid of windows and
columns. The top floor, which houses elements of the building's utilities, is emphasized
as a concluding attic storey. His typical ideal multi-storey building therefore features
a base, shaft and capital, as in a classical column. Sullivan's argumentation ends
in the much-analyzed conclusion: "It is the pervading law of all things organic, and
inorganic, of all things physical and metaphysical, of all things human and all things
superhuman, of all true manifestations of the head, of the heart, of the soul, that
the life is recognizable in its expression, that form ever follows function. This is the
law. . ." The representative value of a house was nevertheless a function which he

Opposite page:
George Herbert Wyman
Bradbury Building in Los Angeles, California
1889–1893
Photo Julius Shulman
This brick and sandstone office building with its
only five floors seems conservative on the outside. Its inner courtyard, with glazed roof, exposed staircases and free-standing hydraulic
elevators is, however, a triumph of iron architecture. Forms of access have here become autonomous elements of movement and communication.

Ernest Flagg
Singer Building in New York, 1906–1908
Photograph taken during construction
From: History of the Singer Building
Construction
The Singer Manufacturing Company proudly
declared their new office building to be the
"highest building in the world". Its 612 feet indeed made it taller than the Washington
Monument, the Philadelphia City Hall, Cologne Cathedral and the Gizeh Pyramids. The
Eiffel Tower was quietly ignored. The old part
of the building, dating from 1897, was integrated into the new section and expanded.
The wind bracing on the tower – steel crosses
in the corners – is clearly visible. The foundation work employed pneumatically-sunken
boxes which produced atmospheric overpres-
sure and were supposed to prevent the intrusion of water during excavation.

took seriously. Ever taller buildings now sprang up at great speed. Highly-specialized
teams of workers erected their steel scaffolding at dizzying heights, with Chicago
and New York alternately outdoing each other. Meanwhile the streets below grew
darker and darker until, in 1898, architect Ernest Flagg suggested that only the base
sections of buildings should be permitted to extend as far as the street, while any
projecting towers should be restricted to one-quarter of the total site size. This idea
was adopted in 1916 as part of New York's new construction regulations, and was
not without impact on architectural design. The rigorous exploitation of maximum
permitted building volumes led to unproportioned, tiered buildings which rose like
wedding cakes from massive bases. Therefore the structural clarity of earlier high-rises
was completely destroyed, and it would take a long time before comparable achievements were once again reached.

Opposite page:
New York skyline of 1914
Photo Joseph P. Day / The New York Histori-
cal Society
The Singer Building by Ernest Flagg and the
Woolworth Building by Cass Gilbert (1911–
1913) can be seen in the background, and in
the foreground the Adams Building.

1892–1925

Hector Guimard
Métro entrance pavilion in Paris,
1900
From: Möhring, Architektonische Charakterbilder II
The "Métropolitain" was officially opened to coincide with the Paris Exposition Universelle of 1900. The floral motifs of its entrances and cashier booths were standardized and compiled from a repertory of normative cast-iron panels, lattices, bars and arches. They exhibited a correspondingly limited degree of conformity to their respective surroundings, shocking lovers of the traditional Paris cityscape.

L'Entrée du Siècle

The artistic movement at the turn of the century had many names: Nieuwe Kunst, Stile Liberty, Jugendstil and Art Nouveau. Even within regional centres of artistic activity there were often fundamentally-opposed stances, even bitter disputes, and at all events divergent departures. The only common factor was the conscious desire to be "modern" – whatever that might mean. This desire finally led architecture away from the now dubious terrain of traditional values and towards fashionable, current trends which – as with Art Nouveau – were frequently only short-lived.

The late nineteenth century saw the middle classes, feeling more and more politically threatened, escape into the world of decoration. The Makart style in Vienna, Alban Chambon's theatres in Brussels, London and Amsterdam, Charles Baudelaire's poetry in "Les fleurs du mal" and Ludwig II's greenhouses and fairy-tale castles built to motifs by Richard Wagner all represent a post-Romantic flight from the overpowering world of industry. Obsession with decoration seems a form of self-deception on the part of a middle class in the face of responsibility for the social upheavals which were already clearly making themselves felt, even though their effects were still hardly imaginable at the time. Unusual flora under filigree glass domes were a set piece of exoticism. Towards the end of the century, romantic nostalgia sent tourists fleeing to the cult and cultural centres of Italy and Egypt. Meanwhile, discussions on architecture were dominated by theoretical exchanges on the aims of the Arts and Crafts movement in Great Britain, on Eugène-Emmanuel Viollet-le-Duc's "Entretiens" and Gottfried Semper's writings and works. The vehemence and passion of these discussions had many causes. Immense population expansion and increasing mobility had precipitated the building of numerous railway stations, town halls, covered markets, post offices, apartment buildings, schools, hospitals and prisons. These various building categories led to the emergence of a typological architectural order. Pavilions served as hospitals, the model of the panoptical prison building prevailed, cultural centres were built in primarily classical styles, while new solutions needed to be found for railway stations, department stores and indoor swimming pools. Ornamentation, it seemed, was a sine qua non, and aesthetic postulates such as "Functional buildings should be without ornamentation" was simply an excuse for budget cuts by French hospital administrators.

The achievement of architecture in the nineteenth century lay above all in its methodical development of building programmes. Stylistic specifications were often decided by central administrative bodies and reflected standards communicated nationally through the many new architectural journals. Architects got used to offering their designs in a number of alternative styles. What were not produced, however, were houses with which the progress-oriented middle classes could identify themselves. This explains the development of new movements, especially in the provinces, which sought to incorporate both regional thinking and modernity. This is true for Nancy, Darmstadt and Glasgow as well as for Barcelona, where Antoni Gaudí designed

highly unusual works in the name of Catalan Modernism. The trend began, however, in Brussels, where an economic boom, combined with the strength of the middle class and the Socialist party, produced a new breed of architectural patron. Rich from profits made in the colonies, and yet in no way opposed to the ideas of Socialism, these sponsors awarded building contracts to their young architect friends. Since the city of Brussels incorporated many rural land plots, building sites were quite small. The street front of the van Eetvelde house, for example, was only nine metres wide. Attempts to redesign the city on the basis of Georges-Eugène Hauss-mann's Paris model failed. The large multi-storey buildings which had become the rule in other metropolises were unsuccessful here. Brussels remained characterized by the narrow bourgeois residence. Its form was rigidly governed by municipal building regulations. The heights of building and rooms, the measurements of plinths, cornices and balconies, even the sufficiency of insulation were all monitored. But it was precisely such limitations in the basic form and the lack of overall town planning which challenged the architectural imagination.

Many theoreticians had already taken a stance against the – now somewhat moderated – doctrines of academic architecture and the ornamental arbitrariness

Paul Hankar
Ciamberlani Studio House in Brussels,
1897–1898
From: Möhring, Architektonische Charakterbilder I
Compared to Horta's houses, this façade
seems opulent and yet planar. The large
omega windows on the first floor contrast with
the window band on the second. Murals by
Adolphe Crespin fill the stucco surfaces between the brick columns.

of the handicrafts industry. Viollet-le-Duc in France for one. In arguing for a return to the ideals of antiquity, and particularly of the Gothic, he propagated a philosophy of "honest" building appropriate to materials used. His writings were widely known. William Morris and John Ruskin opposed the evils of industrial production with their ideals of an arts and crafts culture, which did not prevent them, however, from designing machine-printed fabrics and wallpaper. John Ruskin, too, found the Gothic the only style worth emulating besides the Pisan Romanesque. At the same time he wrote, in "The Seven Lamps of Architecture" in 1849: ". . .the time is probably near when a new system of architectural laws will be developed, adapted entirely to metallic construction." Viollet-le-Duc expressed a similar sentiment. In practice, however, Ruskin shied away from the consequences, for "true architecture does not admit iron as a constructive material, and. . .such works as. . .the iron roofs and pillars of our railway stations. . .are not architecture at all."

The new theories and approaches allowed the use of all available building materials, as long as they were openly exposed and their integration within the building was logical and stylistically harmonious. The basic concept of the building was hardly questioned. Victor Horta's split levels, for example, were thoroughly common in their

Victor Horta
La Maison du Peuple in Brussels, 1896–1899
From: Moderne Städtebilder I. Neubauten in
Brüssel, plate 25
This ambitious project, which housed offices,
shops, a large café and an auditorium, was
commissioned by Emil van de Velde and the
Belgian Social Democratic Worker's Party. Con-
tributions by party members themselves were
considerable.

Auditorium
From: Moderne Städtebilder I. Neubauten in
Brüssel, plate 28
The auditorium was located on the second
floor, which proved a relatively unhappy
solution.

Antoni Gaudí
Casa Batlló in Barcelona, 1904–1906
Stairwell
Photo François René Roland
Zoomorphic forms dominate the house of
textile manufacturer Josep Batlló i Casanova.
The roof ridge recalls the dorsal comb of a li-
zard and the façade, too, has the skin of a rep-
tile. The interiors are softly modelled, with flowing transitions without corners and edges. The
stairwell is characterized by fine green crazing
and pastel-coloured tiles.

Antoni Gaudí
Güell Park in Barcelona, 1900–1914
Promenade
Photo François René Roland
Industrialist Eusebi Güell i Bacigalupi,
Gaudí's influencial friend and sponsor, was
intending to build a model estate on what
was then still a desolate, hilly site. But his
plans collapsed, and in the end only the accompanying park was created. Paths follow
the ground contours or are tunnelled like
caves out of slopes, while earth is stayed by
slanted, rough-jointed retaining walls and pillars. Their angle corresponds – as in other of
Gaudí's buildings – to the lines of force.

day. His façades blended quietly into their surroundings and were relatively incon-
spicuous and reserved. Only once inside, in interiors usually featuring glazed roofs
and generous lighting, were their novelties first revealed: sweeping trains of ornamentation, a sensitive use of colour and surprising material combinations of steel,
marble and precious woods. Flat iron was coiled into artistic banisters and lamps,
while load-bearing supports were revealed to the world.

Inspiration for this new ornamentation, its enthusiastic curves masterfully developed
by Henry van de Velde in particular from constructive elements, came from the
graphic art of the day. In France Henri de Toulouse-Lautrec was designing posters
in a new style, while in England artists such as Arthur Heygate Mackmurdo and
Walter Crane were working on the revival of book illustration within the framework
of the reform movement. Nor should the refined erotic fantasies of Aubrey Beardsley
for example be ignored. New design impulses also came from the pictorial world
of the Far East, and decorated the salons and studies of countless contemporaries

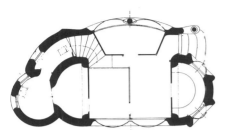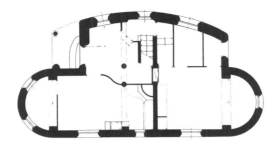

Plans of the Keeper's House and
Administrative Building

in the form of floral graphics. Colour woodcuts by the Japanese artist Katsushika
Hokusai were available as reproductions, and his motifs were to be found in many
Art Nouveau works.

Against this background of orientalism and historicism, Ruskin and Morris's reform
ideas may be seen as a call to honesty in design. Art Nouveau was therefore hardly
able to provide a satisfying response to this challenge in the long term. All too often
it created artificial forms which, although cloaked in the language of mystic-sounding
thoughts on artistic unity, were nothing more than decoration. Which is precisely
what earned Art Nouveau its popularity.

The fashionable character of Art Nouveau emerges particularly clearly in its French
development, its history virtually inseparable from events at the Ecole des Beaux-Arts.
After the crisis in 1863, when Viollet-le-Duc had to abandon his official lectures and
teach in a privately-organized circle, discussions between formalists and non-con-
formists intensified, albeit without bearing particular fruit. It was not until Hector

Park benches
Photo François René Roland
A wide, level terrace was laid on top of a deep
columned hall. Its snake-like parapet is
moulded into seating. Decoration as well as
protection against the weather are provided by
the mosaics of tile and glass fragments, executed in part by Gaudí himself and in part by
workers involved in the construction.

Hall on the ground floor
From: Dekorative Kunst, Vol. XI

Guimard used a modified version of a Viollet-le-Duc drawing from the 70's during the new construction of the Ecole de Sacré-Coeur that it become clear to all that the concept of visible ironwork was not alone a success. In his first house in the "new style", the Castel Béranger, Guimard went further: he exchanged the ornaments of the neo-Gothic planning for florally-animated motifs similar to those he had seen on Horta's buildings, and placed an asymmetrical wrought-iron gateway in the main entrance. As arbitrary as this may seem, it illustrates the proximity of the Gothic Revival and Art Nouveau. This preference for Gothic Revival was one shared by patrons commissioning middle-class homes all over Europe. Its relatively plain façades, natural stone brickwork and expressive details seemed to express the mood of the times as successfully as did Art Nouveau. But the artist-architects of Art Nouveau rose above rigid, conventional plans in the rich fantasies of their open interiors.

At all events, the liberality of Art Nouveau made it excellently suited for commercial purposes, and many large department stores exploited its potential to great effect. The artistic products of this symbiosis, geared towards profit and fame, were palaces

Henry van de Velde
Academy of Fine Arts in Weimar, 1904–1911
La Cambre Archives

such as Frantz Jourdain's "Samaritaine" in Paris. In Berlin, the "Warenhaus", as the Wertheim brothers called their new department store, became a veritable den of temptation. Sales spaces took up entire floors, and the whole street front was made into one large shop window. "Liberation! That's the feeling with which the layman cranes his neck at this magnificent façade, more impressive than a hundred public edifices", as an overwhelmed Alfred Lichtwark described it. The arbitrarily-compiled, mainly neo-Gothic ornamentation had nothing to do with Art Nouveau, but rather with the abandonment of stale design maxims. The awkwardness of its combination of technical structure with flamboyant form became even clearer in its successor, the Tietz department store. While all the elements of a new architecture were present, it was still lacking the masterly fusion of its diverging aspects which would unite technology and form into a single picture.

The Paris Exposition Universelle of 1900 also saw the official opening of the Métro. Its entrances and cashier's booths are the high point of Hector Guimard's work and masterpieces of Art Nouveau. Many contemporary observers criticized the inadequate integration of its serially-conceived architecture into the traditional cityscape. Typical

Severe, factory-type studio windows with exposed steel lintels dominate the main façade. The brickwork between forms powerful pillars which end abruptly and without transition to the sloping roof. In the central projection they extend above the height of the eaves; where an architrave might be expected, there is simply an empty space.

Charles Rennie Mackintosh
Glasgow School of Art, 1897–1909
West front
Museum Bellerive, Zurich

North front
Glasgow School of Art Archives
The left wing with the entrance was completed
during the first construction phase from 1897 to
1899. Seven years later, the School of Art was
extended to the west in conjunction with additions to the original building.

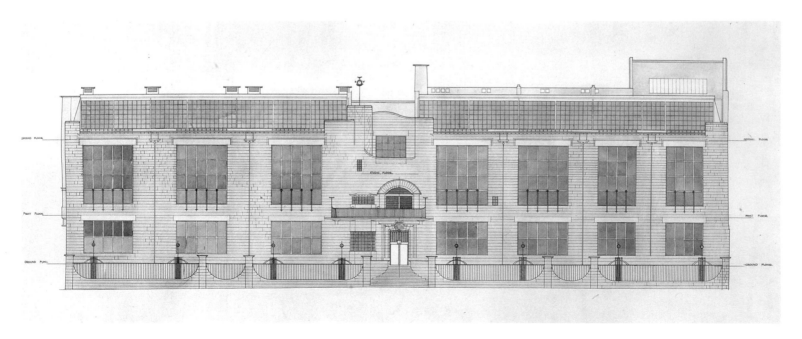

for the Métro stations was their use of standardized elements of cast iron. Unlike Horta, who rejected the material, these elements were Guimard's speciality. His own foundry distributed cast-iron products under the name "Fontes Artistiques pour Constructions, Fumisterie, Articles de Jardin et Sépultures, Style Guimard."

As would later become evident, this bold entrée into the new century was more the glittering end of an epoch than the birth of a new era. The age of so many imitated styles and forms appeared to have provoked no momentous beginnings. The future lay not with the pleasing works of such as Jules Lavirotte and Paul Saintenoy, but with the systematic reductions of Hendrik Petrus Berlage and Henry van de Velde. Count Harry Kessler noted in his diary in 1901: "Breakfast at Frau Richter's. . .spoke about van de Velde. His style in furniture, everybody agreed that he is not suited to luxury rooms. . . Axel Varnbühler: Why luxury art for aristocrats? That's practically a thing of the past."

Fashionable and rational design were also in conflict in the Netherlands. Although many architects here were expressing themselves through curved lines, the works of a group calling itself "Architectura et Amicitia", centred around Berlage and

Smith and Brewer were members of the Art Workers' Guild and worked, as in this London welfare institution, together with other artists in the Arts and Crafts movement. The house had dining halls and common rooms, a gymnasium, a library and private rooms. Its decor was simple but not sparse, its exterior rurally friendly.

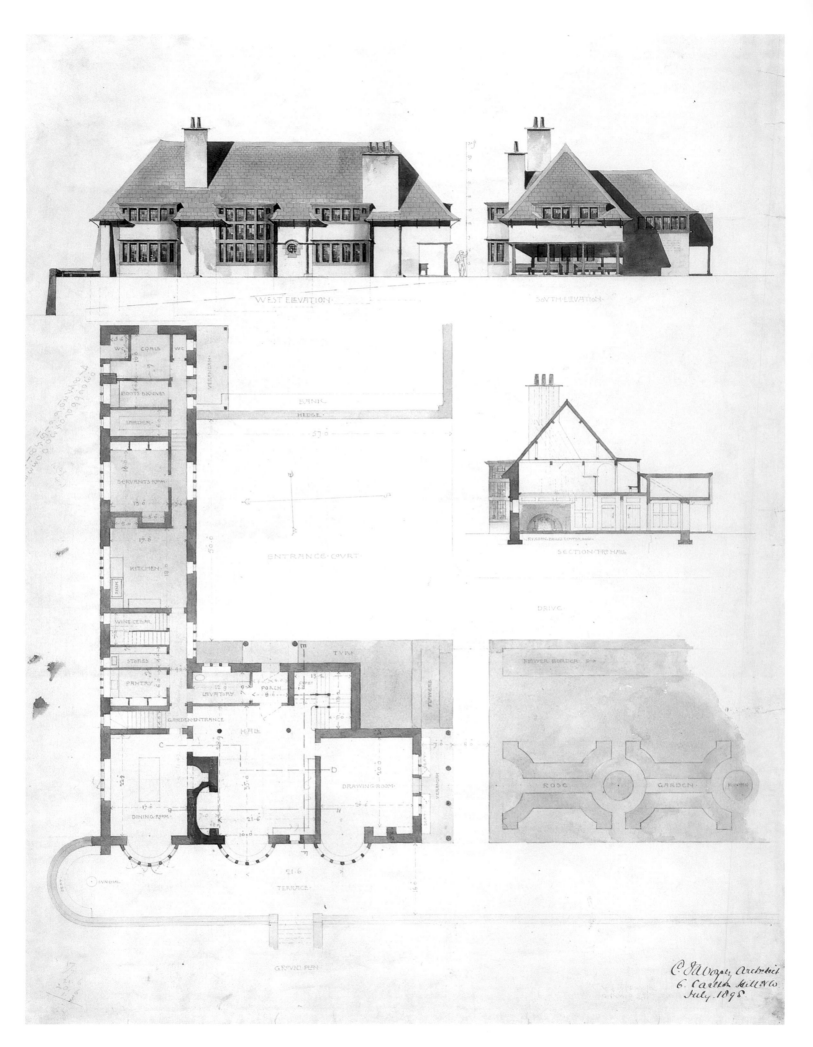

WEST ELEVATION·

SOUTH ELEVATION·

SECTION·TO·HALL·

ENTRANCE·COURT·

ROSE GARDEN

DINING·ROOM·

DRAWING·ROOM·

HALL·

KITCHEN·

TERRACE·

GROUND·PLAN·

C.F.A. Voysey, Architect
6. Carlton Hill N.W.
July 1898

Opposite page:
Charles F. A. Voysey
House for A. Currer Briggs, Lake
Windermere / Lancashire, 1898
Victoria & Albert Museum, London

Hendrik Petrus Berlage
Henny House in The Hague, 1898
View from the north-east
From: Moderne Städtebilder II. Neubauten
in Holland, plate 23
For Carel Henny, president of the insurance company "De Nederlanden van
1848", Berlage built not only office buildings in Amsterdam and The Hague but
also this private residence. Its plan is developed from overlapping, mutually offset
square forms around a cruciform hall and
complicated by calculated rotations. The
dimensions of the small rooms next to the
stairs correspond to the module underlying
the entire plan. The unplastered brick walls
in the interior of the house were also unusual.

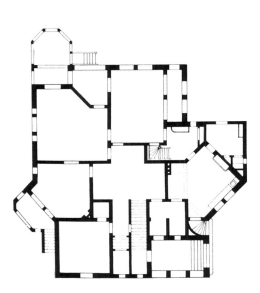
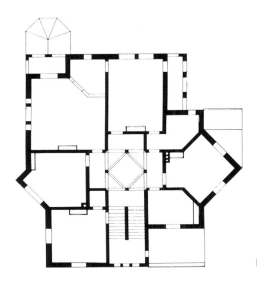

Plans of the ground and first floors

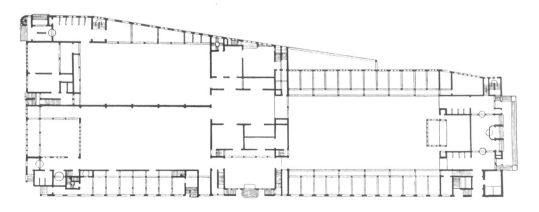

A competition for the rebuilding of the Amsterdam Stock Exchange, which had been destroyed by fire, was announced in as early as 1885; but work on the new building was not started until the turn of the century. Its reserved exterior belies the generous expansiveness of the halls within.

Plan
Behind the entrance front with its powerful corner tower lies the Commodity Exchange. Attached to it – skilfully exploiting the widening of the site – are two smaller halls for the Grain and Stock Exchanges. Although Berlage based the design on a uniform grid system, which also calculated height development according to the proportions of Viollet-le-Duc's "Egyptian Triangle", there is nothing schematic about the building.

Petrus Cuypers, were closer to the rectilinearity of their English and Austrian colleagues, although they, too, dismissed the Vienna Secessionists as "upholsterers, wallpaperers and furniture makers". Interior design was, in fact, the most important field of activity for the young Viennese. Perhaps that explains why their architecture is occasionally reminiscent of a giant item of furniture. The Viennese guest house "Die Traube" frequently saw Josef Hoffmann, Max Kurzweil, Theodor Gottlieb Kempf, Karl Moll, Koloman Moser and Joseph Maria Olbrich discussing architecture together. Here, too, Max Fabiani, who had awarded the contract for the celebrated Café Museum to the young Adolf Loos, finally ended up calling even Olbrich a "decorativist".

Such dismissive attitudes, which long remained widespread, failed to acknowledge the stimulus that Art Nouveau had given the stagnating art world. Even Walter Benjamin saw the confrontation of new artistic will and old ideology as an internal conflict of the age still awaiting resolution: "Van de Velde's houses are an expression of personality. Ornamentation is to these houses what a signature is to a painting. The true significance of Art Nouveau is not revealed in this ideology. It represents the last attempt by art to escape from an ivory tower besieged by technology."

Opposite page:
Bernhard Sehring and L. Lachmann
Tietz Department Store in Berlin, 1899–1900
Kunstbibliothek, Staatliche Museen
Preußischer Kulturbesitz, Berlin
The huge shop windows, 25 x 18 metres respectively, ran through all the floors. The supporting pillars were recessed two metres behind this front. A glass globe with a diameter of over four metres was lit up from within at night.

Alfred Messel
Wertheim Department Store in Berlin, 1896
Main entrance
Kunstbibliothek, Staatliche Museen
Preußischer Kulturbesitz, Berlin
The tall main façade, articulated by slender granite columns, indicates a classical height development; projecting shop windows at its base, tall areas of finely-partitioned glazing above these, and neo-Gothic bronze tracery as concluding frieze. The three central bays were decorated with elliptical oculi, phials and other sculptural historical ornaments. This "artistic" approach to the entrance area was to recompense the unusually large volume of glass.

Max Fabiani
Portois & Fix Furniture Store in Vienna, 1899–1900
From: Architektur des XX. Jahrhunderts, plate 37
The entrance on the right led directly to the sales rooms, while the passage on the left led to the rear courtyard and the furniture store-room in the back building. Since the passageway cut through the ground floor, this latter was reached via the mezzanine level. The shop façade was clad in polished Swedish granite, the three following storeys with an orthogonal mosaic of light green and brownish "pyrogranite" tiles. The top floor containing the workshops was given a Parisian-style sheet metal roofing

Opposite page:
Otto Wagner
Majolika House, Vienna, 1898–1899
From: Moderne Städtebilder IV. Neubauten in Wien, plate 8
Linke Wienzeile 40, a six-storey apartment house, merged with Wagner's recently-completed Linke Wienzeile 38 corner house to form a single block. Glazed earthenware slabs covered the entire façade. The blossoms of the climbing decoration were painted a delicate red, the buds turquoise and the lush foliage of the balcony niches a rich green. Contemporary critics described the results of this ambitious design as "wildly Secessionist". Loos sarcastically termed it "tattooed architecture".

Plans of Linke Wienzeile 38 and 40

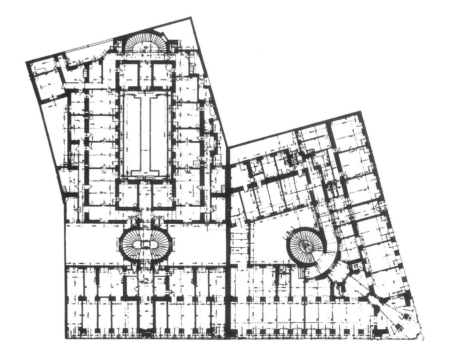

Joseph Maria Olbrich
Exhibition Building for the Secession in
Vienna, 1897–1898
From: Moderne Städtebilder IV. Neubauten in
Wien, plate 20
Behind an entrance framed by massive
cubes lies an exhibition hall with podiums
and a generously glazed ceiling. The words
engraved over the portal – "Der Zeit ihre
Kunst, der Kunst ihre Freiheit" (To the Age its
Art, to Art its Freedom) – formed the motto
of the Vienna Secession, which here created
a forum for its member artists, who included
Gustav Klimt, Josef Hoffmann and Koloman
Moser. The unbroken frontality and monumentality of the building, which was crowned
by a dome of laurel leaves, was a reflection
of how the Vienna avant-garde saw itself
around the turn of the century.

Joseph Maria Olbrich
Habich House on the Mathildenhöhe in
Darmstadt, 1900–1901
From: Architektur von Olbrich I, plate 27

Josef Hoffmann
Palais Stoclet in Brussels, 1905–1911
Bildarchiv Foto Marburg
The exterior of this Art Nouveau jewel, built for Belgian banker Adolphe Stoclet, is costly, exclusive and designed right down to the last detail just like its interior. Smooth surfaces of Norwegian marble are framed with bands of bronze. The windows of the upper floor break through the line of the eaves, emphasizing the weightlessness of their pure, crystalline planes.

Plan

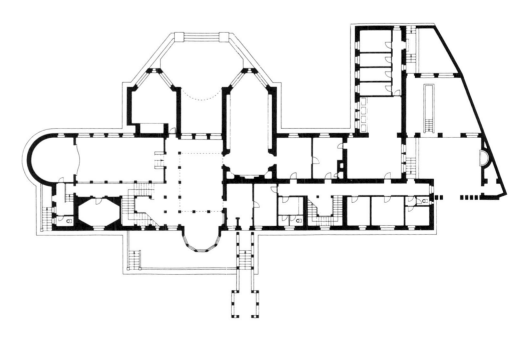

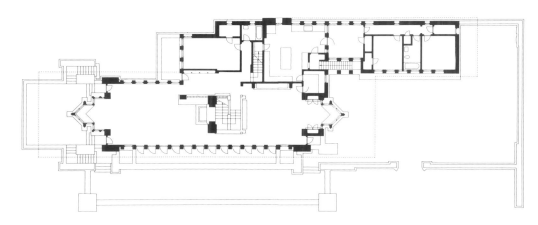

In the Far Landscape

Frank Lloyd Wright
House for Frederick C. Robie in Chicago,
Illinois, 1906–1910
Street front
Photo Hedrich-Blessing
Four longitudinal welded steel beams, approximately 30 metres in length, run through the roof and permit its broad overhang. Extended terraces, low storey heights, continuous parapet bands – of which only some border balconies, others simply delimiting "holes" – and elongated enclosures all take up the dynamic horizontals of the roof and make the house appear larger than it actually is.

Plan

Although Chicago at the turn of the century was, as Frank Lloyd Wright noted soberly after returning from a trip to Europe, a fairly cultureless place, full of slaughter-houses, blast furnaces and George M. Pullman's factories, there was nevertheless one place in this rapidly expanding city which seemed to be a melting-pot for Modernist ideas. This was the office of Dankmar Adler and Louis Sullivan's successful architecture practice. The young Frank Lloyd Wright as well as Irving John Gill worked as draftsmen here.

In 1893, the year that Frank Lloyd Wright left Sullivan's office, the Columbian World Exposition took place in Chicago. With its white stucco orgies and propagated ideal of the "city beautyful", it dealt a fatal blow to those functional ideas still germinating in purpose-built architecture and heralded the triumphant advance of academic architecture in America. The Japanese Pavilion, a replica of the Ho-o-den Temple, attracted Wright's particular attention. Here was an opportunity to study Japanese architecture, with its overhanging roofs and geometric wall slabs, in a full-scale model.

Even before the turn of the century Wright had formulated, in numerous articles and lectures, some of the fundamental principles underlying his entire oeuvre. Anything "which has no real use or purpose" was to be avoided; even necessities such as radiators were to be invisible, were to vanish into the construction. Visible elements, however, were to have their own character and nonetheless relate to the whole. Individuality was one of his favourite catchwords. "There are as many different houses as there are people." Wright's mistrust of industrial stylization was based on his personal experience with the materials available in the building trade. It was not possible to get plain-dyed fabrics for curtains, plain rugs, groove and tongue boards without modelling nor posts without carvings, making a wealth of detailed drawings necessary which were not reflected in the architect's set fees, which were based solely on the use of available materials.

There was in the United States no movement of opposition. The weak Arts and Crafts scene had its forum in the magazine "The Craftsman", published by furniture-maker Gustav Stickley. He also published individual works by Wright, Gill and the Greene brothers, but response was weak. The brothers Charles Sumner and Henry Mather Greene probably came closest to the ideal of the craftsman. Since they worked only with wood, their buildings were very detailed and divided into emphatic single structural elements. They showed lines, angles, projections and recesses instead of closed surfaces. Their building methods were developed directly from wood-joining techniques. The houses were not to be covered with climbing plants; they harmonized with their surroundings at a respectful distance from nature. Wright had set up his own office in Chicago's suburban Oak Park in 1889. He participated intensively in middle-class socializing and spoke at women's club meetings. His most important programmatic articles appeared not simply in the magazine

Frank Lloyd Wright
Stables of the William H. Winslow House
in River Forest, Illinois, 1894
The Art Institute of Chicago
The Winslow House was Frank Lloyd
Wright's first own commission, and thus his
first opportunity to realize his architectural visions fully and completely. The annex shown
here, with its staff apartment, hen house, stables and garage, displays a whole series of
design features which were to prove characteristic of Wright's work: the horizontal emphasis, the low-pitched roof, the entrance
arch and the projecting, often stained-glass
bay window. A tree which stood "in the
way" was left where it was, and the roof
built around it.

"Architectural Record", but also in the widely-read "Ladies' Home Journal". His article "A Home in a Prairie Town" appeared in the latter in February 1901 as part of a series on low-cost housing models.

Wright's early houses were named after the flat prairies of the American Midwest. Their exteriors are influenced by his respect for quiet stretches of countryside and transcend the actual lack of space in suburban areas. He used low-pitched, over-hanging roofs, low eaves, wide-set fireplaces and outreaching garden walls to achieve his effects. The houses are multi-storey despite their obvious horizontality. Narrow stairs emphasize the layered floor levels rather than citing the impressive entrances found in traditional villa architecture. His entrances have no forceful character whatsoever. They are usually hidden, narrow and set at an angle, reflecting Wright's belief that a house should be a "shelter". Colour, which he liked to employ in autumnal shades, took second place behind effects achieved with vegetation. He usually integrated bowls and troughs into parapets. He devoted much attention to fenestration, usually aligning his windows in long bands. He rejected the American guillotine window, preferring instead the European casement. Wright introduced a surprisingly strong ornamental note into his interiors through geometric glasswork. Light filtered through coloured glass whose rising organic patterns symbolized natural growth. In his plans, where the rooms were often grouped in a cruciform arrangement with staggered axes around a large central fireplace, Wright employed typical motifs from the country-house architecture of the nineteenth century, using deliberate asymmetries as a means of artistic design. But the only loose division of his rooms, whereby one seems to flow into the next, goes much further. His plans are balanced and free of obligation to symmetry.

Frank Lloyd Wright
House for William Fricke in Oak Park,
Illinois, 1901
Photo Peter Gössel
Wright also accentuated the verticals in a
number of details here, and experimented
with cubic volumes. The "Tower Room" was
originally a billiard room.

West and north views

Frank Lloyd Wright
House for Avery Coonley in Riverside,
Illinois, 1907–1908
Part of the west façade
Domino's Center for Architecture and
Design, Ann Arbor
Wright spoke of a one-storey house "with
the basement above ground level". All the
rooms except the entrance hall and a play-
room are situated on this raised level. Col-
ourfully-glazed tiles form geometric patterns
on the façade.

Plan
The slender, wide-spread wings organize
themselves around the living area, the core
of the house: the dining room in the north,
the kitchen with domestic staff wing to the
east, the bedrooms along a long southern
axis and the guest rooms in an annex parallel to the utility rooms to the east.

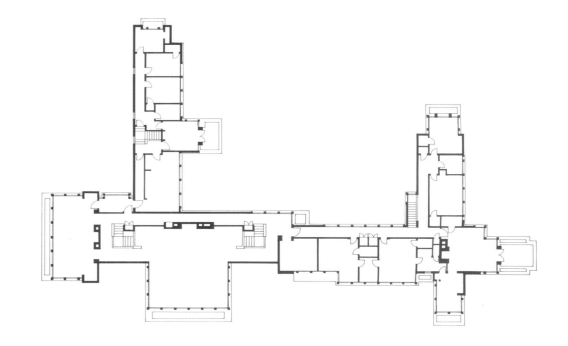

Frank Lloyd Wright
Coonley Villa Playhouse, 1912
Domino's Center for Architecture and
Design, Ann Arbor
Mrs. Coonley had founded a so-called Cot-
tage School in which theatre was also per-
formed. This small Playhouse was built for re-
hearsals and productions. Its plan is strictly
axial-symmetric and is thereby related to the
Gale House. For the tall windows Frank
Lloyd Wright designed colourful glass mo-
saics on the theme of balloons and confetti.

Living room in the Coonley House
Chicago Architectural Photographing
Company
The large fireplace forms the mainstay of the
room; the ceiling climbs towards the centre,
following the line of the roof. This is a "shelter" in the wide expanses of America. The furnishings, also designed by Frank Lloyd
Wright, are kept to a modest scale and do
not obscure the spatial design.

Frank Lloyd Wright
House for Ward W. Willitts in Highland
Park, Illinois, 1901–1902
The Art Institute of Chicago
The stuccoed wood construction sits on the
property upon no distinct base. The cruciform plan organizes the hall and entrance,
living area, dining room and kitchen and service areas into four wings around the central
fireplace.

"The old structural forms which up to the present time have spelled 'architecture' are decayed. Their life went from them long ago and new conditions industrially, steel and concrete and terra cotta in particular, are prophesying a more plastic art wherein as the flesh is to our bones so will the covering be to the structure, but more truly and beautifully expressive than ever." In such statements Wright revealed himself as a visionary who always wanted more than he was able to create. His goal was architecture as a unity created by man, based on practical but not merely pragmatic considerations. His Prairie Houses reach their climax in the Robie House in Chicago. It is situated in the city and therefore cannot be compared to the "real" Prairie Houses such as those he built for Willitts or Coonley. The garden courtyard lies directly on the street and is fully visible to passers by, while the view from the balcony was never impressive. It was perhaps precisely these handicaps which made the house a programmatic statement in itself. Here the prairie was effectively built into the house as part of the architectural philosophy. The interior directly reflects the horizontality of the roof. Particularly flat Roman bricks were laid so that in the vertical joints the mortar was flush, while in the horizontal joints it was recessed, creating long shadow joints. The living room and dining room, separated by the stairs and the fireplace, are reconnected through the wide window band which optically enlarges both rooms.

Charles Sumner and Henry Mather Greene
House for David B. Gamble in Pasadena,
California, 1907–1908
Photo Ezra Stoller/Esto
This country estate is without doubt a
masterpiece of craftsmanship. Carefully-
jointed, meticulously-finished beams form the
supporting skeleton and structure the building volumes. Gentle rounding and polishing
was designed to heighten the colour play of
the wood in sunlight. The teak interior is just
as magnificent as the exterior. The Greene
brothers also designed the entire furnishings.

Plan

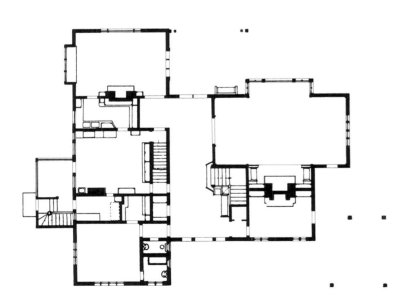

Robert van't Hoff
Henny House in Huis ter Heide near Utrecht,
1915–1919
Photo Frank den Oudsten
Frank Lloyd Wright's German publication of
1910, "Ausgeführte Bauten und Entwürfe",
made a considerable impact in Europe. The
young van't Hoff travelled to America in person in order to meet the master, and subsequently built this house. The horizontal
slabs of its reinforced-concrete construction
are picked out in light grey paint, while sky-
lights brighten the centre of the house.

In 1909 Wright left Chicago and his family and went to Europe; it was during this
time that he produced his German-published book "Ausgeführte Bauten und Entwürfe". This was the conclusion of a personal epoch and at the same time a stimulant
for the many young European architects who saw in his work healthy alternatives
to the vainglorious excesses of their own countries. The Dutch architect Berlage
travelled to the USA shortly afterwards, and subsequently reported his still fresh
impressions to the Zurich Association of Engineers and Architects: "I could hardly
tear myself away from these rooms, whose great originality is probably best described
by the word 'plastic', in comparison to European interiors, which tend to be more
flat."

For their part, the Americans were also familiar with the European avant-garde. The
English magazine "Studio" was published in the USA under the name "International
Studio", and Irving Gill was among its subscribers. He was a great admirer of Adolf
Loos, as can be detected in his works. In his office in San Diego, which at that time
had only 25,000 inhabitants, he nevertheless employed six draftsmen and a clerk
of works. His houses were simple, plastered boxes in the beginning, but later he
grew increasingly interested in concrete construction methods, even experimenting
in his own workshop. He went from hollow bricks to reinforced concrete. Wall
segments were prefabricated in shallow moulds and erected after hardening. Gill
preferred cubic masses and flat surfaces whose severity was softened by round
arches in the traditional local Spanish mission style. "The simple cube-shaped house
with cream-coloured walls, clean and smooth, rising powerfully towards the sky,

undisturbed by cornices or a projecting roof, has something calming and satisfying about it." Constructive components were not emphasized; the façade geometry asserted itself in the equilibrium of often irregular window openings. Gill preferred concrete composition floors painted ochre or tan which curved upwards at the walls. His concept of a hygienic house included a small waste incinerator and a built-in vacuum system. He employed frameless doors in as early as 1902 and also tried to reduce the number of individual components in windows. Gill fully rejected ornamentation.

Frank Lloyd Wright
Gale House in Oak Park, Illinois, 1909
The Frank Lloyd Wright Foundation
Its overhanging surfaces and continuous window strips make this small wooden house seem larger than it is. In the meantime, however, the balconies and projections have mellowed into a positively relaxed mood.

Irving J. Gill
"Horatio West Court", row of terraced
housing in Santa Monica, California,
1919–1921
Photo Peter Gössel

Irving J. Gill
House for Walter Luther Dodge in Los
Angeles, California, 1914–1916
Side view
Photo Julius Shulman

Garden front
Photo Julius Shulman
Mr. Dodge, for whom Gill built this villa with
its extensive spatial programme, made his
money as a manufacturer of patent me-
dicines. While the entrance façade, with its
large arched porch, appears relatively traditional, the house opens onto the garden in a
sophisticated play of asymmetrically-bal-
anced volumes. A flight of steps leads from
the garden to the patio between the kitchen
and billiard room.

Plan

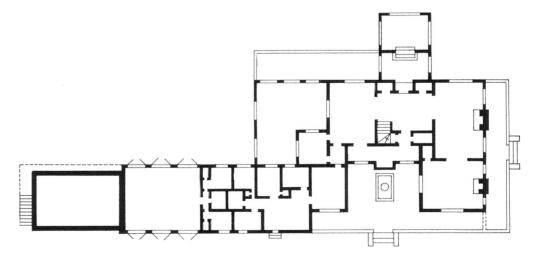

VILLA WAGN

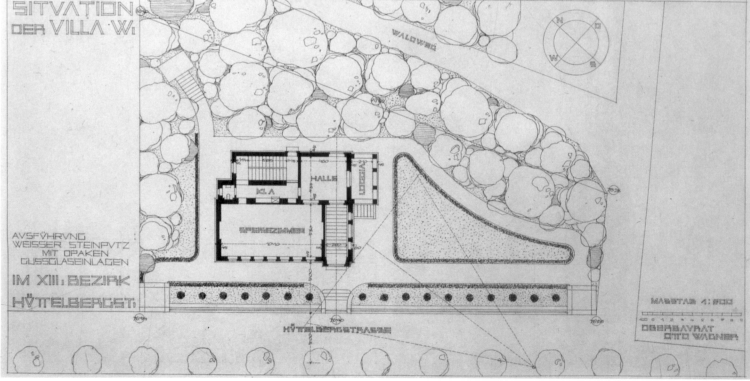

SITVATION
DER VILLA·W₁

WALDWEG

AVSFÜHRVNG
WEISSER STEINPVTZ
MIT OPAKEN
GVSSGLASEINLAGEN

IM XIII. BEZIRK

HÜTTELBERGST.

HALLE

KL·A

SPEISEZIMMER

HÜTTELBERGSTRASSE

MASSTAB 1:200

OBERBAVRAT
OTTO WAGNER

78

Circle and Square

In his book "Line and Form" published in 1902, Walter Crane – a master of book graphics and a pioneer of the English reform movement – traced the vast family of ornaments back to its geometric forbears of circle and square, whose union was achieved in the description of the circle by the square, dissected by diagonals. Dutchman Jan Hessel de Groot rediscovered and employed a related diagram, the "quadrature", in his design work in about 1900. Instead of the diagonals he placed a second square inside the circle, in such a way that the ratio of the lengths of its outer and inner edges was $1:\sqrt{2}$. For De Groot, as for J. L. Mathieu Lauweriks whom he inspired, it was a question of more than just decoration. The figure was nothing less than the key to the underlying order of the cosmos, which could only be expressed in geometric terms. From the point of view of architecture, they believed they had found a "starting-point" from which all styles, preferences and individual tendencies originated and which could serve as a rule for modern architecture – as Lauweriks explained in the journal "Architectura".

Peter Behrens, very interested in the Nieuwe Kunst of the Dutch architects, not only used the circle-and-square motif for many of his two-dimensional designs, but also brought Lauweriks to the Düsseldorf School of Art in 1904 to teach architectural theory. Their discussions on the significance of geometry in "proportional" designs strengthened Behrens in his relinquishing of Art Nouveau and his search for the substantial principles of "monumental art", which he celebrated in 1908 in a speech to the Hamburg Kunstgewerbeverein as the "highest and true expression of the culture of an age. . . It naturally finds expression at the point most suitable for a people, which most deeply affects it, from which it may be moved." He also made it clear that there was no correlation between spatial size and monumentality. "Monumental size cannot be expressed materially; it works through mediums which touch us more deeply. Its medium is proportionality, the regularity which expresses itself in architectural relationships." Behrens' path eventually led him to a purified form of neo-classicism. The plan of the Obenauer House in Saarbrücken features a relatively large number of components developed from two intersecting squares. The plan of the Cuno House in Hagen is simpler and – apart from an interruption on one side – strictly symmetrical in its axes. Its rigid severity is disturbed only by the clear-cut lines of the cylinder inserted in its front.

The Viennese Adolf Loos also published a work in 1908, entitled "Ornament und Verbrechen" (Ornament and Crime), in which he declared war on all superfluous decoration irrelevant to its age. "Ornamentation is wasted manpower and therefore wasted health. It always has been. Today it also means wasted materials, and both together mean wasted capital. . . Modern man, the man with modern nerves, does not need ornamentation; it disgusts him." Loos had already rejected the Secessionist sweeps and flourishes of his colleagues in his starkly elegant design for the interior of the Café Museum – derided in its own day as the "Café Nihilism" – of 1899. In

Otto Wagner
Villa Wagner in Vienna, 1912–1913
From: Einige Skizzen, Projekte and ausgeführte Bauwerke, Vol. IV
Designed in 1905, this second Villa Wagner, planned as a widow's residence, was not actually built for another seven years.

Otto Wagner
Austrian Post Office Savings Bank in Vienna,
1903–1912
Banking hall
Bildarchiv der Österreichischen National-
bibliothek, Vienna

the new Goldman & Salatsch building on Vienna's Michaelerplatz he had his first opportunity to declare his faith in formal purity in a large building exposed to the public eye. Owners Leopold Goldman and Emanuel Aufricht had originally held a competition for the building's design, but were dissatisfied with the results and thus commissioned Loos to execute the project. "Comparative assessment" led to agreement being quickly reached on Loos' proposed plans, and after some manoeuvring his façade design too received his clients' approval, although it went on to provoke an unsuspected outcry. Following the partial removal of the scaffolding, clusters of curious onlookers gathered round the new building whose "more than outsize plainness" would, according to the press, strike passers-by from afar. In the words of a Viennese council member, it was nothing short of a "horror of a house". The relevant authorities called a halt to its construction. Goldman and Aufricht, their confidence shaken by the uproar, held another contest for the façade. Unnerved, Loos eventually proposed an "appeasement design" featuring bronze flower boxes; this appeared to calm tempers, and after a few more skirmishes, the – still pending – permission for use was granted.

Plain façades were in themselves nothing new, and were familiar from cheap tenements and factories. But its location in such a prominent area – right next to the Hofburg –, together with its use as the business premises of an exclusive tailor's studio, made the Michaeler House an eyesore. Its street fronts were divided not into three, as classical models demanded, but into two visually distinct zones: the business

Acroterion on the central projection of the
Post Office Savings Bank
Photo Hans Wiesenhofer/Austria

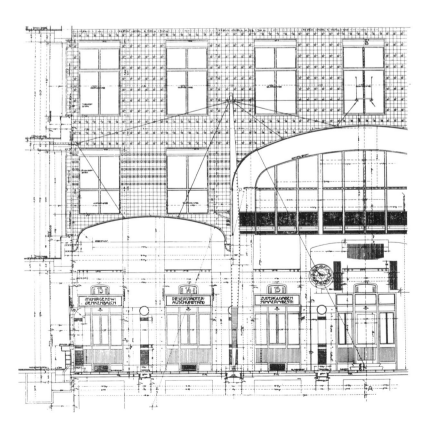

View of the main façade
The Post Office Savings Bank was built in
two phases. The first section was built in record time on the broad side of the trapezoidal
site, between 1904 and 1906; the second
was completed between 1910 and 1912.
Wagner responded to the request for "maximum solidity" with a façade of marble panels, whose anchorage points remained
visible and were indeed even emphasized by
the fat aluminium heads of their rivets. There
are classical references in the height gradations and symmetrical divisions, although accentuation takes place for the most part within the plane — via sunken glass fillets, for
example, or concentrated metal trimmings as
on the face of central projection.

Sectional view of the banking hall
The columns in the banking hall pierce the
roof and end in masts from which the glazed
canopy is suspended. Glass blocks in the
floor permit light to reach the basement
below.

Auguste Perret
Apartment House in Paris, 1902–1903
Façade overlooking the Rue Franklin
Studio Chevojon
Although the principle of the reinforced-concrete skeleton frame can be
read in the façade, Perret disguises his
concrete infills with ornamental panels.
The deep-pleated façade and large
windows onto the park opposite en-
sure that the apartment floors are
pleasantly well-lit. Glazing was particularly generous on the ground floor,
where for a long time Perret kept his
own office.

establishment below, clad in costly marble, and the smooth-stuccoed living floors above. Only a fine caesura below the roof overhang marks a thin concluding frieze. At the flatter corners of the building the plaster is somewhat pointed, thereby "sharpening" and emphasizing the edges. Within the surface of the façade, columns which truly function as such – rather than acting as the usual decoration – bear the weight of the upper floors. Their corporeality and stone cladding, the finely-crafted detail of the mezzanine windows and the inviting entrance recess provide a conscious contrast to the taut and sober surface above.

During the heated debate over the Michaeler House Loos built a private house for Lilly and Hugo Steiner in Vienna which, possibly due to an article in the magazine "Der Architekt" towards the end of 1910, was also caught up in the controversy and at the beginning was repeatedly hailed with stones. Leaving aside the disproportion of the street and garden sides, the complex reflects a problem which occurs again and again in Loos' later houses. Tiered interiors of complex organization are packed almost violently into rigidly stereometrical and symmetrically-arranged building blocks, leading to "left-over space" and often to noticeably forced access to the rooms.

The general use of asymmetrical and decorated façades in Historicism and Art Nouveau lost favour. The search for clarity and coherent order once again looked towards classical rules of proportion by which constructive elements of modern building could be brought into harmony. This is illustrated particularly well in the works of Frenchman Auguste Perret, who translated the regularity of ferroconcrete construction logically and consequently into the articulation of his façades. In accordance with his principle that "Not to show a support is a mistake; to feign a support is a crime", the classical tripartite façade of a large garage in the Rue Ponthieu in Paris is structured by the plain concrete skeleton with recessed fields of glazing. Since it was only a secular, functional building, Perret escaped the bitter suffering which Loos underwent in Vienna. But he, too, met with scepticism and reservations. Loans were not granted for the house in the Rue Franklin which hid its concrete supports under flowery slabs. The extensive glazing planned for the ground

Auguste Perret
Garage in Paris, 1905
Bildarchiv Foto Marburg
Here, for the first time, Perret risked openly displaying the concrete skeleton: pillars and joists stand out from their infills. There are classical elements in the articulation of the façade; the large central window at the front of the basilica-like automobile hall in particular recalls sacred architecture.

Henri Sauvage
Apartment House in Paris, 1911–1912
Sächsische Landesbibliothek, Dept. Deutsche Fotothek, Dresden
In 1903 Sauvage and his partner Sarazin founded the "Société des logements hygiéniques à bon marché", dedicated to healthy and affordable housing. Influenced by the drawings of Tony Garnier he designed a light-tiled terraced house, which was, however, subsequently reserved for wealthier tenants.

Peter Behrens
House for Gustav Obenauer in Saar-
brücken, 1905–1906
Cross-section

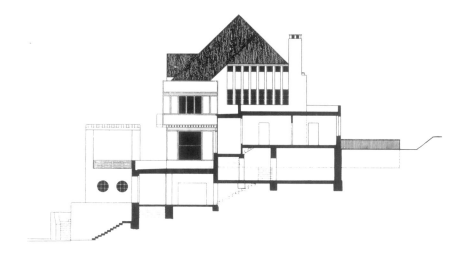

"Its location on a slope was a fundamental factor in the architectural development of the Villa Obenauer. . . Along the road Behrens built a retaining wall, topped by a balustrade and interrupted by the wrought-iron gate located to one side. On the far left a large pavilion, the wing of the massive columned hall, thrusts itself forward like a bulwark. . . From this massive base rises – somewhat set back to create a second, upper terrace running the full front of the house – the powerful cube of the two upper floors, the second jutting forward over a characteristically strong line of denticulation, and barely covered by the low pyramid of the roof. From the right and the rear, side buildings with hipped and gable roofs slide themselves against the main building, along with a larger piece of architecture, also ending in a flat terrace, which together with the other frequently-offset horizontals of the rear front towards the garden express the stereometrically layered nature of this house."
(Fritz Hoeber, 1913)

View from the Trillerweg
Photo Gollas / Konservatoramt Saarbrücken

Joseph Maria Olbrich
"Wedding Tower" and Exhibition Building
on the Mathildenhöhe in Darmstadt,
1905–1908
From: Architektur von Olbrich III, plate 1
The marriage of Grand-Duke Ernst Ludwig of
Hessen gave Olbrich the opportunity to
crown the artists' colony on the Mathildenhöhe with a tower. The gable reaches upwards like a hand; glazed clinker bricks give
its five merlons a golden gleam in the sunlight. The brick masonry is not smooth-
bonded, but animated by small projections
and recesses. The panoramic tower is connected to the exhibition complex via concrete
pergolas.

View

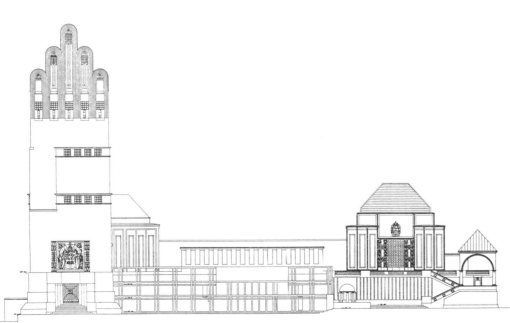

Peter Behrens
Cuno House in Hagen, 1908–1910
Photo Klaus Frahm

floor, so absolutely incompatible with the traditional appearance of solid statics, unnerved his financial backers.

Otto Wagner, the great teacher and doyen of Viennese Modernism, also found his way from historical designs to a functional form of architecture which emphasized its constructive elements. He developed ornamental forms from technical components. Thus the slim, cylindrical heating vents in the central hall of the Austrian Post Office Savings Bank stand like sculptures against the walls. The mounting pins in the glass and marble cladding have shiny aluminum heads which – inside as well as on the façade – add a fine plastic touch to the smooth surfaces. A spectacular solution was found for the glazed vault of the banking hall: the columns pierce the transparent skin and end – invisible to the observer – in poles from which the ceiling is hung.

Otto Wagner defined responsible architectural culture in his acceptance speech at the Vienna Academy in 1894: "You may have heard it said, or seen for yourself, that I am a proponent of a certain practical direction. . . Almost all modern buildings aim to achieve in their outward appearance, more or less happily, as exact a copy as possible of a stylistic trend. Such successful replicas, for which much is usually sacrificed, are then described as stylistic purity and usually serve as standards by which other buildings are judged. . . The starting-point of any artistic creation must, however, be the needs, the abilities, the means and the characteristics of 'our' time.

Adolf Loos
House for Lilly and Hugo Steiner in Vienna,
1910
Garden front
Loos-Archiv, Albertina, Vienna
As the authorities would only grant planning
permission for a one-storey house with a
converted mansard roof, while the clients
wanted a comprehensive spatial programme, the compromise was this unusual
piece of architecture. Loos arched a metal
roof down to the ceiling of the ground floor
at the front of the house, but turned it into a
flat wood-and-cement roof at the apex. It
was thus possible to develop the garden
front on three storeys. The rear façade is
smooth and symmetrical like the front; the
two outer window axes protrude like projections.

Street front
From: Der Architekt XVI, 1910

Detail of the façade
Photo Johanna Fiegl
The house is for the most part a skeleton structure infilled with large bricks. The first to fourth floors are plastered with a smooth, light-coloured stucco; the ground floor and mezzanine are clad in green Greek Cipollino marble, the base in granite. The pillars are monoliths of the same marble, their bases and capitals sections of tombac or cast zinc, overlaid with brass. Loos found a functional justification for the textured zones of the mezzanine oriels: if he used less substantial transoms, he argued, people might be frightened of falling onto the street below.
Inside, the sales rooms of the exclusive tailor's studio are differentiated by podiums and galleries. Tall pillars of precious wood surrounded by formal glass cabinets accompany the main axis. The accounts department and cashier's office were located on a dais, sectioned off by a brass grille, at the rear of the mezzanine. The workrooms were also distinguished by height: 2.07 metres for the seated stitchers, 3 metres for the standing cutters and 5.22 metres in the ironing room.

'Artis sola domina necessitas'. You should therefore ask, when considering the solution to a problem, how appropriate is it to its contemporaries, the task, the genius loci, climatic conditions, the available materials and pecuniary means? Only in this way can we hope to gain general acclaim. The works of architecture, today regarded with incomprehension or a measure of fear, will become generally accepted, even popular. The realism of our time must permeate the work of art."

The Modern Factory

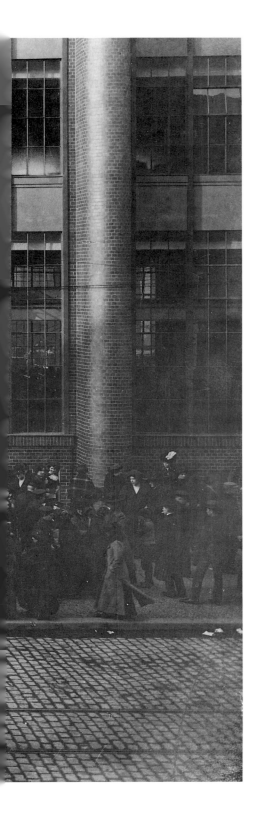

Peter Behrens
AEG Small Motors Factory in Berlin,
1910–1913
Gate entrance at a change of shift
Kunsthistorisches Institut der Freien
Universität Berlin
The long façade front was clad in violet
clinker bricks; the massive columns extend
through five floors with a total useful area
of 35,000 square metres.

View

Unlike France and the United States, where Auguste Perret and Frank Lloyd Wright combined in their thinking new compositional avenues with rational clarity, efforts in Germany following the decline of Art Nouveau produced almost nothing of a valid Modern Style before World War I. Architecture was dictated by a largely uninterrupted commitment to imperial pomp and neo-classical monumentality. Even the works of a man as outstanding as Peter Behrens — his Berlin villa for archaeologist Theodor Wiegand, for example, and the Petersburg Embassy — showed a more than slight tendency towards stolidity. The much-discussed garden cities and country houses of Heinrich Tessenow, Richard Riemerschmid and Hermann Muthesius were characterized by conservative fussiness and solidity. Values such as "soundness, truthfulness and simplicity" were of more importance than the joy of experimentation. Different building requirements were met with different styles; the architectural Utopia such as Tony Garnier created in France with his "Cité industrielle", where factories, communal facilities and apartments were designed along uniform principles using the most modern methods of concrete construction, was a singular departure. The search for new form remained for the most part restricted to the industrial sector. "It is first and foremost", wrote Walter Müller-Wulckow, "the powers of modern economic life who attract new creative personalities and allow them to develop." Fundamental criticism of production conditions was considered "left-wing" and party-political. It was possible, however, for a middle-class organization such as the Deutscher Werkbund to encourage change within the bounds of existing manufacturing structures. The Werkbund was founded in October 1907 by twelve artists and twelve factory owners with the declared intent of improving the form and quality of consumer goods. Largely influenced by the English Arts and Crafts movement, it nevertheless adopted a more flexible attitude to machine manufacturing. This openness to industry was one of the main reasons for its success. For William Morris on the other hand, the pioneer of the Arts and Crafts movement, the principle cause of unsatisfactory work conditions was not merely the alienation which resulted from the division of the production process, but the very existence of mechanized production. His subsequent anachronistic call for pure craftsmanship was adhered to not even by Morris himself — he too designed products which were produced by machines. The logical solution was to transfer the satisfaction given by a perfectly-crafted product to an industrialized setting. Fritz Schumacher formulated this idea on the occasion of the Deutscher Werkbund's foundation in 1907: "We must recreate the joy of work; this is tantamount to an increase in quality."
In a discussion of Walter Gropius' Fagus Factory in the journal "Der Industriebau", it was stated that many factory owners would "admit that artistic collaboration on plant construction can produce what industry can no longer do without — publicity of a most sophisticated kind." Widespread criticism of industry overlooked the fact that it was in precisely this sector that decisive contributions towards innovative

Peter Behrens (arch.), Karl Bernhard (eng.)
AEG Turbine Factory Assembly Hall in
Berlin, 1908–1909
Bildarchiv Foto Marburg

The supporting system of three-hinged arches with beam ties has an apex height of some 25 metres. The supports appear in the side façade as full-wall girder sections, with the large glazed areas between them slightly recessed. The gable front is flanked by two corner pylons which narrow towards the top. The polygonal gable zone displaying the company emblem seems to sit astride the central window. But the apparently weighty, solid façade elements are in fact composed of only a thin concrete skin held by a steel lattice. They represent spatial conclusions, not load-bearing elements. The slim bends in the joints of the corner pylons and the fine metal framing of the tympanum point to the artificiality of the materials used.

Cross-section through the main and side halls

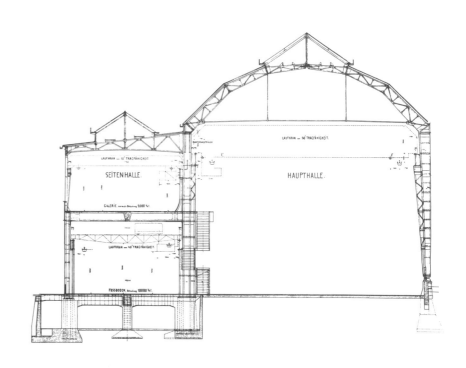

Peter Behrens
AEG High-tension Plant in Berlin,
1909–1910
Perspective drawing
From: Der Industriebau 6/1911
A glass-roofed double hall was inserted between the two parallel, six-storey wing buildings. A four-storey crossbar containing administrative offices runs across the top of the
halls to connect the two main sections.

Peter Behrens
AEG High-tension Plant in Berlin,
1909–1910
Perspective drawing

factory and product design were being made, whereby product design and factory architecture were two aspects of the same goal. An outstanding example here was the Berlin electrical giant AEG (General German Electrical Company). In 1907 the company appointed Peter Behrens as artistic advisor and designer of its entire product range, thereby pursuing and institutionalizing the efforts it had previously invested in presentational form. In addition to lamps, ventilators and catalogues, Behrens designed numerous factories for the AEG, whose aesthetic programme – most clearly apparent in the famous assembly shop of the Berlin Turbine Factory – was fittingly described as "nobilization". An industrial plant, its technical structures already specified, is here transformed into monumental architecture. For Julius Posener, the significance of this monumentality was twofold: "One the one hand, the building should naturally make an impression, be an advertisement", should illustrate in a magnificent gesture the success and self-confidence of the company. Then "secondly, and more importantly, it should publicize internally. It should impress the workers." They should feel part of a company of which they could be proud.

Peter Behrens
Gasworks in Frankfurt am Main, 1911–1912
Water tower and overhead tar tank
Bildarchiv Foto Marburg

Leaving aside the "beautification" of engineering products – a secondary activity which is today called "design" and was harshly criticized by architects such as Adolf Loos –, a certain hierarchy of design is visible in factory architecture: production processes are just as precisely specified as the static requirements calculated by engineers for factory halls. Industrial buildings created without the help of architects, such as the Steiff Company's soft toy factory, were in no way the worst of their kind. Architects were clearly aware of this fact. Their goal was to create not just a technical shell but, as Walter Gropius expressed it in 1913, "a dignified guise" which would impress passers-by and increase the efficiency of the workers, by giving them not only "light, air and clarity" but also the impression of an overall concept which would help them – fully in the interests of the industrialist – to rise above the stupidity of factory work. "They will work more happily towards the creation of great common values in workplaces which are designed by artists to satisfy the sense of beauty with which we all are born and which enliven the monotony of mechanical work." In his turbine factory Peter Behrens employed well-known methods to achieve this desired effects: a huge gable and broad corner pylons are merely grandiose façades. The principle works, but is still tied to old attitudes and takes their conventions into consideration. Even Gropius, whose Fagus factory showed him to be the most progressive architect of the time, still emphasized the entrance portal with a projecting

Hermann Muthesius (arch.), Karl Bernhard (eng.)
Michels & Cie. Silk Weaving Mill in Neu-babelsberg, 1912
Machine hall
Akademie der Künste, Sammlung Baukunst, Berlin
A grand, marble-panelled vestibule was sited in front of the factory hall. From here it was possible to look into the hall through a curved glass wall.

Hans Poelzig
Sulphuric Acid Factory in Luban, 1911–1912
End with stepped gable; views
Plansammlung der Technischen Universität
Berlin

The brick walls are only partly load-bearing, partly not. The difference is revealed by the windows, which are semicircular in the real wall bond, square and without lintels otherwise.

superstructure. Hermann Muthesius described this relationship between tradition and perception in a metaphor: just as the thin metal spokes of a bicycle wheel did not immediately inspire confidence, but nevertheless represented the best solution for such a lightweight construction, so the delicacy of iron in structural engineering, now accepted in practice, would prove itself aesthetically articulate only once the eye had grown accustomed to it.

Leading architects agreed that monumentality and art were mutually inseparable. Gropius collected photographs of industrial buildings and was especially impressed by the large grain silos in American agricultural centres. He believed their geometric forms to be "heralds of a coming monumental style". In a slide lecture in Hagen in 1911, he sought "to consider the field of the secular industrial building within the sphere of monumental art". He noted that "force, severity and stringency" naturally correspond to the organization of the working world. But purely functional arrangement – and here he also meant pure civil engineering – could not produce an artistic result; this required the intervention of "creative will". Gropius then took a decisive step towards a definition of the special nature of industry: "Modern materials such as iron and glass, with their transparent incorporeality", seemed incompatible with "the goal of corporeality in architecture". But Gropius believed – as he demonstrated in his Fagus Factory in Alfeld – that "here, too, artistic will sweeps away seemingly insurmountable difficulties and, with inspired artfulness, wrests the impression of corporeality from unsubstantial materials. . . Artistic potential lies in every material. Modern products such as rubber, linoleum, paper and concrete were at first unjustly viewed as inferior surrogates for other materials."

Industrial construction became one of Gropius' main fields of activity after leaving Behrens' office, whereby he succeeded in realizing his ideas in a convincing way with his first commission for the Fagus shoe last factory. Architect Eduard Werner

Eisenwerk München AG
Margarete Steiff Factory in Giengen/Brenz, 1903
East front
Margarete Steiff GmbH Archives
A double-skinned curtain wall covers the entire three-storeyed eastern wing of the teddy-bear factory. The outer skin hangs the full height of the supporting structure, while the inner layer reaches from floor to ceiling respectively. The frame with the curtain wall rests on a concrete base. Friedrich Steiff, himself the builder of the first iron bridge over the river Brenz, may have been extensively involved in this design.

Opposite page, above: Building extension of 1904
The long outdoor ramp on the main building was built for Margarete Steiff, who was confined to a wheelchair.

Opposite page, below: Factory complex in 1908

Walter Gropius, Adolf Meyer and Eduard Werner
Fagus Shoe Last Factory in Alfeld/Leine, 1910–1914
Entrance on the west side
Photo Klaus Frahm
Flourishing trade meant that expansion was necessary only shortly after the completion of the first new buildings in 1912. The west wing with this entrance porch was added during the extension work in 1914.

Vestibule in the extension wing
Photo Klaus Frahm

had already submitted the final plans for the new factory when building sponsor Carl Benscheidt brought in Gropius, finally making him responsible for the "architectonic-artistic building design". In other words, the plan and "constructive layout" were to be left untouched, but the building's "appearance" was to be "tastefully" redesigned. The façade of the main building is clearly distinguished from its more self-contained neighbours. Iron frames are inserted between narrow yellow brick columns which support generous glazing and grey-painted metal sheets in the parapet area. As an "art form" it differs substantially from both the purely "technical form" and from Werner's more conventional proposals. Its characteristic features suggest a reinterpretation of motifs from Behrens' turbine factory; it is now the columns, rather than the glazed surfaces, which recess inwards, while – in a radical reversal of traditional practice – emphatic, solid corners are abandoned in favour of a fully transparent solution in which corner supports are omitted altogether. The Fagus Factory illustrates, like few other buildings of its time, "that character of precise, clear, material beauty" of which R. Rose wrote in the journal "Deutsche Bauhütte" in 1919, "which our art is developing more and more clearly and which will stand in later times as witness to our way of thinking, a symbol of our work".

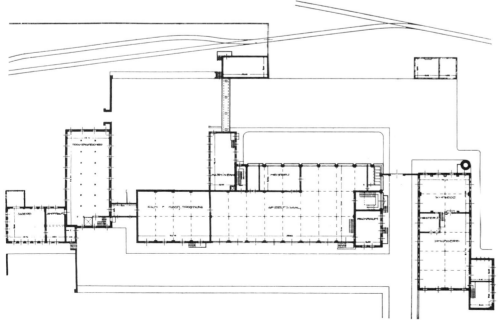

View from the south, 1912
Bildarchiv Foto Marburg

Site plan
The buildings are arranged along a north-south axis in accordance with the production process. The delivered wood is transferred from the saw mill to the large drying store. The artificial drying plant and the finishing hall are located in the main building. On the other side of the road, the toolshop, with its smithy and fitter's shop, conclude the complex to the south.

Walter Gropius
Model factory at the Werkbund Exhibition in Cologne, 1914
Rear of the office building
Busch-Reisinger Museum, Harvard University, Cambridge, Massachusetts
An experiment along the lines of the Fagus Factory: below, a hint of Peter Behrens, in the middle, artistically-interpreted technology, and pure Frank Lloyd Wright on top. It is clearly a designer's design.

Front of the office building
Busch-Reisinger Museum, Harvard University, Cambridge, Massachusetts

Albert Kahn
Ford Motor Company Glass Plant in Dearborn,
Michigan, 1924
Albert Kahn Associates Archives

The sheet-glass plant had four large melting furnaces to which was connected a long shed.
Here the glass was cooled on conveyor belts
and then cut and polished. Each piece
travelled the length of the hall a full three times
during processing. Characteristic for Kahn was
the symmetrical layout of the shed, generous
sections of whose glazing could be opened to
release heat.

Cross-section and plan

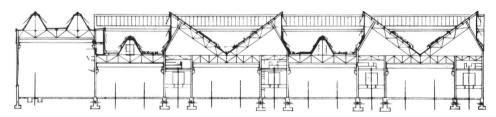

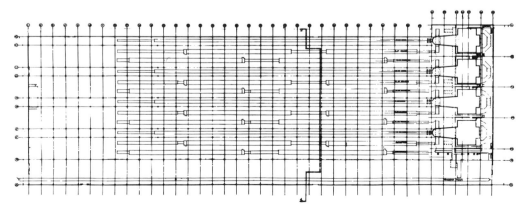

Creative in Concrete

Le Corbusier recorded the following incident from the Paris Ecole des Beaux-Arts in 1909. The professor of structural design was sick, and his place had been taken by the chief Métro engineer who, when he announced he would be lecturing on the possibilities of reinforced concrete, was booed out of the room by outraged students. Clearly, for these young architects, concrete was a material which might be used for tunnels, dams or factories – but not for serious, artistic works.

Although the Englishman J. B. White had built a house completely out of concrete in as early as 1837, and the French businessman François Coignet had patented the insertion of "tension rods" in cement in 1856, the history of reinforced concrete only truly began with an invention by gardener Joseph Monier. He was looking for a frost-resistant material for water pipes, and thereby discovered the advantages of ferroconcrete. Combining liquid cement with iron produces an intimate compound with an organic character. The cement surrounds its iron bones just as muscles surround a skeleton. Monier did not appreciate the importance of the correct positioning of the iron cores and hence the distribution of tensile and compressive forces within the concrete. His 1867 patent for concrete flower pots, and his subsequent later additional patent of 1878 – the "Monier Patent" which he registered in a whole series of countries – nevertheless brought him profitable trade, since they covered almost every use of iron in mortar and concrete. This led among other things to a lengthy legal battle with Berlin master mason Rabitz, who had patented his own metal mesh inserts for plaster surfaces. Monier himself pursued increasingly eccentric ideas, even considering the possibility of ferroconcrete coffins.

His invention was made public through exhibition architecture such as that built in Trier in 1884, where businessman Conrad Freytag first saw the system. He acquired utilization rights for Southern Germany, while Gustav Adolf Wayss assumed the patent rights for Northern Germany. As a form of safeguard, Wayss performed extensive load tests on Monier vaults under scientific conditions and published the results in 1887 in a work entitled "The Monier System and its Application to the Construction Industry as a Whole". This "Monier Brochure" was widely published and encouraged hesitant construction authorities to approve its structures. In 1900, however, in the "Handbook of Architecture", it was noted that its expensive nature would continue to delay "its widespread use in civic building" for as long as "Portland cement gets no cheaper and the process is protected by patent".

Further development stagnated; it was not until Frenchman François Hennebique applied the principle to all the essential elements of architecture – to supports, beams and slabs – and combined these into a "monolithic construction", that decisive advances were possible. Hennebique saw the fireproof nature of the material as its main advantage, and therefore abandoned the previously exposed iron girders of the Monier construction system. Concrete protects corrosive iron and provides a "fireproof shell". Reinforced concrete further proved particularly suitable for use in

Walter Bauersfeld, Dyckerhoff & Widmann
Planetarium in Jena, 1924–1925
Cupola netting during construction
Dyckerhoff & Widmann AG Archives
The hemisphere of the Jena Planetarium achieved a span of 25 metres at a thickness of only six centimetres. The assembled net of iron rods was covered with a thin wire mesh, and concrete then gunned from outside into a movable mould in the interior.

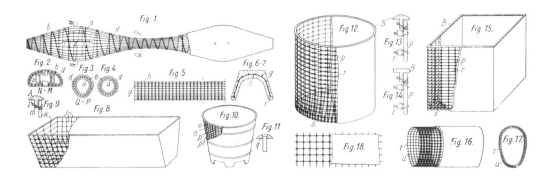

Joseph Monier
"Process for the Production of Objects
of Various Natures from a Combination of
Metal Ribs and Cement"
Drawing from his German patent specification of 1880
Although Monier did not fully understand the
functional principle of reinforced concrete,
and even in later applications failed to place
the iron rods within the tension zones as
structurally required, it was still necessary to
pay his licence fees when building reinforced-concrete structures.

Hildebrand and Günthel, Drenckhahn &
Sudhop
Roland Mills in Bremen, 1910
Foundation slab with reinforcing rods
From: Der Industriebau 8/1910

factories in which steel structures were insufficiently resistant to corrosive fumes. This
applied above all to the textile and chemical industries. In 1896 Hennebique produced
transportable prefabricated houses, made in one piece, for level-crossing watchmen.
By 1902 his successful company, together with its licencees, had planned over 7 000
commissions. An important factor in this success was undoubtedly Hennebique's
own flexibility: in executing house façades, for example, he would seek to incorporate
his clients' every imaginable wish. One result was that, in the early stages of many
ferroconcrete structures. the material was not visible at all.

The Dyckerhoff and Widmann company developed from owning a simple concrete
goods factory to becoming specialists for gasometer basins, water reservoirs and
ceiling vaults. These initially employed chiefly compressed concrete, as in Germany's
first concrete bridge, exhibited at the Düsseldorf Trade and Art Fair of 1880 The
use of concrete increased substantially after the turn of the century; in 1913 company
profits in the building sector increased from 4 to 31 million Marks, aided by such
important buildings as the Breslau Jahrhunderthalle. The form of its ribbed ferroconcrete dome, with its impressive 65-metre span, is nonetheless that of a supporting
steel framework. Its articulation into singular ribs produced significant moments of
bending in the trusses and rings and thus required strong cross-sections, with the
result that the weight of the overall building, despite its apparent lightness, was still

Harbour front of the silo building
From: Der Industriebau 8/1910
"Simply compare the neighbouring industrial buildings and warehouses in this photograph, with their battlements, towers and innumerable details, with the calm and impressive volumes of this work, standing with an almost defiant power as though it had grown out of the earth below, and directly stating its purpose – quite unlike the other buildings, which give absolutely no clues to their function."

The silo building was designed for the storage of a maximum 14,000 metric tons of grain in 24 cylinders. The fireproof advantages of reinforced concrete led to its choice as construction material.

Sections

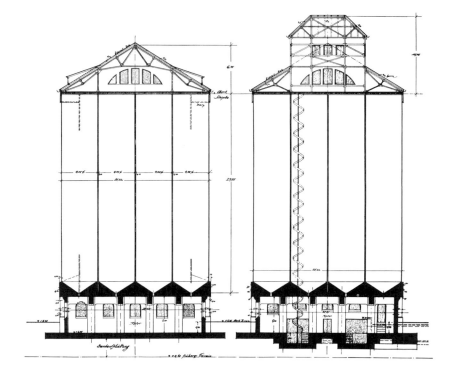

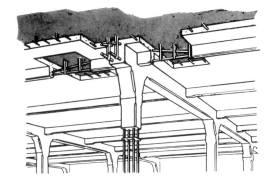

François Hennebique
Drawing of a Monolithic Concrete
Construction
Hennebique saw the advantages of reinforced concrete above all in the opportunity to combine supports, walls and ceilings into one unit which displayed greater stability than achieved with previously-known construction methods. France – unlike other European countries – refused to recognize the patent for composite construction which he submitted in 1892. This had no adverse effect on the success of his business which produced, among other things, transportable prefabricated houses for level-crossing watchmen.

Heinrich Zieger, Wayss & Freytag
Hall of an Enamel and Metal Goods
Factory in Ligetfalu, 1912
Interior view
Wayss & Freytag AG Archives
A large hall with a 30-metre span and a small hall with an 18-metre span, both 150 metres long, are bridged by a three-stayed arched roof truss. The aesthetic possibilities of concrete were illustrated here in the architectural unity of supports and ceiling joists.

Opposite page:
Auguste and Gustave Perret
Esders Ready-made Clothing Studio in
Paris, 1919
View inside the large hall
Bildarchiv Foto Marburg
The task of providing the tailors with the maximum amount of light was solved with the aid of a large glazed roof, whose joists rest on impressive concrete arches determining the spatial impression.

Max Berg
Jahrhunderthalle in Breslau, 1911–1913
Interior view
Bildarchiv Foto Marburg
This magnificent dome with its light-filled 65-metre diameter rests on four arches, below which are four apses. These can be closed off with heavy curtains during conventions, or opened during exhibitions to allow more light into the hall. 32 ribs merge like the arms of a star to form the cupola. The vertical windows stand in concentric circles.

Sections

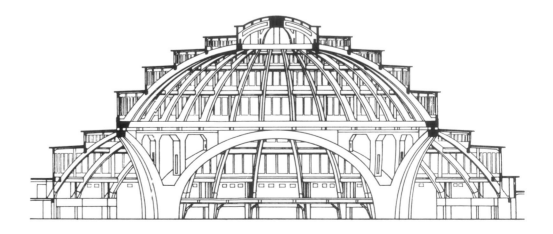

considerable. The exposed concrete surfaces indicate, however, an extraordinary mastery of mould techniques.

Architects such as Auguste Perret and, later, Erich Mendelsohn sought to exploit the advantages of concrete. In 1905 Perret, together with his brothers Gustave and Claude, even founded the company "Perret frères entrepreneurs" specializing in concrete construction. Their works succeeded in deploying the structural advantages of reinforced concrete in particularly economical buildings with sensible solutions to detail and balanced proportions. But it was left up to engineers such as Robert Maillart to find a way from traditional post and joist structures to practical new concrete forms. In 1912, for a grain store in Switzerland, he designed a joistless mushroom ceiling in which the supports converged in an organic, funnel-shaped curve into the flat ceiling. However, this only further heightened the difficulties of executing crucial details: were the transitions to the ceiling inadequately resolved, fine cracks could form which weakened the structure and enabled moisture to corrode the iron.

When building his first bridges, engineer Eugène Freyssinet discovered just how inaccurate structural formulae regarding concrete behaviour still were. Contrary to the estimations of the regulations on reinforced concrete construction published in France in 1906, the bridges when built displayed dangerous settling tendencies

Max Berg had insisted that the outside of the building should appear "just as it left its mould". He justified his choice of concrete thus: "After the experience of the Brussels exhibition, a thoroughly fireproof housing was demanded for the valuable objects loaned for historical exhibitions. Such a construction could only be made of reinforced concrete or of iron with a fireproof sheath. The first solution was chosen since it not only proved more economical from the point of view of tenders, but also because it allows for a more meaningful architectural and constructive design."

112150

Eugène Freyssinet
Airship Hangers in Orly, 1921–1923
Erecting the mould scaffolding
Roger-Viollet, Paris
17-metre-high concrete sections were first
completed on both sides, then the roof vault
connecting them was completed in segments
of 7.5 metres in width. Once one segment
was completed, the mould was lowered,
shifted along and re-erected.

Construction drawing
The hangars are 175 metres long, 91 metres
wide and 60 metres high. The front elevation
shows the inserted glazing; on the right can
be seen the cross-sections of a rib with a
width of 7.5 metres and a front rib with
mould.

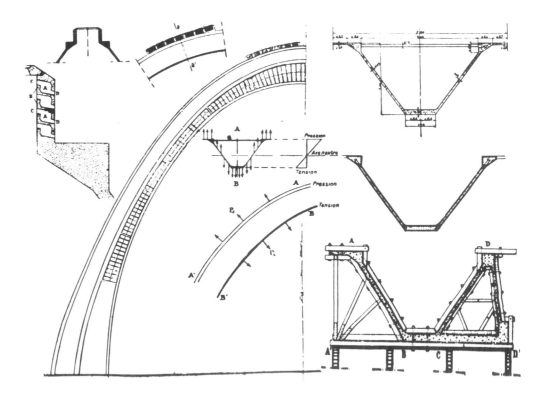

which had to be corrected in subsequent alterations. Numerous innovations can be traced back to developments introduced by Freyssinet: vaults with rib superstructures, sliding formwork and, above all, decisive steps towards the introduction of pre-stressed concrete, in which initial stress enables tension members to carry much higher loads and to counteract the slow deformation of concrete. The airship hangers in Orly were built as large parabolic folded-slab constructions, whereby Freyssinnet — as in the Paris Hall of Machines of 1889 — abolished the distinction between walls and ceiling. The principle is similar to that of corrugated iron or cardboard and enables extraordinary strengths to be achieved at low weight. The cross-section of the hangers corresponded to the central line of thrust of the dead loads, with the ribs broadening towards ground level. Function and form, like material quality and economic construction planning, were understood and executed as a uniform whole. While the first planetarium device, destined for the Deutsches Museum in Munich, was receiving its finishing touches at the Zeiss works in Jena in 1922, it was suggested that a dome suitable for projection trials should be built on the factory roof. The structure therefore had to be especially light, while still creating as exactly as possible a dome with a sixteen-metre diameter. Planetarium inventor Walter Bauersfeld had the idea of building the dome out of a mesh of thin iron rods, whose juxtaposition in combinations of numerous small triangles would approximate the shape of a dome. Franz Dischinger of the Dyckerhoff and Widmann company succeeded in designing a dome surface composed of almost 4,000 rods having only 51 different lengths. With the aid of the newly-developed shotcrete method, the assembled mesh netting became a concrete shell whose surface of 400 square metres had the

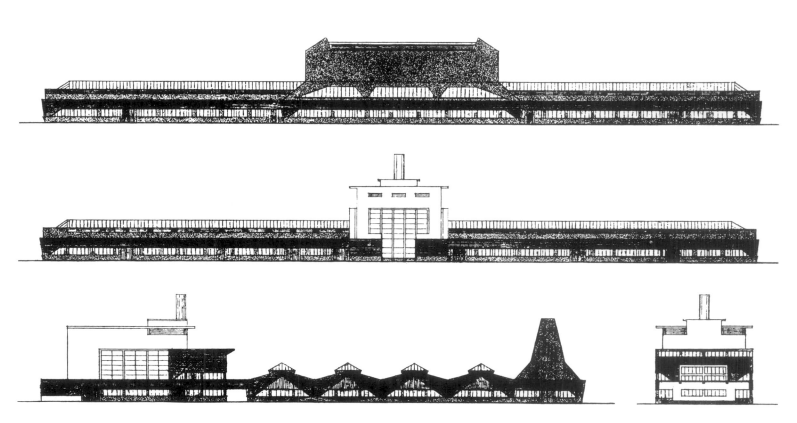

Erich Mendelsohn
Friedrich Steinberg Hat Factory, Herrmann
& Co. in Luckenwalde, 1921–1923
Opposite page: Dye works
Below: Interior view of the spinning mill
Österreichische Ludwig-Stiftung für Kunst und
Wissenschaft, Museum Moderner Kunst,
Vienna
Hats of both hair and wool were produced
in this factory complex in two parallel produc-
tion processes. The dye works and power
station served both work chains and hence
lay within the symmetrical axis of the plant.
In the dye works Mendelsohn tested a new
ventilation system, which extracted poison-
ous fumes via a shuttered shaft-like attachment. This "cap" made the dye works the
dominant feature of the inner courtyard.

Elevations of the factory complex
The striking dye works lies to the south of the
four-aisled factory hall, with the power plant
to the north. The halls and dye works were
sited in such as way that the longitudinal
axes could be extended without difficulty.

unbelievably low weight of three and a half metric tons. This same new method
seemed appropriate for a new glass-cutting plant which the Schott Works were
planning to build in Jena. Since the shape of the plant was not important, a round
structure was again chosen, albeit this time with an extremely flat shell dome. At a
diameter of forty metres and a rise of barely eight metres, the shell was only six
centimetres thick, which represented less than one-sixhundredth of its span. As in
the municipal planetarium built in Jena in 1925, the mesh netting was laid in a system
of parallel circles. The number of different rod lengths was greater than required by
the earlier trial dome, but since the rods were assembled from the outer edge it was
easier to build. This Zeiss-Dywidag construction method, as it came to be known,
opened up entirely new avenues in architectural design.

1912–1939

Erich Mendelsohn
"Einstein Tower", Observatory and Astrophysics Laboratory on the Telegrafenberg in Potsdam, 1920–1921
Sächsische Landesbibliothek, Dept. Deutsche Fotothek, Dresden
The building was commissioned by the Einstein Foundation for the purposes of spectroanalytical research, in particular to prove Einstein's theory of relativity, and went into operation in 1924. The coelostat in the cupola reflected rays from cosmic light sources vertically through the tower into the underground laboratory. Here they were deflected by a mirror angled at 45° and thereby guided to instruments for generation and comparative measurement of spectra.

Elevations and details

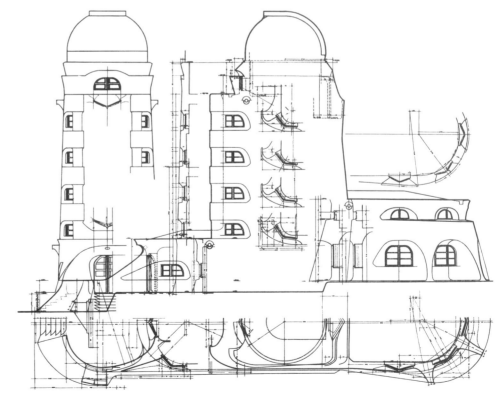

The Return of Art

The years between 1914 and 1920, the years of the First World War and the political confusion and radical changes that followed, were bitter ones for many German architects. "My drawing-board here in the office sits empty, every day the same nothing. . . I'm hanging about as an 'imaginary architect'", wrote Bruno Taut in 1919 in a letter to Karl Ernst Osthaus. During the War, that "epidemic of derangement", he built a fictitious, better world for a future society in visionary designs and rapturous Utopias. His "Stadtkrone" of around 1916 were drawings of fantastically tiered city crowns; these were followed by a series of sketches of "Alpine Architektur", hymnically crystalline objects to wreath alpine peaks. "Crystals in eternal ice and snow — covered and adorned. . . with areas and blocks of coloured glass — mountain blooms." Taut offered a practical illustration of such crystalline form in the Glass Pavilion which he built for the 1914 Werkbund Exhibition in Cologne.

Loose groups and organizations were one means by which artists, writers and architects attempted to overcome their isolation. Taut himself sought comrades-in-arms who shared his belief in an artistic architecture with the highest ideals and who strove for freedom from material obligations and purposive rationalism. In 1918 he was among the founders of both the Arbeitsrat für Kunst, an "art soviet" seeking a politico-cultural voice, and the Novembergruppe, a small group of progressive artists. In 1919, together with like-minded artists and architects, he organized the Gläserne Kette (Glass Chain), a circle whose members communicated with one another in so-called chain letters signed under pseudonyms. Thus Bruno Taut was "Glas", Hermann Finsterlin "Prometheus", the brothers Hans and Wassili Luckhardt "Angkor" and "Zacken", and Walter Gropius "Maß". Their common goal was to overcome ossified academic architecture with fundamentally new forms taken from animate and inanimate nature. A forum for these ideas was also provided by Taut's journal "Frühlicht", which also published Mies van der Rohe's first design for a glass skyscraper. They were "tired of the dry tone" and the "respectable form", as Adolf Behne noted in his book "Wiederkehr der Kunst" (The Return of Art), written during the war.

The spectrum of published visions ranged from Paul Scheerbart's rhymes — "ohne einen Glaspalast ist das Leben eine Last" (Life is a burden without a glass palace) — to the "biomorphic fantasies" of Hermann Finsterlin, who wrote in 1921: "Inside the New House we will not only feel ourselves the inhabitants of a fairy-tale crystal cluster, but also the internal occupants of an organism, wandering from organ to organ, a giving and receiving symbiosis of a 'fossile giant womb'. A small fragment of the translatory multi-clause sentence of the world's forms lies in the sequence of city, house, furniture and vessel: one grows out of the other, like the gonads of an organism. . . As 'outside', soft hollows will sink themselves around the rest-seeking body, but the foot will wander across glass-transparent floors, allowing the antipodean bas-relief to be fully experienced, pushing into the illusionary the necessary but

Johan M. van der Mey, Michel de Klerk,
Pieter L. Kramer
"Scheepvaarthuis" Shipping Office in
Amsterdam, 1912–1916
Left: Part of the façade
Opposite page: Stairwell with glasswork by
W. Bogtman.
Below: Wrought-iron ceiling lights by
H.J. Winkelman
Photos Klaus Frahm

A brick façade with rich plastic decoration was placed in front of the reinforced-concrete building. Since the building was used by six shipping companies, the themes of the appliqué strips, reliefs and sculptures are ships, sea and trade. These analogies are continued in many details in the interior. The artistically-designed light fittings on the stairwell ceiling display a wealth of nautical motifs, with lamps suggesting the gaping mouths of predatory fish and recalling exotic creatures of the deep in their bizarrely-serrated contours.

terrible horizontal which, were it solid and dense, would cut though the new space and building like a pathological membrane. Through the transparent flooring, however, an omni-dimensional sense of space is diffused, maintaining the occupant in an unsuspected equilibrium. . . Thus the house could become an experience, a living marsupial mother who lovingly nurtures and forms us like the fluid sack of a baby gall-fly, a grail which fills itself daily anew with the forces of our pulsating earth, and not a coffin for cloth dummies set – and cut – to size four in a Procrustean bed, transplanted, foreign creatures whose accusations we have hourly to absorb." Finsterlin illustrated his concepts of such organic housing in sensual, colourful sketches, solutions which were naturally never built.

Erich Mendelsohn's career also began with drawings of architectural fantasies – "data, contour specifications of a sudden face", as he called them in a letter. A series of these sketches was exhibited in 1919 in Paul Cassirer's famous Berlin gallery under the title "Architecture in Iron and Concrete". The first drafts for the Einstein Tower in Potsdam were shown here; it was to make him famous just a few years later. Although the internal organization of this laboratory complex was largely

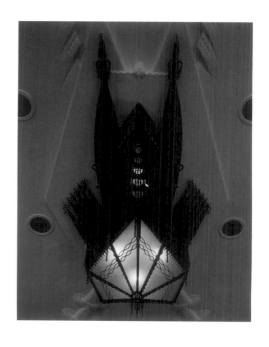

Michel de Klerk
Apartment Block on the Sparndammerplatsoen in Amsterdam, 1913–1914
From: Nieuwe-Nederlandsche Bouwkunst I,
1924

determined by scientific requirements, Mendelsohn had full freedom in its architectonic design, something of which he took full advantage. The extraordinarily dynamic
outline of the bodies and surfaces Mendelsohn called "the logical motive expression
of the powers inherent in the building materials iron and concrete". The tower is
actually a simple brick building, but covered with a thick cement stucco to make it
look as if it was cast purely of concrete. After a series of attempts it had simply
proved too difficult and too expensive to build the formwork required by its irregu-
larly-curved forms.

Compared to the modelled surfaces of Mendelsohn's earlier designs, Otto Bartning's
buildings and designs from the same period seem ceremonial and controlled. The
dominant forms in his architecture are crystalline fractures and angular folds. The
plan of probably the most beautiful of his executed rooms, the Music Room in the
Wylerberg House near Kleve, shows the complicated – but not agitated – figurations
which he was capable of creating. The construction is irregularly polygonal and at
the same time stabilized by a strong axial symmetry towards the extreme tip of the
bay.

Michel de Klerk
"Het Scheep" Housing Complex in Amsterdam, 1917–1921
End building with Post Office
From: Nieuwe-Nederlandsche Bouwkunst I, 1924
Because this wedge-shaped block sliced into the neighbourhood like the hull of a ship, the occupants nicknamed it "Het Scheep" – The Ship. The housing complex, which lies between the Zaanstraat, the Oostzaanstraat and the Hembrugstraat near the Sparndammerplatsoen, was commissioned by the house-building company "Eigen Haard"("Own Stove").

Post Office hall with telephone booth
Photo Klaus Frahm

Michel de Klerk
"Het Scheep" Housing Complex in
Amsterdam, 1917–1921
Chimneys over the roofscape; entrance
with projecting overhead bay.
Photos Klaus Frahm

"Stern" of the "Het Scheep" housing
complex
Bildarchiv Foto Marburg
The obelisque-like tower was originally intended to be crowned by a rooster, then the
symbol of Dutch Social Democracy.

Plan of the complex

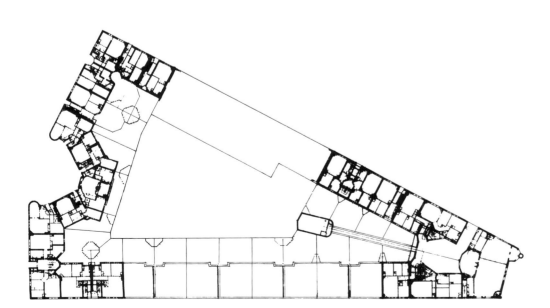

Fritz Höger
Chile House in Hamburg, 1922–1924
View of the huge shipping office complex
from the south-west
Bildarchiv Foto Marburg
The name of this shipping office was inspired
by the man who built it, Henry Brarens Slo-
man, who made his fortune trading saltpetre
with Chile.

Plan

Opposite page:
The "sharp" eastern tip
Kunstbibliothek, Staatliche Museen
Preußischer Kulturbesitz, Berlin

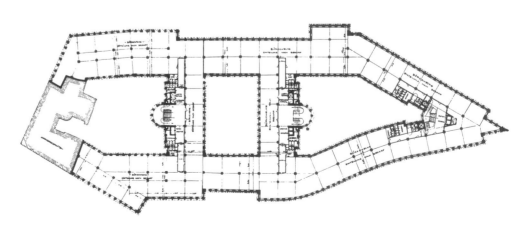

126

Hugo Häring
Cow Shed on the Garkau Farm Estate near
Lübeck, 1924–1925
Burkhard Verlag Ernst Heyer Archives
The supports for the steel construction lie inside the building. Parts of the horizontal
frame appear as bright strips in the brickwork. Originally left natural, the vertical
weather boarding on the hay lofts and silo
were subsequently painted green in the late
1930s.

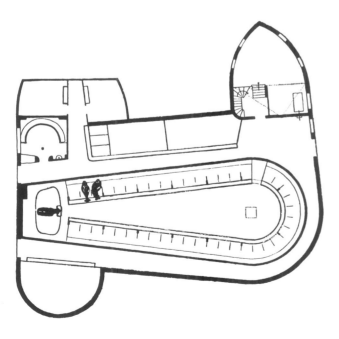

Plan sketch
The heart of the "organ-like" stall is the pear-
shaped byre for one bull and 41 dairy cows.

Otto Bartning
Water Tower of the Roof-tile and Lignite
Works in Zeipau, Silesia, 1923
Österreichische Ludwig-Stiftung für Kunst und
Wissenschaft, Museum Moderner Kunst,
Vienna

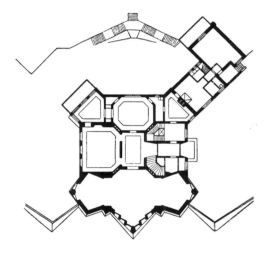

Otto Bartning
Wylerberg House near Kleve, 1921–1924
Photo Theo Schafgans / Österreichische Ludwig-Stiftung für Kunst und Wissenschaft,
Museum Moderner Kunst, Vienna
The rooms of this house are angled and
folded like the roof and façade. The bedrooms are pentagonal, the library heptago-
nal and the dining room octagonal. The
most complex room is the polygonal music
room with its multiple fractures. Even the windows in the pointed bay turn away from the
wall plane and stand angled in their soffits.

Plan of the ground floor

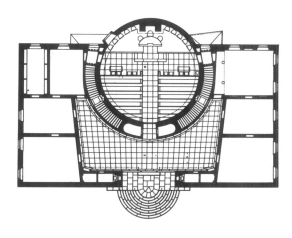

Gunnar Asplund
"Listers Härads Tingshus", County Court in
Sölvesborg, 1917–1921
Plan of the ground floor
The lobby and court room are laid out strictly
symmetrical to the axis running between the
entrance and the magistrate's chair. The
round chamber is encircled by stairs; the
floor tiles in the lobby are perspectively cut.

Main façade with flat gable and glazed
entrance portal at the end of an avenue
Photo Klaus Frahm

Hugo Häring countered such artistic-formalistic solutions with his theory and practice
of "organ-like building". He demonstrated this concept in a cow stall for the Garkau
farm estate in Schleswig Holstein. The cattle stand not in the usual long rows next
to each other, but around a pear-shaped feed table. The hay loft lies above the
stall, so that food can be delivered directly to the feed table through a ceiling hatch.
The ceiling pitches inward for optimal ventilation. Rising warm air is thus channelled
towards the outer wall and released through a slit between the ceiling and walls.
The high windows cannot be opened and serve only to let in light. According to
Häring, the goal was "to find the form which most simply and directly served the
functional efficiency of the building", a form which in each case needed to be

Side entrance to the court room
Photo Klaus Frahm
Many of the wood fittings are painted ir a
soft matt grey and pleasantly rounded, like
the grandfather clock which Asplund designed specially for this court-house.

Court room
Photo Klaus Frahm
The plaid wall hangings and the chairs for
judge and assessors were altered during
general renovations and hence no longer
represent the original models.

"discovered". "Organ-like building has nothing at all to do with the imitation of organs of the natural world. The fundamental demand we make from an organic viewpoint is that the shape of things should no longer be determined from without, but that it must be sought within the essence of the object." Häring thus identified the essence of architecture as a developmental process leading to the goal of "efficient form". The fact that the cow stall does not employ a strictly utilitarian form based solely on agricultural operating procedures can nevertheless be seen in a number of formal details, such as the pointed semicircle of the silo porch, in the shape of a heart, quite apart from considerations of cost-efficiency when compared to conventional stabling. These buildings are thus often more a criticism of conventions in building form than logical, mature architectural solutions. Although traditional elements are adopted, they are set in motion via expressive structures reaching beyond the building itself.

There was expressive building in other European countries during these same years, although with greater reference to traditional local styles and with fewer idealistic trimmings. Particularly in the Netherlands, which had remained neutral during the

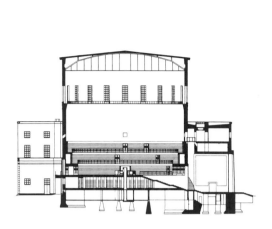
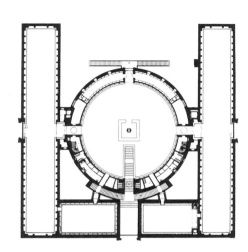

Main façade
Photo Klaus Frahm

Section and plan of the first floor

Erich Mendelsohn
Schocken Department Store in Stuttgart,
1926–1928
Landesbildstelle Württemberg, Stuttgart
The complex is grouped on an asymmetrical
plan around an inner courtyard. The fronts of
the façades – whose varying heights reflect
local building regulations – run to two contra-
puntal stair towers which absorb and pass
on movement like points of inflection. This
photograph shows the fully-glazed main stair
tower.

First World War, social-democratic building policies provided challenging opportunities for young architects in the form of municipal commissions. House-building
associations, too, were awarding contracts for large-scale housing estates. Many
of these contracts went to architects such as Melchior van der Mey, Pieter L. Kramer
and Michel de Klerk, members of the Amsterdam School, which had created a
powerful organ in its "Wendingen" magazine. Their façades are probably the most
impressive aspect of their buildings – suggestive, imaginative creations of ornamental
brickwork with vital plasticity.

In his buildings, with their initially conventional appearance, Swedish architect Gunnar
Asplund developed a symbolic repertoire of details which he employed to very
deliberate effect. He thereby entirely omitted the usual ornaments, cornices and
emphases. The front façade of his Lister District Court is an entertaining composition
of more or less clearly encoded elements, which thematically illustrate both the
principle of the façade and the function of the building. The course of the earth with
sun and moon appears in the large, bright round of the entrance and the dark clock
in the pediment, while the entrance steps appear as if folded down from the matching
opening in the façade. A light wave motif creates an optimistic mood, and only a
few serious details recall the extravagance of those classical appendages usually
attached to law-courts.

Opposite page: Design sketches
Kunstbibliothek, Staatliche Museen
Preußischer Kulturbesitz, Berlin

Volumetric Experiments

In Weimar the State Bauhaus was created in 1919 under the directorship of Walter Gropius from the Grand-Ducal Saxon School of Arts and Crafts founded by Henry van de Velde in 1906 and the Grand-Ducal Saxon Academy of Fine Arts. Its early years were still clearly influenced by the impassioned introspection of post-war Expressionism, as could be read in the first manifesto of 1919: "Let us therefore create a new guild of craftsmen without the class divisions that raise an arrogant barrier between craftsman and artist! Let us together desire, conceive and create the new building of the future, which will combine everything in a single form: architecture, sculpture and painting. . . a crystalline symbol of a new and coming faith."

After only a few years, however, signs of a polarization emerged at the Bauhaus which was viewed and described inside the school as a conflict between Itten and Gropius. Itten was thereby equated with "Indian cult, Wandervogel movement, vegetarianism", and Gropius with "Americanism, progress, the wonder of technology and invention". The Bauhaus production principles of 1925 revealed no further trace of the mysticism of the Gothic stonemason's lodge. Gropius spoke instead of future crafts determined equally by technology and form and acting as a "medium of experimental work for industrial production". "The Bauhaus wishes to contribute to the development – appropriate to the times – of housing, from the simplest appliance to the finished dwelling. Convinced that house and furnishings must relate to each other rationally, the Bauhaus seeks – by means of systematic theoretical and practical research into formal, technical and economic fields – to derive the form of an object from its natural functions and limitations. . . The nature of an object is determined by what it does. Before a container, a chair or a house can function properly its nature must be studied. . . Such research into the nature of objects leads to the result that forms emerge from a determined consideration of all the modern methods of production and construction and of modern materials, forms which diverge from existing models and often seem unfamiliar and surprising."

With the removal of the Bauhaus to the City of Dessau, Walter Gropius – or rather his private architectural practice – was given the opportunity to tailor a brand new building for the institute. In fitting with Gropius' analytical standards, the entire complex was organized according to function. There was a workshop wing, an accommodation and studio block for Bauhaus students and a teaching wing for the Dessau Technical College, which was also to be housed in the Bauhaus complex by wish of the city magistrate. These three main sections, clearly differentiated in their external appearances, volumes and heights, Gropius linked via a raised administrative section and a lower connecting wing with auditorium, theatre and canteen to create a balanced, rectangular structure. The most spectacular element of the complex was the central workshop wing, clearly visible from afar. A delicate skin of glass held in a regular grid of slender black steel bars covered three sides of its

Walter Gropius
Bauhaus Building in Dessau, 1925–1926
Workshop wing and driveway
Bildarchiv Foto Marburg

Willem Marinus Dudok
Dr. Bavinck School in Hilversum, 1921
Nederlands Architectuurinstituut,
Amsterdam

The front two rows of windows belong to the corridors leading to the classrooms. The gymnasium connects at a right angle on the left, with the tower-like corner architecture containing the stairwell. The right wing contains rooms for teachers and teaching materials and the library. The angular volumes, rhythmic smooth surfaces and the emphasis upon horizontals and verticals recall works by De Stijl architects. But Dudok was not a member of this group and was also less dogmatic in the wide range of building commissions which he executed, chiefly for the City of Hilversum. He built symmetrical façades, arches and softly-rounded thatched roofs all with the same disciplined surety.

Plan of the upper storey

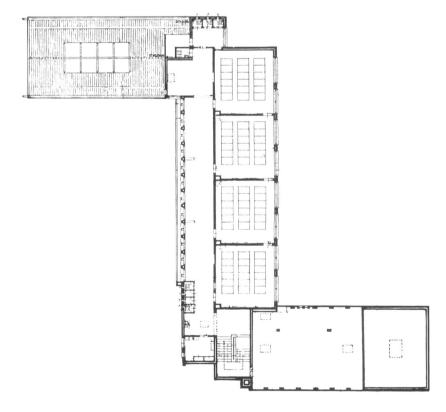

reinforced-concrete frame. Its large prismatic body thus assumed a light, crystalline transparency. In addition to the new Bauhaus building, Gropius also built a Director's House and three semi-detached houses for the Bauhaus Masters; these were conceived as models of a new lifestyle in keeping with the machine age. They were based on the modular system of a "large-scale set of building blocks: houses which are composed of combinations of variable prefabricated off-the-shelf pieces." Although the goals of standardization and the industrialization of construction were not achieved in Dessau – the houses were in fact built in entirely conventional manner –, the formal handling of volumes nevertheless convincingly demonstrates the aesthetic presence that can be achieved in the reduction to a few basic cubic forms.

In Holland in 1917 the De Stijl group formed with the aim of creating a style valid for the "new consciousness of the age", which would replace the "individual" with the "universal". In painting this meant the rigorous rejection of all representational reference, including the Cubist and Purist. Nature was too material, too individual. "Universal" art allowed only for abstract composition, as an "equilibrium of position and weight of colour". The pictures by Piet Mondrian, the most important painter in the group, were reduced to straight black lines in rectangular arrangements, in conjunction with the primary colours of red, blue and yellow, supported by much white and some grey.

The architects of De Stijl were concerned with the calculated distribution of unequal masses in an anti-cubist system which exploded the closed contours of volumetric

Willem Marinus Dudok
Municipal Baths in Hilversum, 1920
Nederlands Architectuurinstituut, Amsterdam
Rising through the central façade axis, the chimney of the heating system marks the division between the women's and men's baths.

bodies. In 1918 Jacobus Johannes Pieter Oud, then city architect in Rotterdam and a founder of De Stijl, described the role played by Frank Lloyd Wright and his ideas on the "destruction of the box": "Wright created the bases for a new plasticity in architecture. Masses shoot in all directions – forwards, backwards, to the right, to the left. . . In this way, modern architecture will increasingly develop into a process of reduction to positive proportions, comparable to modern painting."

One of the few buildings to consistently adhere to these maxims is the Schröder House built in Utrecht by Gerrit Rietveld, who joined the group in 1918. The basic form is cuboid, but is "de-composed" by horizontal projections and vertical wall slabs, parapet panels and supports. The right angle which Mondrian elevated to the level of dogma governs even the details: windows opening outward can thus only be secured in one position, namely exactly 90 degrees to the façade. The colour scheme is that of Mondrian: all linear elements are red, blue or yellow, while surfaces are white or grey.

The large popularity which De Stijl achieved within just a few years was due above all to the painter and architect Theo van Doesburg, spiritus rector, organizer and driving force behind the group. He ran its magazine, organized exhibitions and travelled through Europe with his programme of lectures. It was his initiative, for example, which led in 1923 to an important exhibition in Leonce Rosenberg's avant-garde gallery "L'Effort Moderne" in Paris where, in addition to De Stijl projects, works by Mies van der Rohe could also be seen. Contacts with the Soviet Russian avant-garde were strengthened that same year when artist-architect El Lissitzky (who saw himself as an "artist-engineer") joined the group. Van Doesburg's attempt, in 1922, to cleanse the Weimar Bauhaus of its "Expressionist degeneration" through a full-scale "siege" failed miserably, however.

Adolf Loos' primary concern lay not with abstract, formalist principles – he rejected drawing-board experiments – but with human proportions and requirements, around which he sought to develop space. He designed room sequences not along the usual horizontal plane, but instead organized his plan on different levels. He found the rigid convention of regular storeys too narrow a strait-jacket; varying floor heights were subsequently among the most significant results of his thoughts on the "Raum-plan" (volumetric plan). He "solved the plan in space", as he himself put it. Low, private niches thereby correspond via "neutral" intermediate levels to an open hall. The access to the living quarters is often very complicated and not always successful.

Jacobus Johannes Pieter Oud
Café "De Unie" in Rotterdam, 1924–1925
Façade design
Nederlands Architectuurinstituut, Amsterdam

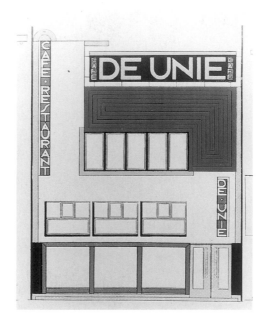

Opposite page: Street view
A. Oud-Dinaux Archives
The façade – all that Oud actually designed, and squeezed between two solid blocks of historicist architecture – proved the provocation it was supposed to be. Conformity to its neighbours was not planned. "It seemed best to view the café as an autonomous body and to try to establish the validity of both the café and its surroundings through logical contrasts. We have been taught – and not by the Ultramoderns, either – that only that which develops organically from the essence of the epoch can coexist with that which has arisen from the essence of another age." (J.J.P. Oud)

141

Gerrit Th. Rietveld
House of Interior Designer Truus Schröder-
Schräder in Utrecht, 1924
View from the south-west
Photo Frank den Oudsten

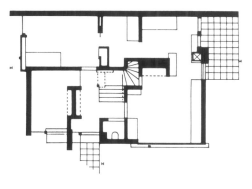

Plans of the ground and first floors
The upper floor can be divided into single
rooms by means of sliding walls.

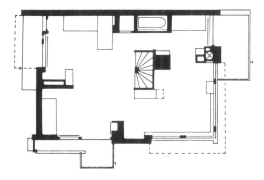 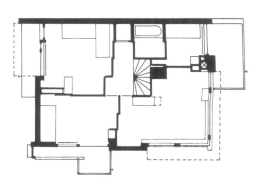

142

Living and dining area on the first floor with
furniture by Rietveld
Photo Frank den Oudsten

View from the south-east
Photo Frank den Oudsten

Konstantin Melnikov
Soviet Pavilion at the "Exposition
Internationale des Arts Décoratifs et
Industriels Modernes" in Paris, 1925
Overall view
Musée des Arts Décoratifs, Paris

Before reaching the so-called "small hall" in the Moller House, for example, the visitor will have gone round in at least one full circle, during which time he may have got rid of his hat and coat but will not have seen much more than the narrow vestibule behind the front door and the closed walls of the staircase. For it is necessary to pass the service flat, domestic quarters and garages before gradually approaching the centre of the house. The strict cube-symmetrical enclosures with which Loos clad his houses led, understandably if not inevitably, to a contradiction between interior and exterior. In his few completed houses, however, he pointed out the restrictions still affecting the designs of his contemporaries.

Opposite page: Stair passage
Musée des Arts Décoratifs, Paris
This glazed wooden skeleton structure in the
Constructivist tradition of Vladimir Tatlin was
one of the most progressive buildings of the
exhibition. A staircase cut diagonally through
the building, rectangular in plan. The lettering and tower scaffolding corresponded to
agitprop architecture.

144

Walter Gropius
Bauhaus Building in Dessau, 1925–1926
Busch-Reisinger Museum, Harvard University,
Cambridge, Massachusetts

On the right, behind the curtain wall, lie the
"laboratory workshops" of the Bauhaus
classrooms, and on the left the wing containing the City of Dessau "Technical College".
The raised section above the road housed
the administration offices and Walter Gropius' private architecture practice.

Stairwell in the workshop wing
Photo Klaus Frahm

View from the south-east
Bauhaus-Archiv, Berlin
On the right the student accommodation
block with 28 studio flats, baths and a gymnasium; in the flat section leading to the
workshop wing lay the canteen, auditorium
and theatre. These could be opened up to
form one continuous "party level".

Plan of the first floor

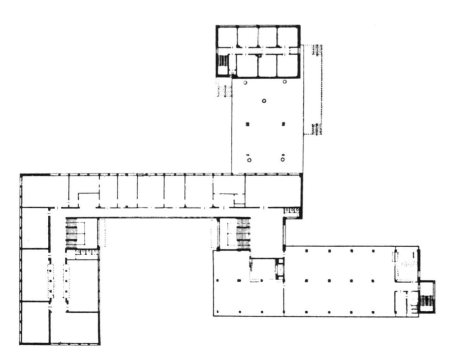

Walter Gropius
Director's House in Dessau, 1925–1926
South front
Photo Lucia Moholy / private collection

Walter Gropius
Semi-detached Master's House for László
Moholy-Nagy in Dessau, 1925–1926
East front
Busch-Reisinger Museum, Harvard University,
Cambridge, Massachusetts
Gropius designed three generously-sized
semi-detached houses for Bauhaus Masters
Paul Klee and Wassily Kandinsky, Georg
Muche and Oskar Schlemmer, Lyonel Fei-
ninger and László Moholy-Nagy.

Ludwig Mies van der Rohe
Villa for Silk Manufacturer Hermann Lange
in Krefeld, 1928
Garden front
Photo Christoph Bürkle

This widely-spaced cubic body, with its smooth, clearly-structured façade and materials of red brick, white-painted concrete, glass and black metal, recalls the brick country house which Mies designed in 1923. The present floor plan, however, falls far short of the progressive standards set by the country-house project. There, under the influence of De Stijl, Mies had conceived the interior as a continuum with inserted wall panels and angles. The inner organization of the Villa Lange is conventional in comparison: a bourgeois spatial programme of dining room, lounge, women's and men's rooms is arranged around a central living area. The doors and windows, however, are related in such a way that long visual axes are created through the suites of rooms and out to the landscape garden. Since the 1950s the house has been a museum and art gallery.

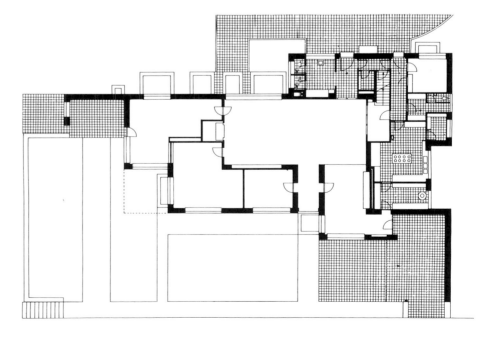

Plan of the ground floor

Adolf Loos
House for Tristan Tzara in Montmartre,
Paris, 1925–1926
Street front
Loos-Archiv, Albertina, Vienna
The symmetrical street front curves slightly inwards. Both the base, which extends through
two storeys, and the retaining wall, which is
needed to stay the sloping site, employ
visible ashlar masonry, while the wall above
is smoothly stuccoed. The entrance – the
right-hand of the two doors; the one on the
left leads to the garage – opens only onto a
small hall. From here, a straight flight of narrow, ravine-like steps leads past a lodger's
flat to the studio apartment of the owner himself.
The Romanian writer and Dadaist Tristan
Tzara, a "master of the art of living and lan-
guages with a fiery vitality and aggression"
was at that time, together with André Breton,
head of the Paris avant-garde which in turn
lead the field in literature and art in Europe.
The Tzara House introduced Adolf Loos, too,
into this circle, but did not in the end lead to
the further commissions he had probably
hoped for. Although consulted for advice,
and even requested for designs – as by the
American Joséphine Baker, for example,
who enjoyed great success in the mid-1920s
with her "Révue Nègre" on the Champs Ely-
sées –, when it came to actual building, Loos
found himself passed over in favour of
French colleagues.

Section
In introducing split levels within individual
floors and offsetting rooms one against the
other, Adolf Loos demonstrated his concept
of "solving the plan in space".

Adolf Loos
Villa for Hans and Anny Moller, Vienna
1927–1928
Street front
Loos-Archiv, Albertina, Vienna

Raised seating area in the bay window overlooking the street
Photo Christoph Bürkle

Jacobus Johannes Pieter Oud
Spangen Estate, Rotterdam, 1919
Rear view of Block 8
A. Oud-Dinaux Archives

Housing Estates

The First World War saw a drastic worsening of the housing crisis already affecting the metropolises of Central Europe. Urban development and house building had practically come to a standstill, while many new families were begun after the War. Even more people had to be crammed into the soulless tenements of the pre-war period and in the – already overcrowded – older city districts, with their catastrophic hygiene conditions. Massive migration to cities and industrial centres sent property prices through the roof, and the lack of state and municipal control mechanisms opened the door to speculative land development.

The loss of its hinterland left "Red Vienna" in particular financial straits. To strengthen the position of social democracy and earn the loyalty of the electorate, however, every possible effort was devoted towards a successful municipal building policy. 64,000 apartments were built in the ten years between 1923 and 1933, albeit – with very few exceptions – in densely-crowded apartment houses connected via a succession of inner courtyards. Three-quarters of these apartments had a total surface area of less than 40 square metres. In Amsterdam in 1914 F. M. Wibaut, a member of the Social Democratic Workers' Party, became city councillor for public housing, and was able to substantially increase the scope of urban building. In the twenties, the "Schoonheidscommissie" – a committee which assessed the artistic value of buildings on city property – was largely composed of young architects from the Amsterdam School, whose offices subsequently benefitted from large commissions and who in turn brought new design ideas to housing. Their influence was, however, broadly restricted to façades; the new formulation of ground plans was resisted through lack of interest, by the building contractors. In Rotterdam J.J.P. Oud became city architect in 1918. Although a member of the De Stijl group at the time, the housing he completed was extensively free of the De Stijl influence that might have been expected. His rejection of Theo van Doesburg's proposed colour schemes for the Spangen Estate in Rotterdam even led to a rupture between the two friends. In his Hook of Holland projects and Kiefhoek Estate in Rotterdam Oud found solutions which, despite the cramped nature of their plans, displayed great clarity of overall design.

Bruno Taut went on to make masterly use of colour as a means of organization and spatial tension. He developed the bold Expressionist experimentation of his days as municipal architect in Magdeburg in the housing-estate projects of which, as architectural adviser to GEHAG (Gemeinnützige Heimstätten-, Spar- und Bauaktiengesellschaft) in Berlin, he was in charge. Berlin's municipal building surveyor was Martin Wagner, who had already called for the public running of housing affairs in a memorandum of 1917. And indeed, 1918 saw the broadening in Prussia of municipal competence for city planning.

As city planning advisor in Frankfurt, Ernst May – together with artistic director Martin Elsässer and a large, newly-acquired staff – was given extensive opportunity as

Jacobus Johannes Pieter Oud
Housing Complex in Hook of Holland,
1924–1927
A. Oud-Dinaux Archives
The flat, emphatically horizontal housing
rows found a dynamic conclusion in their
rounded end buildings, which were designed
for small shops selling daily necessities.

from 1924 to implement the concept of normative building. The declared aims of the large estates planned for the "New Frankfurt" was the "unification of maximum fulfilment of function with minimum form" and the rejection of superimposed artistic detail. Only through the conscious "alignment of uniform parts" was "existence-minimum" housing to acquire an aesthetic quality, through which Bruno Taut, too, believed it would contribute to the moulding of a "collective mentality". Such trains of thought, coupled with the sober final appearance of long rows of houses with flat roofs, naturally supplied conservative observers with plenty to criticize. The repeated appearance of structural defects – and in particular caused by damp – due to lack of experience with the new construction methods was triumphantly cited as proof of their misguided nature. The improvement of hygienic conditions was precisely one of the most important arguments for new building, with "Light and air for all" the battle-cry against tuberculosis. The logical consequence was the rejection of back-to-back block building around courtyards and its replacement by long lines of row housing in green areas, which allowed each apartment to receive an equal amount of sunlight.

Earlier far-sighted precautions had ensured that the land situation in Frankfurt was better than that in other comparable major cities. A second major obstacle on the path to healthy and cheap housing were building costs. Ernst May therefore attempted to industrialize building methods, having standardized elements such as wall panels manufactured in central works. Although this made it necessary to employ expensive

Dick Greiner
Community Centre in Watergraafsmeer
Garden City, Amsterdam, 1922–1926
Photo Klaus Frahm

W. Greve
Houses in Watergraafsmeer Garden City,
Amsterdam, 1923–1925
Photo Klaus Frahm
This estate, which later became known as
"Betondorp" (concrete village), was an experiment employing prefabricated concrete
elements on a large scale for the first time.
Old photographs showing the houses in their
original, unplastered condition clearly reveal,
however, that this meant not slab construction but concrete-block masonry. The name
"Betondorp" was probably sooner inspired
by the contrast between this and the more
familiar building materials being used in
other Amsterdam estates of the day.

Ernst May, H. Boehm, C.H. Rudloff
Höhenblick Estate, Frankfurt am Main,
1926–1927
End houses on the Kurhessenstraße
Österreichische Ludwig-Stiftung für Kunst und
Wissenschaft, Museum Moderner Kunst,
Vienna

The accentuated corner buildings with their small stores announce the entrance to the estate. The deceptively simple terrace façades hide comparatively lavish interiors: with five rooms, built-in "Frankfurt Kitchen", central heating and garden or roof-top terrace, the apartments were well above normal "New Frankfurt" standards. The wind screens on the front doors were highlighted in light blue, as part of a colour scheme which laquered the window frames in a variety of vibrant shades and which offset the darker corner architecture against the luminous lightness of the terraces.

cranes, the use of pre-fabricated parts reduced the lengthy drying time required by masonry walls. With the rapid rise in interest rates at the end of the twenties, however, the race for affordable housing was lost in Frankfurt, too. It had to be resignedly accepted that even an idealistic will to build and ingenious methods of rationalization could not beat inflation.

In addition to its enormous volume of newly-built living space, Frankfurt was distinguished by the care with which it carried design ideas into interior details such as fittings, handles and windows. Under the motto "First the kitchen – then the façade", the "Frankfurt Kitchen" designed by Grete Schütte-Lihotzky became a model of improved household organization. On a space of only 3.5 x 1.9 m it contained all the necessary household appliances. The possibility of educating tenants in the choice of more functional and appropriate furnishings found its echo in the "Frankfurter Register", a supplement to the magazine "Das Neue Frankfurt", which illustrated furniture, lamps, ovens and other "functional and functionally-beautiful" items alongside details of manufacturers and prices.

Large-scale exhibition projects were intended to overcome prejudices and at the

Bruno Taut, Martin Wagner
Britz Estate in Berlin, 1925–1927
View of the Liningstrasse, now the
Dörchläuchtingstrasse
Landesbildstelle Berlin
Red and blue façades gave greater spatial
tension to those parts of the estate built during the first construction phase. Particularly-
exposed walls, such as those of the corner
shops, were executed in robust visible clinker
masonry.

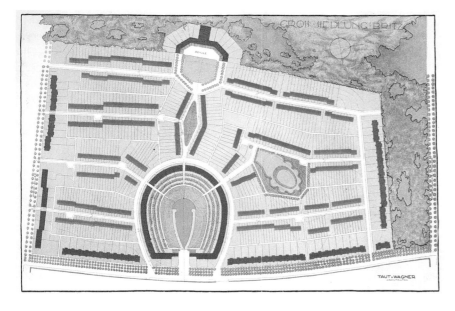

Second layout design of 1925/1926
Akademie der Künste, Sammlung Baukunst,
Berlin

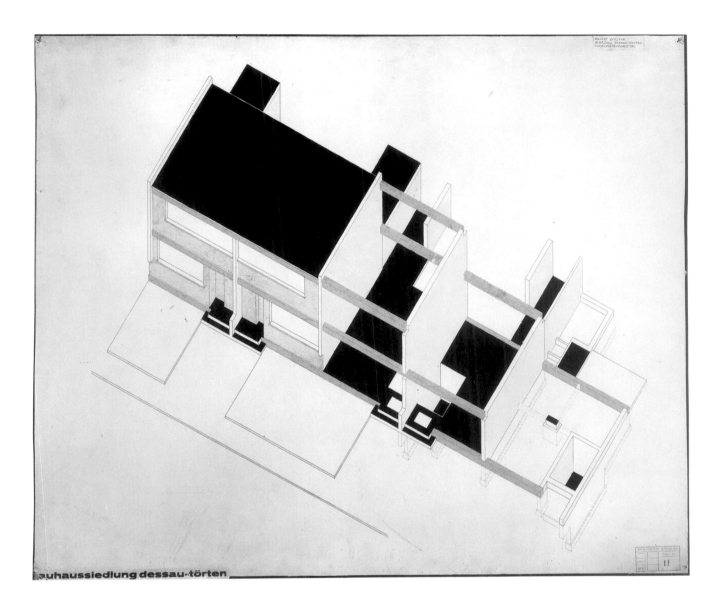

auhaussiedlung dessau-törten

Walter Gropius
Törten Estate, Dessau, 1926–1928
Axonometric projection
Busch-Reisinger Museum, Harvard
University, Cambridge, Massachusetts
The drawing reveals that only the fire walls
of slag concrete blocks have a load-bearing
function. The concrete ceiling joists, which
were cast on site, thereby lie parallel to the
façade. A report by the Imperial Research
Society for Cost-Efficiency in Building and
Housing Affairs censured this – and countless other – aspects of the design, since it
could potentially lead to uncalculated sub-
sidence. The same applied to the pumice-
stone, aerated and cellular concrete walls
employed as infills, whose behaviour was un-
reliable and which probably explained the
serious cracking which appeared only shortly
after completion.

Plan of the entire complex

same time widen housing vocabulary through the fertile confrontation of different design approaches. The Deutscher Werkbund initiated three important exhibitions. The first, entitled "Die Wohnung" (The Apartment), took place in Stuttgart in 1927, its Weißenhof Estate intended as an "experimental colony to determine the principles of modern serial construction". But in line with the beliefs of its artistic director, Ludwig Mies van der Rohe, the exhibition featured – alongside Mies van der Rohe's own apartment house and the row housing by J. J. P. Oud and Mart Stam – predominantly small, one-family houses. The planners of the 1929 Dammerstock Estate in Karlsruhe, Walter Gropius and Otto Haesler, employed rigidly schematic row housing. For Gropius, the "high-rise was not a necessary evil, but a healthy form of city living appropriate to our age. . . Only the multi-storey high-rise – with grassy areas for recreation and relaxation – can make life easier and more pleasant for its occupants via its central domestic facilities and communal rooms. . . Instead of in a sea of stone" the city dweller should live "in ten to twelve-storey houses with sufficient room for light, air, sun and quiet. Central facilities for heating and hot water, laundry, elevators, refrigerators, and central community kitchens diminish the work. Dining halls, club, sport, bathing, and entertainment rooms for adults, Kindergartens and day care centers for children – all create a pleasant living atmosphere." With its provisions for a "commune", the high-rise had the advantage of the promise of social Utopia over the five-storey apartment block whose economic advantages were purely mathematical. 1929 also saw the opening of the exhibition "Wohnung

View of a street showing the improved type of housing of 1928
Photo Musche/Bauhaus-Archiv, Berlin
Since the standardized plans took no account of the respective alignment of each house, interior lighting was not always optimal. The windows, which were hung on the upper crossbraces before the front was sealed, could only be opened partially, and then only outwards – a bizarre design feature which made them difficult to clean. In the improved type of 1928 they were replaced by pivoting windows which left a gap of ten centimetres, just enough to reach through and clean. The houses were impractical in other ways, too. The patented "Metroclo" earth closets, for example, which allowed faeces to be used as garden fertilizer, were only accessible via the small outhouse.

Wilhelm Riphahn
Kalkerfeld Estate in Cologne, 1927
Photo Werner Mantz / Rheinisches Bildarchiv,
Cologne

Opposite page:
Ernst May, H. Boehm and C.H. Rudloff
Römerstadt Estate, Frankfurt am Main,
1927–1928
View of the "Shoemaker's Block"
Historisches Museum Frankfurt am Main

Plan of two flats in the "Shoemaker's
Block"

Adolf Rading
Apartment block at the "Wohnung und
Werkraum" Werkbund Exhibition in
Breslau, 1929
Kunstbibliothek, Staatliche Museen
Preußischer Kulturbesitz, Berlin
Rading's "high-rise" was the most spectacular and controversial building of the
exhibition. Originally planned to be higher,
the abridged final version revealed proportional imbalances. Two symmetrical wings,
each containing four apartments per floor,
met at a stairwell lit via glass blocks. The
wide corridors were to promote community
life, a somewhat implausible justification for
wasted space.

und Werkraum" (Living and Work Space) in Breslau, although this featured no
self-contained estate complexes. Its – in part highly unusual – buildings remained
isolated experiments and were unable to supply new models.

The achievements of Swiss Werkbund members Max Ernst Haefeli, Werner M. Moser
and Emil Roth in the Neubühl Estate built in Zurich in 1930 were, on the other hand,
outstanding. The Estate illustrated "not attempts but results", "a not emerging but
so to speak consolidated modernity" as a co-operative housing model for the middle
classes. Already the Weißenhof Estate had effectively ended optimistic hopes for
functional housing for the broad masses. A wealthier breed of citizen moved into
the new housing type. The frugality of earlier functional solutions was replaced by
the idealized white city of the "1930 style".

At the centre of the Weißenhof Estate rises
the block of 24 apartments by Ludwig Mies
van der Rohe. This core of the Stuttgart exhibition, Mies van der Rohe planned in his
capacity as artistic director. Seventeen architects from Germany and abroad designed a
total of 21 individual buildings. Following the
curving Rathenaustraße from right to left are
the houses by Hans Scharoun, Josef Frank,
Max Taut, Richard Döcker, Hans Poelzig.
Ludwig Hilberseimer and Le Corbusier.

Overall plan of the complex

Le Corbusier and Pierre Jeanneret
Duplex for La Roche and Jeanneret-Raaf in
Auteuil, Paris, 1923
Living room of banker and art collector
Raoul La Roche
Photo Christoph Bürkle

Machines for Living In

In 1921, in other words two years after Gropius had founded the Bauhaus, four years after De Stijl had first appeared in the Netherlands and a whole seven years after the first sketches for his "Dom-ino" frame system, Le Corbusier employed a concept in an article in the magazine "L'Esprit Nouveau" which expressed nothing less than the re-invention of the house: the "machine for living in". "L'Esprit Nouveau" was a platform which he had created himself, and which he used, along with Amédée Ozenfant, to attack the – in France still dominant – traditions of the Ecole des Beaux-Arts, the "falsity, make-up and tricks of the courtesan" which it taught, and the "barren flourishes of its plans. . . the foliage, pilasters and crowns" in which it immersed itself. "We have acquired a taste for clean air and full sunlight. . . The house is a machine for living in, bathrooms, sun, hot and cold water, temperature which can be adjusted as required, food storage, hygiene, beauty in harmonious proportions. A chair is a machine for sitting in: Maple showed us the way. Basins are machines for washing in: Twyford invented them. With the exception of the lime-blossom or camomile teatime hour, modern life, the world of our activity, has created its own objects: clothing, the fountain pen, the razor blade, the typewriter, the telephone, wonderful office furniture. . . the 'Innovation' suitcase. . . the limousine, the ocean liner and the airplane."

Le Corbusier demonstrated in comprehensive sets of drawings how his passionate calls for a new contemporary architecture could be realized in practice. He firstly applied the industrial principle of factory buildings to a framework for individual design. In his Maison Dom-ino, a grid of supports and continuous load-bearing ceilings formed a skeleton which, with the insertion of as many walls as desired, enabled an endless variety of plans to be created within the same construction system. In 1920 he designed the Maison Citrohan, in which two load-bearing walls delimited the sides of a cuboid, opened in between by generous windows and entered via an outside staircase. In 1922 Le Corbusier published a design for a new city entitled "Une Ville contemporaine". The commercial centre comprised cruciform office towers grouped around an airport, and was surrounded by grassy shopping arcades, leisure facilities and slim apartment blocks. But with its long avenues and the rigid central symmetry of its visual axes, the overall plan remained almost baroque and the whole a Utopian fantasy. Le Corbusier built only single houses in the twenties, which only came together to form a estate in Pessac. After much dispute he succeeded at least in demonstrating his concept of Immeubles-Villas in the scale model of a housing unit shown at the Paris Exposition Internationale of 1925. He recommended visitors to picture the pavilion fifteen metres above the ground as part of a concentrated block system.

For Le Corbusier, the only conceivable basis for an architecture corresponding to the precise world of machines was geometry: prisms, cubes, cylinders, pyramids and spheres as "pure volumes". Concept and rhythm should obey equations just

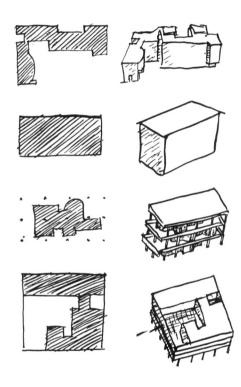

Le Corbusier
"Les quatres compositions", 1929
The top two sketches show the La Roche-Jeanneret duplex, an "artistically-animated" composition according to a note in the margin. The next two sketches show the "pure cube" of the Villa Stein in Garches, the third pair the "Dom-ino" system of the gridded reinforced-concrete skeleton in which plans can develop freely, and the bottom row the Villa Savoye in Poissy, a smooth prism raised on stilts with a rich interior life.

Le Corbusier and Pierre Jeanneret
"Pavillon de L'Esprit Nouveau" at the
"Exposition Internationale des Arts Décoratifs
et Industriels Modernes" in Paris, 1925
Interior view
Musée des Arts Décoratifs, Paris
This two-storey living space with sleeping gallery was furnished with the "casiers standard" container elements designed by Le Corbusier, Maple armchairs and Thonet chairs. The "Pavillon de L'Esprit Nouveau" was intended as the prototype for a "living unit" for villa apartment blocks. The exhibition organizers took it as an affront and hid it behind high boarding during the opening ceremony.

as in mathematics, while self-imposed "size regulators" should curb the arbitrariness which endangered the "beneficial effect of order". Although the unfamiliar new forms of his buildings and their experimental details at times defeated their builders, often leading to considerable structural defects, they proved that architecture which conforms to mathematical premisses can be more than mechanical stereometry. Examples here include the Maisons La Roche and Jeanneret-Raff in Auteuil, the Villa Stein in Garches and the Villa Savoye in Poissy. This is architecture as the "masterly, correct and magnificent play of masses brought together in light", as Le Corbusier stated in his "Three Reminders to Architects".

In 1927, in conjunction with his buildings for the Weissenhof Estate in Stuttgart, Le Corbusier formulated his "fundamentally new aesthetic", as he humbly called it, in a five-point programme whose essential elements were the pilotis, the roof garden, the free plan, the strip window and the free façade composition. Single posts took the place of walls: "These pilotis are placed at the same specific intervals, without taking into consideration the inner organization of the house. They rise directly from the ground. . . and elevate the ground floor. . . The building site remains the garden. . . This area is regained on the flat roof. . . as a rooftop terrace, a rooftop garden." That the city skyline in the age of reinforced concrete should be nothing but a "tête-à-tête between the stars and the shingles" was sheer anachronism to Le Corbusier's mind. He sought to overcome the traditional contrast of "front" – a façade exposed to traffic – and "back" – crammed into a narrow courtyard –

Exterior view
Musée des Arts Décoratifs

Le Corbusier
"Immeubles-Villas", 1922
Design sketch of a villa apartment block with
120 units
Fondation Le Corbusier, Paris

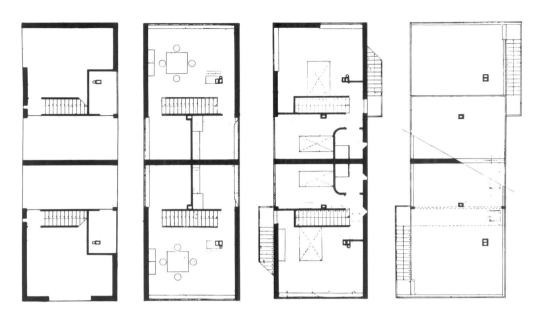

Le Corbusier and Pierre Jeanneret
"Quartiers Modernes Frugès" Estate in
Bordeaux-Pessac, 1925
Plans of the "gratte-ciel" duplexes
The ground floor consists simply of a garage, storage room and a type of shelter,
which runs the full width of the house. The kitchen and living room are situated on the first
floor, the bedrooms on the second floor and
on top the roof terrace.

Views of the "gratte-ciel" duplexes
(above) and a lower housing type with
roof terraces (below)
Fondation Le Corbusier, Paris
These photographs show the houses as plastered shells. The coats of paint they later acquired were apparently unusually modern and
disturbing for contemporary observers. "The
bases of the houses are black, the walls alternately burnt sienna, light blue, light sea-green,
white, bright yellow and grey. Different sides of
the houses have different colours. One side
may be dark brown, the other light green, with
these colours meeting directly at the corner.
This is perhaps the most effective means of
making the walls seem immaterial. The impression is foreign and fantastic, but not chaotic."
(Steen Eiler Rasmussen, 1926)

Le Corbusier and Pierre Jeanneret
House 14/15 in the Weißenhof Estate,
Stuttgart, 1927
Mercedes-Benz AG Archives, Stuttgart
The construction represents a reinforced-concrete frame with outer walls of hollow pumice blocks and internal walls of brick. Garages were originally to be built behind the retaining wall, which was required to stay the loose, sloping ground. Le Corbusier liked to see his houses photographed together with cars, here a Mercedes sports car. Indeed, when commissioning photographs himself he would insist upon the inclusion of a limousine. For him, cars, airplanes and liners were "choice quality products" of the modern machine world, "norms" of maximum precision and perfection which he ranked alongside the "choice quality products" of Classical architecture, such as Phidias' Parthenon.

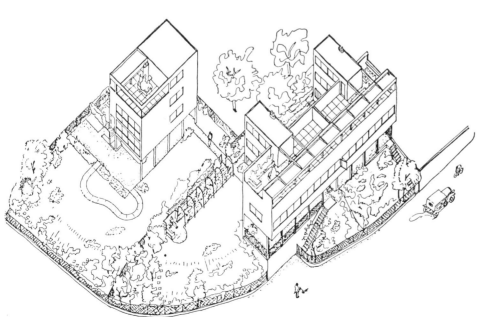

Axonometric projection of Houses 13 and 14/15 in the Weißenhof Estate

Le Corbusier and Pierre Jeanneret
Villa Stein in Garches, 1927
View from the drive
Sächsische Landesbibliothek, Dept. Deutsche
Fotothek, Dresden

through the division into "top" and "bottom". "You simply reverse the plan, you flee the street, you strive towards the light." Le Corbusier increasingly abandoned the use of continuous intermediate ceilings and organized his plans around open, two-storey living halls. Stairs were replaced by ramps, thus creating "architectural promenades". Above all, the outer wall lost its significance as a static element and became a "membrane of any desired thickness". Long, horizontal window bands replaced the traditional tall French windows, an innovation which – today surprisingly – sparked a central debate among French Modernists similar to the discussion surrounding the flat versus gable roof in Germany. Even the progressive Auguste Perret insisted that windows should stand upright "like a man". But Le Corbusier took the destruction of the typical façade even further than this: "Through the balcony-like projection of the floor over the pilotis, the entire façade is extended beyond the building skeleton. It thereby loses its load-bearing character. . . and thus has freedom of composition." A freedom which was only limited by the bounds of the technically possible.

Opposite page: Axonometric drawing
Fondation Le Corbusier, Paris

Le Corbusier and Pierre Jeanneret
Villa Savoye in Poissy, 1929–1931
North corner
Photo Maurice Babey/Artephot

Plans
On the ground floor are the lobby, rooms for domestic staff and garages; behind the strip windows on the first floor are the living rooms, which open onto the terrace garden via sliding glass walls. The roof, with its curved screen walls and "framed" views is a sun terrace. The floors are connected by ramps and spiral staircases.

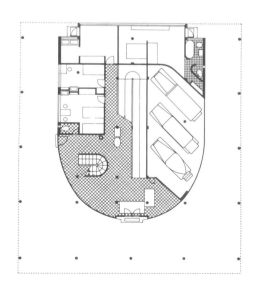

Terrace garden with a ramp leading up to
the roof level
Photo Maurice Babey/Artephot

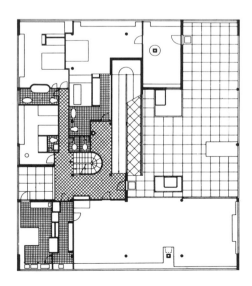
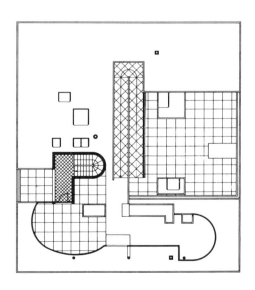

Ludwig Mies van der Rohe
German Pavilion at the International
Exhibition in Barcelona, 1929
Inner courtyard
Photo Klaus Frahm
The pavilion stood for barely six months before being dismantled and all its reusable elements being sold. The photograph shows the reconstruction which has since been built. The pool of its marble-lined courtyard features the sculpture "Der Morgen" (The Morning) by Georg Kolbe.

Plan

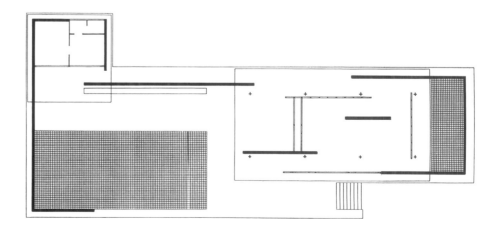

The International Style

The recognition which Ludwig Mies van der Rohe earned from the much-discussed Weißenhof exhibition in Stuttgart probably led to his invitation to design the German Pavilion at the International Exhibition in Barcelona in 1929. This "Pavilion of the German Empire" formed the setting for the official opening ceremony performed by the Spanish royal couple, Alfons XIII and Victoria Eugenia. In its light and generous elegance, it was much more than a mere architectural showpiece. The elongated, flat-roofed building was distanced from the street by a wide travertine terrace with a shallow pool. Vertical slabs of costly marble and metal-framed panels of glass in shades of white, grey and green articulated the flowing spatial continuum, its skilful relationship to the exterior creating an impression of extensive depth.

The architectonic concept underlying the Barcelona Pavilion was first applied to a private residence in the Tugendhat villa. A semicircle of wood screening the dining area and a free-standing panel of onyx doré formed the only partitions within the 250 square metres of living area. To the south and east the room opened onto the garden through wide, continuous glazing, while its street front appeared reserved and withdrawn. The Tugendhat House was considered, along with Le Corbusier's Villa Savoye in Poissy, a pinnacle of modern architecture, but its exquisite exclusivity could hardly serve as a model during a time of economic depression. That role fell instead to office buildings such as Erich Mendelsohn's Columbus House or the Luckhardt brothers' Telschow House on Potsdamer Platz in Berlin. These two dynamic symbols of metropolis and efficiency corresponded far more closely to the search for an economic and self-confident architecture of the present. And yet all these buildings had something in common. But in order to identify their joint characteristics and subsequently to formulate the aesthetic criteria of a new style, distance – not only spatial – was needed. A distance such as that of Henry-Russell Hitchcock and Philip Johnson in faraway New York. In 1931 they prepared an exhibition on modern architecture in the Museum of Modern Art for which an accompanying catalogue, entitled "The International Style", was published in 1932. "The idea of style . . . has become real and fertile again . . . This contemporary style, which exists throughout the world, is unified and inclusive, not fragmentary and contradictory like so much of the production of the first generation of modern architects." Such a subsumption naturally failed to find uniform acceptance in Europe. Thus, in 1935, Walter Gropius said of his position in the twenties: "The aim of the Bauhaus was not to propagate any kind of style, system, dogma, formula or fashion, but purely and simply to exert a stimulating influence on planning."

Bruno Taut, whose work was by no means characterized by Purist severity and who had made masterly use of colour and form in his architectural designs, steered similarly clear of aesthetic considerations in his "Five points of new architecture". For him, beauty arose solely from the agreement of building and function. Materials and construction were subordinate to their best possible usage as the only valid

Ludwig Mies van der Rohe
Villa for Fritz and Grete Tugendhat in Brno
1928–1930
Living room with view into the winter garden
Bildarchiv Foto Marburg
The polished chrome pillars are load-bearing,
while the walls are merely partitions. The furni-
ture is designed entirely by Mies.

Plans
On the upper floor (left) – the level at which
the house is entered from the street – lie bedrooms and sun terraces. The floor below (right)
contains rooms for domestic staff, the kitchen
and the large, open living room measuring 250
square metres. The only dividing elements are
a semicircular screen of lively-grained Macas-
sar ebony in the dining area and a wall panel
of gold-brown onyx doré between the seating
area and library.

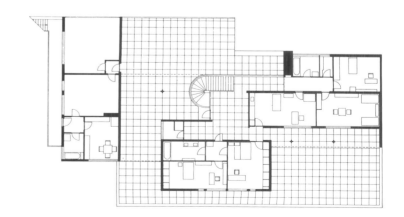

Garden front
Bildarchiv Foto Marburg
Every second pane in the continuous, ceiling-high glass wall could be electrically lowered.

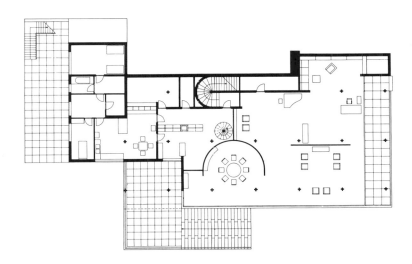

Hans and Wassili Luckhardt with Alfons
Anker
Villa Kluge am Rupenhorn in Berlin, 1928
Photo Arthur Köster / Akademie der Künste,
Sammlung Baukunst, Berlin
The far-projecting living-room terrace and
the line of bedroom windows face west, with
a view of Lake Strössen.

Plans
The living room embraces the whole of the
ground floor (above); bedrooms and secondary rooms are located in the upper and
basement floors (below).

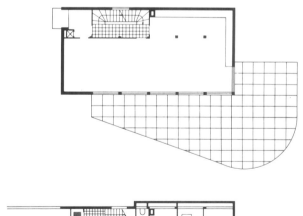

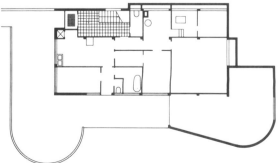

Library and living room
Photo Arthur Köster / Akademie der Künste,
Sammlung Baukunst, Berlin
The two cased pillars are part of the steel-
skeleton structure. The Luckhardt brothers
designed all the fixtures as well as the tubu-
lar-steel seating group.

criterium. Details served the whole. Only the principle of repetition was acknowledged an "artistic means". Hitchcock and Johnson responded indirectly with the objection that it was "nearly impossible to organize and execute a complicated building without making some choices not wholly determined by technology and economics. . . Consciously or unconsciously, the architect must make free decisions before his plan is complete." Thus the aesthetic definition of the International Style differed fundamentally to that of Functionalism, albeit without individually citing truly different buildings. The functionalist principle embraced far more the technical and social aspects of modern architecture. Rationalism was the name preferred in particular by those Italian architects who first formed the "Gruppo 7" in 1926 and later, in 1931, the MIAR (Movimento Italiano per l'Architettura Razionale). Here, too, aesthetics played a minor role, but Rationalism included more than just functional solutions and fell clearly within the tradition of rational and socially-regulated architecture. The "Gruppo 7" attempted to base its modern architecture on the "spirit of tradition"; the MIAR wanted to bring Fascist and modern architecture to congruence, as illustrated by Giuseppe Terragni's Casa del Fascio in Como. Neither were successful, however, although Italian Fascism did not adopt such a vigorously anti-progressive stance as German National Socialism. Official bodies in Italy ultimately still tended towards a homespun neo-classicism.

The concepts of Rationalism and Functionalism stood for an architectural under-standing that sought to free itself from individualism through its belief in a better

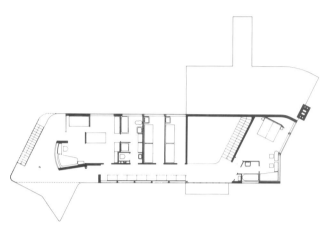

Hans Scharoun
Villa Schminke in Löbau, Saxony, 1933
Photos Akademie der Künste, Sammlung
Baukunst, Berlin
Above: View of the winter garden. The glaz-
ing is angled in order to allow the plants
more sunlight.
Right: View from the north
Opposite page: North-east tip of the house.
Gangway stairs lead to the terrace deck.
The circles in the roof slab are coloured
lights which reflected off the garden pool at
night.

Plans of the ground floor (below) and first
floor (above)
The east-west layout of the building was dictated by its site. To the south lay the road
and businessman Fritz Schminke's factory
complex, and for this reason the rooms open
towards the north onto the old English landscape garden. Rotated 30° around the axis,
the entrance, stairs and utility rooms face
south-west and the dining area in the open
living room north-east.

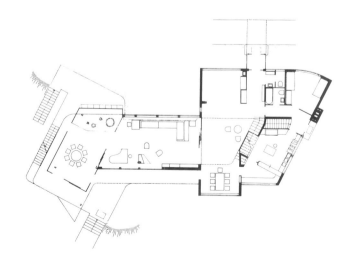

Hans Scharoun
Hostel for Single People and Newly-married Couples at the "Wohnung und Werkraum" Werkbund Exhibition in Breslau, 1929
Entrance front
Kunstbibliothek, Staatliche Museen
Preußischer Kulturbesitz, Berlin

Plan

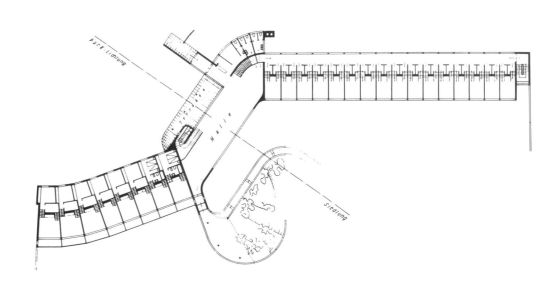

society, and which placed design in the service of social progress. Industrial construction methods, plain façades and standardized plans all contributed to this end. Hitchcock and Johnson, on the other hand, encapsulated the characteristics of the International Style in three aesthetic principles. The first saw "architecture as enclosed space". Since the load-bearing structure is preferably a steel or concrete skeleton frame, not only can the plan be developed more freely but the load-bearing masonry bodies lose their previous significance. The exterior shell merely offers protection against the weather. The ideal material for an outer skin is a façade entirely of glass, such as Mies van der Rohe employed in his 1922 design for a skyscraper. It does not rest on the foundations, but hangs from the inner frame. The impact of such a curtain wall could be further intensified by recessing the piers and securing the façade elements to projecting slabs. The "enclosed space" is comparable to the "pure volume" described by Le Corbusier ten years earlier. With the rejection of secondary, decorative façade elements, fenestration gains new significance. Rather than being placed in deep soffits, glazing is now incorporated as far as possible into the surface, in order to emphasize the character of the skin. In 1930, in a commentary on their buildings am Rupenhorn in Berlin, the Luckhardt brothers compared the changes taking place in architecture with those in the clothing sector: "As clothing, in particular women's clothing, has become more practical and healthier and has adapted itself to the requirements of hygiene and the demand for sporting activity, so too modern architecture will be an expression of such concerns." From

Johannes Andreas Brinkman and Leendert
Cornelius van der Vlugt with Mart Stam
Van Nelle Tobacco Factory in Rotterdam,
1926–1930

View from the driveway
Nederlands Architectuurinstituut,
Amsterdam
Transparent, filigree façades of mirror glass –
and, in the parapet zone, of "Torfoleum" –
curtain the iron construction. A cafeteria was
housed on top of the factory building in a
glazed turret not unlike an air-traffic control
tower. And indeed, the works' landing strip
used by the private plane of the owner could
also be seen from here.

Section and plan

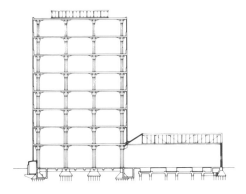

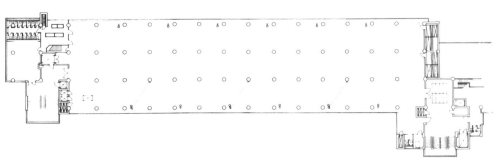

J.A. Brinkman, L.C. van der Vlugt and
Willem van Tijen
"Bergpolder" apartment block in Rotterdam,
1933–1934

this they derived concrete requirements of a "new living form": "Light and air in increased quantities,. . . the 'flexible' plan which allows interior walls to be positioned according to the individual needs of the occupant,.. the possibility of freely designing the size and layout of the openings in the outer walls."

Hitchcock and Johnson declared a second major principle to be the "attempt at modular regularity". The regular grids of skeleton frame constructions resulted naturally from the standardization of building components and had long been common practice in American high-rise construction, since varying support intervals only increased costs. This principle replaced axial symmetry as aesthetic order and was accompanied by a pronounced emphasis upon the horizontal, which corresponded to the storey slabs with interspersed parapets and window strips as well as the dominant flat roof. The grid system invited rectangular volumes, but it was precisely in the exploitation of the elasticity of its order that the artistic challenge lay. In interior design in particular, freely-formed walls promised "a more favourable distribution of available space", whereby the thin supports could remain standing in space.

Some of the attractive and exciting results that can be achieved with controlled fractures and curvatures are beautifully illustrated in the Schminke House built by Hans Scharoun in 1933. In contrast to numerous examples of formal stagnation, he

View from the north-east
Nederlands Architectuurinstituut,
Amsterdam
The clear, linear building was sited amidst the low brick houses of a plain, working-class district of Rotterdam. The economical apartments are linked by outdoor walkways. The glazed end of the construction houses the stairs and a lift – the first in a apartment block in this price range.

Alvar Aalto
Tuberculosis Sanatorium in Paimio,
1928–1933
Main staircase
Photo Welin / Suomen Rakennustaiteen
Museo, Helsinki

Opposite: View from the west
Photo Welin / Suomen Rakennustaiteen
Museo, Helsinki
The Paimio Sanatorium, a co-operative financial undertaking by over fifty communities,
was built in a remote location in the forests
of south-west Finland. The design which won
Alvar Aalto the competition in 1928 was essentially based on two considerations. First,
the clear division of personnel and patient
areas: the nurses, ward attendants, doctors,
administrators and maintenance personnel
living in the same seclusion as the patients
were given their own living and relaxation
areas, fully separate from the running of the
clinic. Second, a better solution to patient accommodation: in a tall, slim block ending in
a terrace wing, Aalto arranged the rooms in
a linear manner which provided maximum ex-
posure to sun and air. The interior sensitively
reflects the long hours the patients spend
lying in bed; thus the ceilings are painted in
deeper shades and the lighting is indirect.
The complex, projecting out into the landscape and with its clearly differentiated functional areas, became a model for hospital
buildings all over the world.

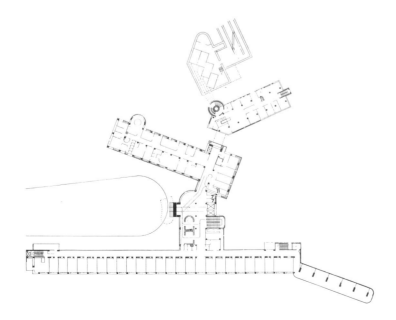

Plan
The elongated main wing contains the patients'
rooms; behind, the connecting section between
this and the second main wing houses treatment facilities and communal rooms. Kitchens,
heating, garages and further technical facilities
are located in the two rear buildings.

here demonstrated opportunities for developing the vocabulary of form by rejecting all dogmatic solutions and extracting organic form from functional relationships. The house refuses clear orientation; rotated axes change its directions of movement. Scharoun countered its marked horizontality with his effective placing of a gang--way-like staircase on the "bow" of the house. Formal variety is here intensified into a bold composition of animated lines. The living room inside this tip is flooded with light through its window walls and is extensively isolated from the protection of the house. Adolph Behne found it especially pleasing that "the panes are etched at a number of points where the eye demands a point of reference".

This bears a direct relation to Hitchcock and Johnson's third principle, the "avoidance of superimposed decoration". Traditional ornamentation was now replaced by the subtle design of window frames, entrances, porches, parapets and even inscriptions. The authors also treat the role of colour in this context. Although crystalline-white surfaces were employed by choice in the thirties, colour design nevertheless played a substantial and indeed decorative role for details. George Howe and William Lescaze explained the interaction of different materials in the example of the Philadelphia Saving Fund Society tower: "The way in which different materials were combined in terms of type, surface structure and colour with the aim of achieving a decorative effect, without the actual decorative forms, has particular repercussions for architecture. These effects are increased through an extensive use of artificial light and the visual distraction of numerous light reflections and refractions, particularly

Eugène Beaudouin and Marcel Lods
Open-Air School in Suresnes, 1932–1935
Roger-Viollet, Paris
The steel-skeleton buildings are infilled with prefabricated reinforced-concrete elements developed in collaboration with Eugène Freyssinet. The teaching pavilions can be instantly transformed into covered outdoor seating areas by simply folding back the glazed concertina walls.

Rudolf M. Schindler
Beach House for Philip Lovell in Newport
Beach, California, 1925–1926
Glass wall of the two-storey living room
with a view onto the Pacific
Photo Tim Street-Porter

View from the north-west
Photo Julius Shulman
The street front is dominated by five power-
ful, constructive reinforced-concrete frames.
Bedroom loggias lie behind the protruding
stuccoed wooden parapets.

in rooms for the public, where stainless steel and yellow bronze were used in conjunction with highly-polished marble. Marble usually served as cladding for large, wide wall surfaces. Stainless steel was chosen in preference to other white metals for its resistance and hardness, this latter allowing the very economical dimensioning of every detail; an extremely appropriate, standard-raising design medium Aluminium was mainly used for the wide window bands of the lower floors, as well as for radiators, ventilation ducts and light fixtures."

Leaving aside the stylistic characteristics listed by Hitchcock and Johnson, a further vital aspect of modern architecture remained its internationalism. On his "Gli elementi dell architettura funzionale", a compilation of hundreds of buildings from around the world, Alberto Sartoris commented: "A further essential aspect of Functionalism is the search for a contemporary style with uniform construction methods which must, however, permit a variety of uses and interpretations. . . The demand for simple, sober and useful forms leads to the development of a uniform aesthetic direction."
International similarities were striking above all in the work of younger architects, as was the rapid spread of the New Architecture.

In Czechoslovakia, Brno became one of the centres of the Modern Style. Architects such as Bohuslav Fuchs, Otto Eisler and Jindřich Kumpošt were active here. Important

Richard Neutra
"Health House", Villa for Philip Lovell in Los
Angeles, 1927–1929
Photo Julius Shulman
A lightweight structure of steel girders on a
projecting reinforced-concrete foundation
forms the basis for this house, built on a
steep hillside in the Los Feliz Canyon. Its balconies are hung from the roof frame and its
surfaces infilled with concrete and glass.

Plan

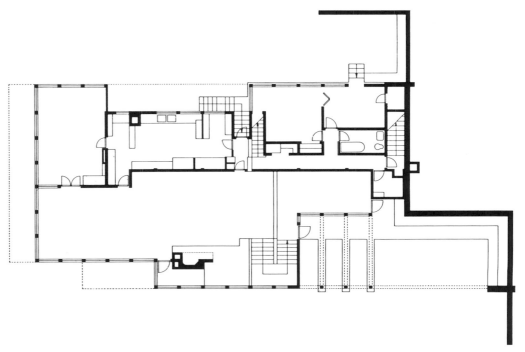

figures in Austria included Ernst A. Plischke and Lois Welzenbacher, in Denmark Arne Jacobsen and in the Netherlands Johannes A. Brinkmann, L. C. van der Vlugt, Willem van Tijen and Johannes Duiker. In Amsterdam Gropius' concept of a high-rise apartment building for workers was partly realized in the Bergpolder Block. It was built out of steel, although its intermediate ceilings, doors and windows were of wood. Inadequate soundproofing, noise penetrating the apartments from the outside walkways and the expensive maintenance required by the exposed metal parts detracted somewhat from its success, but the building proved the benefits of slab housing and encouraged other, comparable projects. Pioneering work in Great Britain was carried out chiefly by young immigrant architects such as Amyas Connell and Berthold Lubetkin, while in France a new generation, which included Eugène Beaudouin, Marcel Lods and André Lurçat, was finding success. In California, Richard Neutra and Rudolf Schindler had already developed their own interpretations of volume and light in the twenties.

The need to identify common directions and to awaken understanding for new approaches in architecture, and hence in urban planning, led to the founding of CIAM (Congrès Internationaux d'Architecture Moderne). Topics discussed by the first congress of 1928 included modern technology, standardization, cost-efficiency,

Gregory Ain
"Dunsmuir Flats" Residential Complex in Los Angeles, 1937–1939
Photo Julius Shulman
The north front of these four two-storey units reveals itself as a staggered sequence of cubes with narrow, high-lying window strips. The south front opens in balconies and terraces into private gardens.

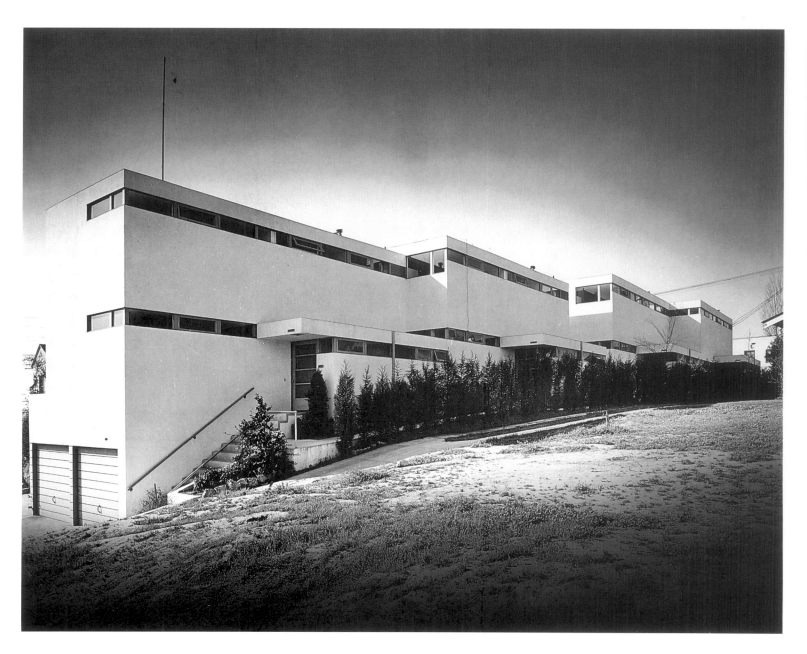

urban planning, youth education as well as architecture and the State. Further congresses followed: the main theme in Frankfurt in 1929 was "The existence-minimum apartment", and in Brussels in 1930 "Rational methods of development". The fourth congress, planned for Moscow, had to be rescheduled following a change in Soviet building policy, which had now fallen back into academic line. It was eventually held on a cruise from Marseilles to Athens. The starting-point for negotiations on "The functional city" were standardized plans and analyses of a large number of major cities, on the basis of which concrete conditions were to be investigated. Functional analysis as a means of design planning was also applied to urban development, and led to the identification of the four primary functions of the city – residential, work, free-time and traffic. The concluding "Principles of the Fourth Congress" demanded that the urban areas corresponding to these four functions should be designed according to their own laws and requirements. They should furthermore be interrelated in such a way "that the regular daily cycle of working, living and relaxing can also be designed to achieve maximum time savings". Numerous finer points detailed the consequences. Roads are thus differentiated according to function: residential streets connect the quieter estates, while wide expressways without intersections allow the rapid flow of rush-hour traffic. The

Rudolf M. Schindler
House for Victoria McAlmon in Los Angeles, 1935
Photo Julius Shulman

194

Frank Lloyd Wright
"Fallingwater", Villa for Edgar J. Kaufmann
in Bear Run, Pennsylvania, 1935–1939
Photos Christopher Little
A stone tower with the central fireplace
group forms the coordinating centre of the
complex horizontal layering. The light-coloured concrete parapets of the terraces and
verandas reach far out into the untamed wil-
derness. Inside, natural rock outcrops form
part of the ambience.

Plan

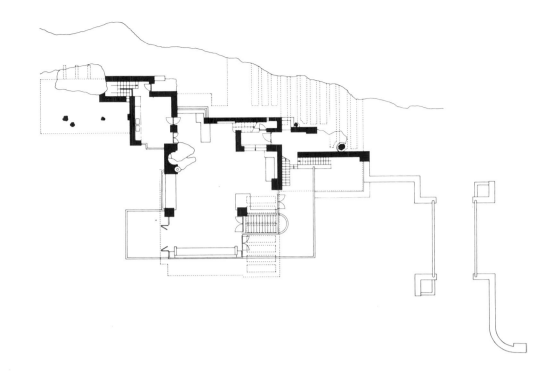

Amyas Douglas Connell
"High and Over", country house for Bernard
Ashmole in Amersham / Buckinghamshire,
1929–1930
View of the house from the valley
Photo Felton / Royal Commission on the
Historical Monuments of England, London
The plans arose in close cooperation with
the customer. He wanted the maximum
possible exploitation of the scant English sun-
shine, best possible protection from the bit-
ing winds and an uninhibited view of the
beautiful Misbourne valley. Connell realized
his wishes in a Y-shaped building with a
glazed inner courtyard, long window bands
and large, covered roof terraces. Small flaps
were built into the window panes to allow
modest, draft-free ventilation. Planning permission for the water tower with look-out
platform and covered playground, which
stood at the highest point of the property
and was visible from far around, was only
granted after a difficult and protracted negotiations with the local authorities.

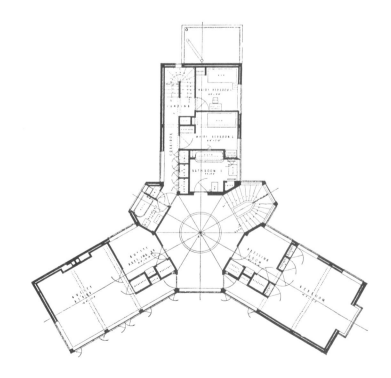

Amyas Douglas Connell and Basil Robert
Ward
Villa for Sir Arthur Lowes-Dickinson in
Grayswood, near Haslemere / Surrey, 1932
Stairwell
Photo Felton / Royal Commission on the
Historical Monuments of England, London
Load-bearing support for the staircase is the
chimney for the house heating system; the
finely-articulated glass skin simply delimits ts
space.

Ground and first floor plans

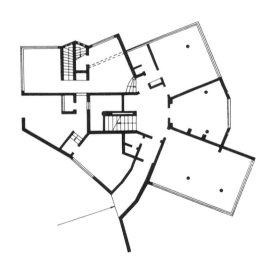 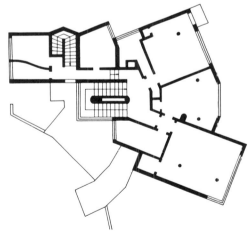

197

Giuseppe Terragni
Casa del Fascio in Como, 1932–1936
Photo Heliograph/private collection

planning of residential areas was to take into consideration the quality and location of building sites and only lead to higher population densities where levels of industrial emissions, fog and damp were relatively low. As a principle there was to be no building along busy roads, while green belts were to surround zones reserved for industry. It proved extraordinarily difficult, however, to formulate the conclusions of the congress. In 1943 the French group finally published an annotated version of the "Principles" as "The Athens Charter"; Le Corbusier was the only author to be named in later editions. In a number of fundamental points the emphasis was shifted; the functional division of city zones thus appeared more rigid and schematic than was originally intended. Le Corbusier thereby unfortunately gave decisive impetus to the increasing dismemberment of cities. The decisive requirement for successful urban planning, namely the municipalization of property, or its rescue from the field of speculation, was a utopia and could thus not be created under the reigning social conditions of the day.

Southern corner
Photo Heliograph/private collection
The building was commissioned by the Fascist Party. Its basic form is a halved cube with edges 33 metres long and 16.5 metres high. The radiant white, marble-clad exteriors of the concrete skeleton construction are plastically interrupted by the dramatic interplay of open and closed surfaces. Terragni had originally conceived this "House of the People" as a horseshoe opening onto the Piazza dell'Impero. In the end, however, he created an inner courtyard with a spectacular, martial entrance, whose sixteen glass-leaf doors could be swung open simultaneously.

Plan

Opposite page:
Ernst Otto Oßwald
Tagblatt Tower in Stuttgart, 1924–1928
Landesbildstelle Württemberg, Stuttgart
After extensive testing, the local Materials
Research Laboratory developed a special
concrete mixture of Rhine sand, Rhine gravel,
porphyry breeze, crushed stones and high-
grade cement for this "bold enrichment" of
the cityscape, which achieved a "good effect
of colour". (Deutsche Bauzeitung, 1929)

H. and W. Luckhardt with Alfons Anker
Telschow House in Berlin, 1928
View from Potsdamer Platz
Photo Arthur Köster / Akademie der Künste,
Sammlung Baukunst, Berlin
The Telschow House resulted from the conversion of three office buildings, their front
spanned by a curving façade following the
line of the traffic and "pointing the way like
a flag". It appeared fully uncompromising towards its Potsdamer Platz neighbours. The
glass of its smooth skin was opaque white,
that of its window connections shiny black,
while its narrow side wall — an important advertising space facing the square — was ultra-
marine blue.

Erich Mendelsohn
Columbus House, Berlin, 1931–1932
Bildarchiv Foto Marburg
The ten-storey steel-skeleton building with its
curtain wall and "flying roof" was a residential and office block with cafés, restaurants
and shops on the ground floor. It was to be
the first step in the transformation of Potsdamer Platz into a "cosmopolitan square".
Other projects planned within the scheme,
such as the Cylinder House by the Luck-
hardt/Anker team, were not, however, executed.

Plans

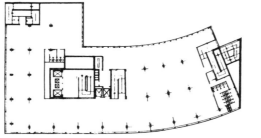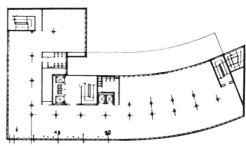

M. Belloc
Gaumont Film Palace in Paris, 1931
Auditorium
Musée des Arts Décoratifs, Paris

The New Deal

Faith in the self-regulating ability of the capitalist system was shattered in October 1929 by New York's Wall Street crash which rocked the financial world and ruined countless careers. Overnight, the luxurious, gourmet style of Art Déco became a symbol of a luckless epoch. Its wasteful abundance was now all too often equated with the decadence of the Prohibition profiteers and their cocktail culture. The proud New York high-rise projects such as the Chrysler and Empire State Buildings and the Rockefeller Center were only completed because their contracts had already been signed; nothing of comparable magnitude was to be built for a long time. The Empire State Building by architects Shreve, Lamb and Harmon remained for the most part unleased, and it was jokingly renamed the "Empty State Building". It was surely no coincidence that the game of "Monopoly", in which players could practice property speculation, was invented in 1929. Some sectors actually profited from the crisis: talking films and radio entertained even the less well-off, and Hollywood's "dream factory" lived well from productions of extravagant melodramas.

The New Deal policy which Franklin D. Roosevelt introduced in 1933 was designed to counter the effects of Great Depression. It was complimented by comprehensive state-financed construction and development projects such as the regulation of the Tennessee River and dam building in the western United States. Recovery began above all in the field of consumer goods production, however, and was substantially encouraged by extensive electrification. Whereas only 24 percent of all households had electricity in 1917, by 1940 this total had risen to 89 percent. Radios thereby sold just as well as refrigerators, vacuum cleaners, toasters and other small appliances. The demand was for functional and useful goods rather than luxury items, and manufacturers, facing increasing competition, began to take a greater interest in product designs which might improve sales. Industrial designers such as Walter Dorwin Teague, Raymond Loewy, Norman Bel Geddes and Henry Dreyfuss put a new face on everyday objects and created the New Deal style – both sensually pleasing and smoothly hygienic at once. The aerodynamic drop shape of airplanes, automobiles and locomotives, such as the 1930 Lockheed Orion, the 1934 Chrysler Airflow and the Burlington Zephyr of 1933, became the omnipresent symbol of the age. Lighters, cocktail shakers, vacuum cleaners and even pencil sharpeners in streamlined forms satisfied the general enthusiasm for speed and technological progress. Everything had rounded corners and chrome trimmings.

A new interest in design had already been aroused towards the end of the twenties as a result of various museum-initiated design presentations. Many of these ambitious compilations were adopted by department store chains and thus reached a broader public. Unlike Hitchcock and Johnson in 1932, still set upon an angular-cut stylistic vocabulary, the exhibition committee of a 1929 design show in the New York Art Center had decorated the only architecture room purely with photographs of buildings by Erich Mendelsohn. Recognizable in his rounded corners was an architectural line

Bernhard Hoetger
"Atlantis" House in Bremen, 1931
Ceiling light
Photo Klaus Frahm

Coffee dealer and patron of the arts Ludwig Roselius had, in the 1920s, purchased a number of properties on Bremen's Böttcherstrasse, a narrow street formerly housing artisans, with the aim of creating a "stronghold of North German culture". He employed as his architect the Worpsweder artist Bernhard Hoetger who, with his "Atlantis" House, gave the ensemble a bizarre centre. His iconography was drawn from the phantasmagoria of historian Hermann Wirth and celebrated the legendary sunken island as the home of the Nordic race. Odin, progenitor of the Asians, appears on the façade in the world ash tree, accompanied by the Norns Urd and Skuld and by Verdandi, Fate of the present and mother of "that which is to come". The interior is dominated by flowing forms in powerful colours; shaded lamps provide subdued lighting. The complex spatial arrangement reaches its conclusion and climax in a chamber in the attic storey, which is vaulted with a sky of blue and white glass blocks.

which announced the arrival of a modern age energetically and without unnecessary decorum. The clear forms of the European avant-garde were increasingly adopted by American architects in the following years, but interpreted more fashionably in their stylistic aspects.

In the "Ladies' Home Journal" in 1930, Norman Bel Geddes had introduced the prototype of a "House of Tomorrow" in which elements of functional architecture were combined to create a new stylistic concept. Smooth surfaces formed vertical and horizontal curves, windows were simply cut, porches projected like rounded "eyebrows" from the façade and balustrades recalled ship's railings. Expanding the picture to include walls of glazed modules, superimposed masts and pastel-coloured coatings, the result was cheerful, unassuming buildings which, particularly in beach resorts such as Miami, grew to become an atmospheric form of recreational architecture.

Such a lighthearted approach was unthinkable in Europe, with its bitter debates surrounding traditional and modern architecture. It was in the field of shop, cinema and night club interiors that combinations of decorative design fantasies and Modernist verve were most likely to be found. In many buildings, however, imaginative decoration remained hidden behind a reserved exterior. The American scene, on

Opposite page:
Spiral staircase with light sculpture
Photo Klaus Frahm

The design, originally drawn up for building
contractor William H. Reynolds, was finally
sold to Walter P. Chrysler, who wanted a
provocative building which would not merely
scrape the sky but positively pierce it. Its 77
floors briefly making it the highest building in
the world – at least until the Empire State
Building was completed –, it became the star
of the New York skyline, thanks above all to
its crowning peak. In a deliberate strategy of
myth generation, Van Alen planned a dramatic moment of revelation: the entire seven-
storey pinnacle, complete with special-steel
facing, was first assembled inside the building, and then hoisted into position through
the roof opening and anchored on top in
just one and a half hours. All of a sudden it
was there – a sensational fait accompli.

Van Alen seemed, even to his contemporaries, to have somewhat overshot the mark
in his interiors. Thus Philip Youtz observed in
the magazine "Architectural Forum" in 1930:
"An effective lighting system is destroyed by
coarse-grained walls in a rich shade of choco-
late. What is possibly an interesting ceiling
design is practically invisible. The coloring
and veigning of the marble used are furthermore so obtrusive that the walls of the corridors seem to close threateningly around their
users."

the other hand, was largely characterized by building commissions which did not
need to take historical urban structures into consideration. Gas stations, snack bars
and cinemas in – often standardized – eye-catching forms sprang up everywhere,
designed to appeal directly to a large, motorized market. "Drive-in" became a
magic word and the future the destination of the journey.

The "Century of Progress Exposition", built on an artifical promontory on Lake
Michigan, opened in Chicago in 1933. The show, originally scheduled to last five
months, was eventually extended by a whole year. By the time it finally closed, 38
million curious visitors had entered this consumer's paradise illuminated by thousands
of coloured neon lights. The pavilions of the major companies set the scene. Their
architecture was to attract potential buyers, and designers were encouraged to give
their fantasies free reign – despite the fact that their buildings would soon be
demolished. Materials such as alumirum, stained glass and bakelite were among
the most popular, along with asbestos sheeting and other technical innovations from

Opposite page:
S. Charles Lee
Academy Theater in Inglewood, California,
1939
Photo Julius Shulman, UCLA
In designing his cinema Lee responded
to the increasing importance of automobile traffic. Meaningful forms targeted
drivers-by; even the few steps to the
entrance were all part of the experience –
"The show started on the sidewalk".
For the streamlined front of the Academy
Theater he used glass blocks and
aluminium sections for the first time.
Under black lighting, the flucrescent-
painted spiral tower at night became
a luminous landmark, visible from
afar.

E.H. Burnett, H. Burnham and J.A. Holabird
Travel and Transport Building at the
"Century of Progress" Exposition in
Chicago, 1933
The Art Institute of Chicago
In the brightly-coloured, neon-lit atmosphere of the Chicago Exposition, the architecture of the Travel and Transport Building
proved outstanding amongst the numerous
company pavilions. Twelve steel towers directed the cables on which the metal roof
was hung, creating a large, support-free interior.

Frank Lloyd Wright
Administration Building for S.C. Johnson &
Son Co. in Racine, Wisconsin, 1936–1939
Exterior view
The Art Institute of Chicago
In his Johnson Wax administration building,
Wright created a self-contained world. The
windowless brick building with its rounded
corners fills an entire block in an area devoid
of charm. The actual entrance lies inside the
complex beside a driveway. The visitor
reaches the central, large office area via a
low, half-lit entrance zone.

Opposite page: Interior view
The Art Institute of Chicago
Circular forms characterize the design of the
interior as well as the exterior: transparent
plastic pipes fill the roof plane between
mushroom-shaped pillars. As lighting strips,
the same pipes connect the outer walls with
the ceiling; they also mould the lift cylinder.

the construction industry. Much-admired novelties included the industrially-manu-
factured Dymaxion Houses by entrepreneur-inventor Richard Buckminster Fuller,
which could be assembled on the building site in just a few steps. Their name was
taken from their principle: dynamic plus maximum efficiency.
Optimistic visions of the future once again reached a high point at the New York
World's Fair held in Flushing Meadow Park in 1939. Automobile companies in
particular took centre stage. In the "Highways and Horizons" pavilion of General
Motors, designer Norman Bel Geddes exhibited the giant model of his "Metropolis
of Tomorrow" – no longer the horrific vision of Fritz Lang's film "Metropolis", but a
radiant city organism, flooded with pulsating traffic. America here demonstrated
that it had finally freed itself from its oft-quoted "colonial" dependence on Europe.

1944–1971

Charles Eames
Case Study House No. 8 for Ray and
Charles Eames in Pacific Palisades,
California, 1945–1949
Photo Julius Shulman
This first steel construction in the Case Study
House Program was originally intended as
more of a bridge construction, and thus as
something of quite different appearance. But
when Eames saw the delivered material lying
on the site, he redesigned the house: it
seemed to him that his first plan wasted too
much steel. This larger, two-storey building
thus resulted from the already specified numbers of beams and supports.

Case Studies

Radical changes can stimulate or stunt growth; for Los Angeles after the Second World War, however, the future looked most promising. Its harbour had become the most important base along the American West Coast. Its legendary film studios and its oil industry were joined by new, innovative businesses such as the aviation industry. Hundreds of thousands streamed into the sun-filled valley, which experienced the largest real-estate boom in its history. Orange plantations gave way to endless rows of uniform detached houses, built by leading development companies in the levelled landscape. Traffic organization within this rapidly expanding man-made environment was based on the 1940 design by the Los Angeles Regional Planning Commission: a generalized network of highways covering the city.

An extreme — but not unusual — example of the speed and scale of post-war building was Lakewood Park, a suburb of 17,000 houses for some 70,000 people commissioned by development tycoon Louis Boyar. First 133 miles of road were built into the countryside, then houses erected, assembly-line style, on both sides. Small, specialized teams operated machines which dug each set of foundations in just fifteen minutes. Wooden walls and ceilings were delivered prefabricated, merely requiring on-site assembly. Finally, conveyor belts moved into the blocks for the tiling of the roofs. There were even machines for hanging doors. Up to 100 houses might be completed in a day; 10,000 were built in the first two years. The results were dreary houses, their uninspired plans repeated ad nauseum, in boring rows on levelled ground without beginning or end.

At the same time, plans by a young generation, which saw architecture as a social responsibility and an essential element of modern, democratic urbanism, lay idle on drawing-boards. Their designs had less to do with the normative urban Utopias of the thirties than with comprehensible model solutions. Their inspiration was not Le Corbusier's "Ville radieuse" or Frank Lloyd Wright's "Broadacre City", but examples such as Ludwig Mies van der Rohe's apartment house in the Stuttgart Weißenhof Estate — steel-frame construction with flexible plans, the open apartment on a generous scale.

Support was no more to be expected from speculative construction companies than from public funds. It was left to John Entenza, committed publisher of the magazine "Art & Architecture", to translate new, unused ideas into practice. He succeeded, entirely without subsidy, in setting up the Case Study House Program. In January 1945 he himself commissioned eight designs by promising architects, which were to be advertised as prototypes and made available to an interested public. After three years a total of six detached houses had been completed and viewed by 370,000 curious visitors.

The results of the Program are among the best built in California at that time, despite the considerable limitations affecting design. Materials newly developed or improved during the War and which could have been used for experimentation were simply

Pierre Koenig
Case Study House No. 21 in Los Angeles,
California, 1956–1958
View from the north
Photo Julius Shulman

not on the market. In the early years, therefore, construction was restricted to the use of the sole available material, namely wood. Floor areas, too, were still regulated. All the more surprising, then, was the generosity achieved by these economical, unpretentious houses. They looked away from the street into private inner courtyards without losing their relationship to the surrounding landscape. The kitchens were not small, separate closets but were integrated into the living area and thus formed a part of the flowing spatial continuum. Although standardized building components were developed, no serial production of any magnitude took place; it involved too much effort and expense. The use of conventional industrial semi-finished products proved more successful.

The first steel-frame construction to be built within the Case Study House Program was the house of designers Ray and Charles Eames on the Santa Monica Canyon. Using elements from the industrial sector for the construction was not in itself unusual, but to show them openly and thereby to achieve elegance was new. An important role in this respect was played by the interior, which featured Eero Saarinen's softly curving "womb chairs" and laminated wood models from Eames' "plywood group", particularly admired by visitors.

The immediate post-war years also saw the development of housing models on a co-operative basis. Many of these initiatives were defeated, however, by "Regulation

Entrance front
Photo Julius Shulman
A flat bridge over the pool leads to the entrance. To the right is the carport. The steel frames are infilled with corrugated metal sheeting, roof projections are avoided for reasons of cost. To improve the microclimate the water is pumped up to the roof, from where it flows back into the reflecting pool via small water spouts.

Living room with free-standing kitchen divider
Photo Julius Shulman

Raphael S. Soriano
**House for Julius Shulman in Los Angeles,
California, 1950**
View from the studio into the residential wing
Photo Julius Shulman

Richard Neutra
**Atwell House in Los Angeles, California,
1950**
Guest room
United States Information Service, Bonn

X", which was intended to prevent racial mixing in city districts and thus made impossible any joint projects by Whites and Blacks.

Outstanding architects such as Craig Ellwood, Raphael Soriano, Pierre Koenig and Richard Neutra managed to find sponsors and commissions which were subject to fewer restrictions. Neutra in particular developed a new, much-imitated type in his villa designs: clear, far-reaching masses with extensive glazing, striking sun reflectors and effectively-positioned mirror walls produce subtle, provocative mixtures of interior and nature. Entrances remain reserved and without magnanimous architectural gesture; but upon opening the unassuming and often hidden door, the gaze falls across the interior to the glass walls on the opposite side and into the landscape. Neutra felt that only architecture built in harmony with its surroundings could serve as a "harbour for the soul", that happiness could only be found in a place which contained "a slice of eternity". Anything fashionable was taboo since only in this way could real art be produced in architecture with a social conscience.

Richard Neutra
Eagle Rock Clubhouse in Los Angeles, California, 1950–1954
East front
Photo Julius Shulman
A multi-purpose hall for parties, sporting events and theatre productions was supplemented by more intimate club facilities in the northern part of the building. As visible in this picture, the outer walls of the hall can be slid upwards.

Richard Neutra
Kaufmann House in Palm Springs,
California, 1946–1947
View from the north-east
Photo Julius Shulman

Entrance from the garage and outdoor seating area
Photo Julius Shulman
Adjustable aluminium blinds protect the seating area from sun and sand. The roof was coated with reflecting ceramic granules to reduce its heat absorption.

View from the pool
Photo Julius Shulman
Pipes circulate below both the floors of the interior and the slabs of the terrace, carrying hot or cold water, depending on the temperature.

Plan

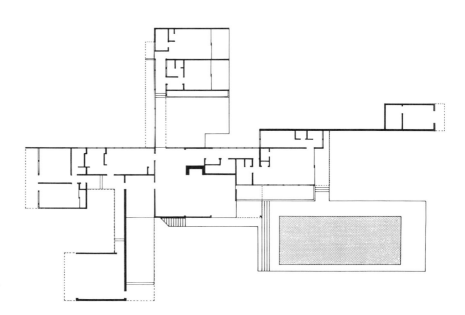

Ludwig Mies van der Rohe
Crown Hall of the Illinois Institute of Technology
in Chicago, Illinois, 1950–1956
Photo Ezra Stoller/Esto

Less is More

Ironically, the developments on both sides of the Atlantic after World War II were equated with a loss of identity. On the one continent reigned the indifferent pragmatism of reconstruction, the specification of whose basic structures was a matter for the county councils, while on the other the native élite grew jealous of the status achieved by German immigrants such as Ludwig Mies van der Rohe, Walter Gropius and Marcel Breuer. In the mood of post-war Europe, nostalgically looking back, modern buildings often appeared too sudden, too violent. Restorations and careful reconstructions of historical edifices using traditional, skilful craftsmanship were considered more valuable than the new buildings of the day. In the absence of clear city contours, contemporary architecture searched desperately for identity alongside the sentimental populistic motifs of arcades, oriels and gables. This "skinny", mediocre architecture of the fifties, precariously balanced between art and kitsch, always had an episodic character.

Unlike the manual orientation of the European construction industry, against which even the successful experiments of Jean Prouvé, amongst others, could make no long-term headway, the major architectural firms in the USA had meanwhile developed a thoroughly industrial philosophy. Priority thereby lay not with apartments, but with strictly economical office design and the creation of company identity. The market demanded mainly two basic variations: the downtown high-rise and the spatious company headquarters in a landscape setting. One prototyp for the latter are Mies van der Rohe's plans for the Illinois Institute of Technology in Chicago, where he himself taught, followed by Saarinen's comparable complex for the General Motors Technical Center in Warren, Michigan. A rapid succession of four buildings inaugurated the development of a new type of skyscraper. In 1948 Pietro Belluschi built the administrative headquarters of the Equitable Savings and Loan Association in Portland, Oregon, in which the reinforced-concrete frame was hung with a skin of glass and aluminium in such a way that no part projected more than two centimetres. In New York in 1950 Wallace K. Harrison and Max Abramovitz completed the secretariat building for the United Nations, an office complex for 3400 employees based on a general plan by Le Corbusier: a slim building with two vast glass façades between windowless end walls of white marble. In New York in 1951 Gordon Bunshaft, working for the Skidmore, Owings & Merrill partnership, designed Lever House for the Lever Brothers, a green glass box which skilfully combined a flat base with a slender tower. In the same year Mies van der Rohe built the famous Lake Shore Drive Apartments in Chicago for construction mogul Herbert S. Greenwald. Following his appointment in 1938 at the Armour – later Illinois – Institute of Technology in Chicago, Mies van der Rohe had the opportunity to plan the new university complex on the outskirts of the city. The concepts he had formulated in Germany he now applied to the situation in America, whereby he became stricter and made greater use of symmetries than in the few houses he had built before the War. Since

Ludwig Mies van der Rohe
House for Edith Farnsworth, Plano, Illinois,
1946–1951
South front
Photo Hedrich-Blessing
Eight white-painted steel beams support the
floor and roof slabs and raise the house above
the flood-endangered river plain. Placed in
front of the house is a laterally-offset terrace
platform; wide steps connect the different levels. The interior, glazed from floor to ceiling
throughout, is articulated only by a core of
precious wood containing kitchen and bathroom facilities. A free-standing wardrobe sepa-
rates the sleeping area from the living area.

Plan

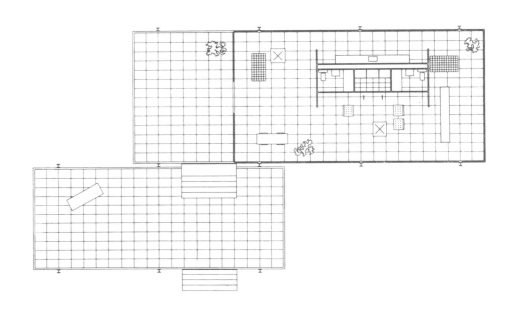

Philip Johnson
"Glass House", Architect's House, New
Canaan, Connecticut, 1949
Photo Norman McGrath

Interior View
Photo Norman McGrath
Mies van der Rohe had designed the couch
for Philip Johnson's New York apartment
back in the early 1930s, and the chairs for
the German Pavilion at the Barcelona International Exhibition of 1929.

fire regulations did not permit an exposed frame, Mies developed an aesthetic of steel, glass and brick which brought the perforce covered structure artistically back to the surface. He thereby paid particular attention to connecting elements and transitions.

Mies devoted himself to two basic forms. First the pavilion, which was to have a support-free interior and which in its ideal form was a floating volume of "air between two plates", as perfected in the Farnsworth House. Second the skyscraper, which he treated as a skeleton construction with identical floors behind a perfect façade of constructive elements which articulate a seemingly unbroken glass surface and rob it of the membrane-like character of usual curtain walls.

His most significant buildings are only inadequately described by phrases such as "almost nothing" or "less is more". These terms would suggest a link with the earlier Chicago School, whose products Mies must have seen almost daily. But the poorly-conceived details of those early high-rises, their cheap construction with changing effects and strange reconciliations of structure and appearance conflicted with his own beliefs. It was rather the perfect industrial buildings of his contemporary Albert Kahn, whose giant bomber factory he transformed into a concert hall in a collage of thin wall and ceiling panels, which formed the typical American starting-points for his work. These confirmed Mies in his denial of the individual and the artistic in architecture.

His houses are not, however, entirely lacking in classical references. Yet the two mutually offset towers of the Lake Shore Drive Apartments differ from typical high-rises of their day in their ground-plan side ratios of three to five. Although, as in the Skidmore, Owings & Merrill Lever Building, curtain walls conceal the structure, it is nevertheless the latter which determines the overall appearance of Mies' buildings. The structure is clearly evident even in the entrance hall. The actual façade starts seamlessly with the first floor; fine I-beams at window-width intervals run its full height. Only one in every four of these regularly-spaced mullions conceals a broader, load-bearing support. The two outer windows of each field are thus always somewhat narrower than their central neighbours. Parapet bands and transoms form a horizontal counterpoint to the emphatic verticals.

The Lake Shore Drive Apartments, with their intelligent construction solutions, were cheaper to build than comparable projects. Once the steel skeleton was erected, the prefabricated façade elements — each two storeys in height and one structural bay in width — were lifted by cranes into position and welded on the spot. The aluminium windows were then installed from the interior. Mies' concern that the perpendicular I-beams should be reassembled in exactly the same order that they left the rolling mills, to exclude even the smallest errors of measurement, reflected both his own perfectionism and the logic of his design. Mies was thwarted in only in one area: his client considered the originally open plans, recollecting the Barcelona Pavilion, too daring; he felt the small rooms of the traditional apartment block would sell better.

What appeared sparingly economical in Chicago became, in the office tower built for Distillers Corporation Seagrams Limited in New York, a luxurious and expensive masterpiece. It was the daughter of the company president himself who halted existing plans for a new building and, following consultations with Philip Johnson, then Director of the Architecture Department of the Museum of Modern Art, put forward the name of Mies van der Rohe. The Seagram Building was markedly different from any other previous New York skyscraper. It stood back from busy Park Avenue, creating an open urban space before it. This "plaza" emerged as both homeless and windy, however, and only really served to introduce and reinforce the towering glass front with its strictly axial entrance. Unlike Chicago, the structural

Skidmore, Owings & Merrill; Gordon Bunshaft
Administration Building for the Lever Brothers Company in New York, 1951–1952
View from Park Avenue
Photo Ezra Stoller/Esto
A low building with an inner courtyard reaches to the very boundary of the site. Out of it grow the 21 office storeys of a second, steep y-soaring architectural body. Lifts, stairs and secondary rooms are concentrated within the narrow end of the building facing away from the street. The curtain wall of green insulating glass and slender, stainless-steel girders embraces the steel skeleton without projections or other forms of differentiation. The opaque parapet bands identify the individual floors, while the rails for the window-cleaning basket emphasize the verticals.

230

Opposite page:
Ludwig Mies van der Rohe with Philip Johnson
Seagram Building, New York, 1954–1958
View from Park Avenue
Photo Ezra Stoller/Esto
Unlike the Lever Building, the Seagram Building stands with its broad side to the avenue. The concept of the pure box is here effectively abandoned: the rear façade projects at its centre by one support bay, while lower, staggered elements ease the transition to buildings in the side streets.

Detail of the façade construction

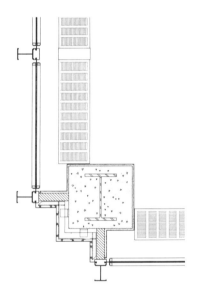

Ludwig Mies van der Rohe
Lake Shore Drive Apartments in Chicago, Illinois, 1948–1951
Entrance area
Photo Ezra Stoller/Esto

Detail of the façade construction
In contrast to the Lever Building, the façades of Mies' high-rises are composed of clearly-displayed constructive elements. The fact that the vertical I-beams dividing the windows are also deployed on the corner supports – entirely unnecessary from a structural point of view – was interpreted by many critics as a declaration of the capitulation of Functionalism. They failed to realize that Mies had never championed that particular cause.

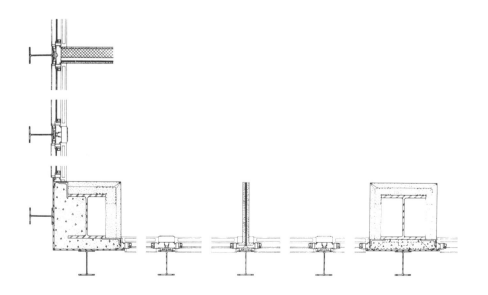

Eero Saarinen
General Motors Technical Center in
Warren, Michigan, 1949–1956
Entrance to the main building of the Design
department; in the background, the steel cupola of its accompanying auditorium.
Photo Ezra Stoller/Esto
The original idea of an office block was
abandoned during the planning phase. The
eye-catching accent was now placed by a
large fountain and silvery water tower in a
central artificial lake. Five corporate depart-
ments were housed around this lcke in buildings no more than three storeys high. Innovations in their design included large, enamel-
led metal panels, neoprene insulction strips
between the façade elements and luminously
colourful glazed bricks, which elevate the
windowless ends of the office wings to the
status of "pictures" in the artistic landscape.

Stairs in the Research department
Photo Ezra Stoller/Esto

Raised walkways linking the buildings
of the Research department
Photo Ezra Stoller/Esto

Overall plan of the complex

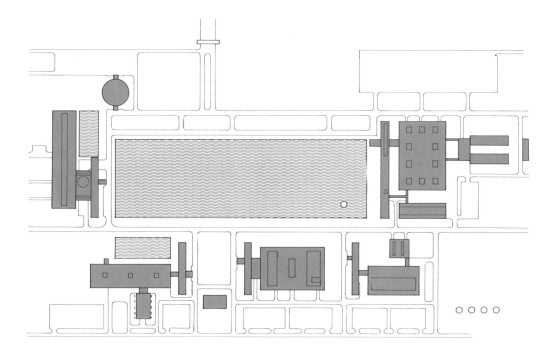

234

Opposite page:
Helmut Hentrich and Hubert Petschnigg with
Fritz Eller, Erich Moser, Robert Walter and
Josef Rüping
Administration Building for Phoenix-Rhein-
rohr AG in Düsseldorf, 1955–1960
Photo Arno Wrubel/HPP
This three-slab building rises – with no apparent starting point – from the grounds of a
park concealing an underground garage.
Flexibility of floor plan was sacrificed to the
emphatically slim form, since in the termina-
tions of the slabs – treated optically as individual compartments – the end rooms were
unavoidably narrow.

Typical floor plan

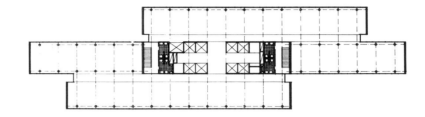

Paul Schneider-Esleben with Egon Schneider
Haniel Garage in Düsseldorf, 1949–1950
Schneider-Esleben Archives
This transparent glass building was the first
multi-storey car park to be built in Germany
after the war. The two outdoor entrance and
exit ramps were suspended from projecting
reinforced-concrete supports. There was
space for up to 700 cars on its five floors.

sections were laid not on but in the glass plane and emphasized via shadow joints. Nor were they the products of serial manufacturing, but special fabrications in bronze. Mies was thus able to modify their profiles. He strengthened the visible, thin edge of the I-beams to give them more optical weight and moved the vertical joists closer together. The office-storey windows run without transverse interruption from floor to ceiling. The façade thus acquires a decisive verticality and thereby gives the same basic design an entirely different appearance.

This building type was developed further in the following years in particular by the architectural firms of C.F. Murphy and Skidmore, Owings & Merrill. Glass boxes – perfect and economical – now characterized modern city skylines all over the world. Serial production led, however, to the loss not only of originality but also of the love of detail which was most important for Mies, and without which the standards of an architecture of "less is more" sadly declined to almost nothing indeed.

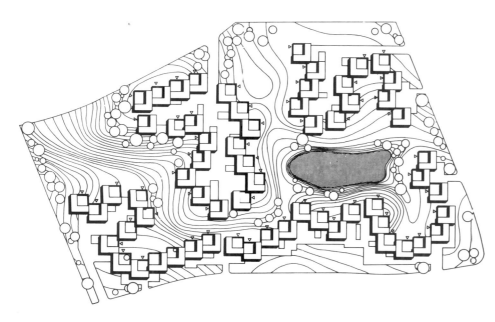

238

Stonebound

Jørn Utzon
Kingohusene Estate in Helsingør,
1958–1960
North front
Photo Keld Helmer-Petersen
The yellow brick buildings with their bold
chimneys fall into meandering lines. They
open onto atrium courtyards, but shut themselves away from the street.

Overall plan of the complex

The schematically functional boxes of the post-war years cemented the primacy of the right angle. Orthogonality is not, however, a synonym for Modernism. Thus Frank Lloyd Wright sought intensively in the forties to determine the status of organic architecture. In his Usonian Houses he tried to develop buildings of maximum possible constructive simplicity as successors to his Prairie Houses, while at the same time continuing the experiments begun in the thirties on honeycomb and circular houses. In his "Testament", published in 1957, he lists his guidelines for a new architecture. It is essentially a summary of his own oeuvre from the turn of the century, but also implicitly incorporates the experiences of his colleagues. Nine somewhat vague postulates address problems of urban planning, such as decentralization, design specifications such as the appropriateness of materials and the deployment of cantilever systems, and questions of building character and expression. "Poetic tranquility instead of a more disastrous "efficiency" should be the consequence in the art of Building."

The second Jacobs House in Wisconsin followed this self-imposed guideline in exemplary fashion. Protected by banks of earth, it offers a "shelter" from the cold wind. The semicircular complex squats against the landscape with its raw, coarse-textured walls and flat roof. Large glazed surfaces facing into the inner courtyard aim at a solar-house effect; a pool dissects this south wall and intensifies the relationship with nature. Inside, the ceiling is lowered to a height of 7 feet; Frank Lloyd Wright held "every additional inch" to be unnecessary, whereby his measurements were guided by his own diminutive stature. Above is a sleeping loft, suspended from the roof. Wright's obligatory fireplace forms the heart of this hideaway. Despite the presence of basic geometric forms, the obvious opening and closing of walls and the flat, projecting roof play their part in the "destruction of the box" which Wright saw as dominating the architectural world to excess.

The Finn Alvar Aalto reached similar conclusions from a different tradition and different cultural influences. For him, architecture was the "play of free forms and animated surfaces" in correlation with appointed task and site environment. The starting-point for his designs were always clearly-arranged bodies, whether a city hall, school, library, large cultural centre or small dwelling. To these he added soft, seemingly non-directed and thus "natural" elements. His Senior Students' Dormitory in Harvard illustrates one such transformation. Here, a serpentine curvature in the flights of rooms ensures that the dense alignment of large numbers of similar – very spartan – cubicles does not result in monotony. Aalto was convinced that this movement would also communicate itself to the person looking out of the window at the Charles River. He felt that, even without actually seeing the form, one could sense that the visual axes lay not stereotypically juxtaposed but at angles to each other. The zigzag façade facing the campus more clearly reveals the basic cubic volumes. Here too, however, the strict stereometry is interrupted and overlaid – to

Alvar Aalto
M.I.T. Senior Dormitory in Cambridge,
Massachusetts, 1947–1948
Façade facing the campus
Photo Ezra Stoller/Esto

Plan

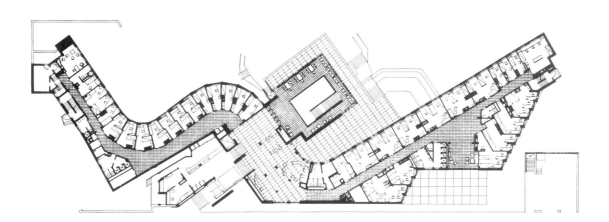

Alvar Aalto
Town Hall in Säynätsalo, 1949–1952
South-east front
Photo Kolmio / Suomen Rakennustaiteen
Museo, Helsinki
Four wings flank a raised inner courtyard.
The western section contains the library, located above shops on the ground floor; in
the eastern section lies the Council Chamber
and municipal administration offices, with
apartments in between. The complex employed traditional building materials: masonry of red bricks, ceilings of wood and
roofs of copper. The window strips blend har-
moniously into the façades with the help of
narrowly-spaced window bars.

Western entrance to the inner courtyard
Photo E. Mäkinen / Suomen Rakennustaiteen
Museo, Helsinki

the sides by staggered offsets, towards the projecting entrance by flights of steps recalling layered rock formations. Misshapen and creased bricks which would normally be rejects were deliberately used in the exterior brickwork. A wall landscape was thus created from a smooth compound. Geomorphic structures are a recurring theme in Aalto's work. The entire display area of his pavilion for the 1939 New York World's Fair quoted the contours of Finnish lakes.

Where Aalto integrated house and Nature, it had nothing to do with that well-known solace of architects, the Green of Atonement, through which less sensitive buildings hoped for long-term intercession and redemption. In his case it meant returning to Nature part of the land that had been built over, such as the steps and the raised inner courtyard of the city hall on the small island of Säynätsalo, and integrating it as an autonomous element into his compositions.

Younger architects – especially in Nordic countries – followed this same practice. Thus Jørn Utzon's atrium houses in the Kingohusene Estate in Helsingør respectfully acknowledge the existing terrain in lines which follow those of the landscape. Intermediate spaces are not filled with artificially-imposed road networks, relaxation or recreation areas, but are carefully integrated. As a decentralized, non-urban housing model it is dependent both on occupant mobility and appropriate infrastructures. Its charm and reconciliatory Utopian character thus remain quite exclusive. Bruce Goff's Bavinger House is determined by an extremely individualistic relationship to nature, in an architecture which assimilates circuitous "personal" details and an arbitrary selection of ready-made materials and in which even kitsch is not taboo. The five-thousand-dollar house which Goff designed together with the Bavingers, an artist couple whose hobby was plant-breeding, stands in an imaginative but somewhat tendentious no man's land. The walls describe a logarithmic spiral. Glass bands between the guyed roof helix and the brickwork emphasize the texture of the rough-layered quarrystones and boulders, while window openings resemble cracks and crevices. The house is approached from the rear; a path down a small hill leads to a sheltered seat lined with stone slabs above the river. This terrace is continued in the house, where it becomes a rock garden with lush plants. Paths wind between grottoes, plant troughs and pools. There are no rooms in the conventional sense;

Alvar Aalto
Cultural Centre in Helsinki, 1955–1958
Auditorium Building
Photo H. Havas / Suomen Rakennustaiteen Museo, Helsinki
This union-commissioned building consists of a large auditorium and an office building. The outer wall of the auditorium follows the curve of the seating rows. The precision of the convex surfaces of masonry was made possible by the use of small square bricks.

Plan

Frank Lloyd Wright
"Solar Hemicycle", House for Herbert
Jacobs in Middleton, Wisconsin, 1944
Entrance
Photo Ezra Stoller / Esto
Protected to the north by an earth mound,
the house opens via extensive glazing onto a
lower-lying garden courtyard to the south.
The bathroom and kitchen are located in the
stone cylinder which overlaps the hemicycle
of the outer wall.

they are replaced by flat, circular elements, built from airplane noses covered with velour. These stand in space like oversized cocktail glasses or are hung from the ceiling as "living lamps". They are positioned at equal intervals and trace the line of a second spiral. The different levels are connected by fragile stairways ending in the light-filled studio at the top of the house. There is a delicate balance between utilized and free space.

The house caused a considerable sensation after its completion and received enthusiastic reviews. The Bavingers allowed public viewings and gave regular tours to thousands of visitors. For them, too, the house was not a temporary living solution but a thing of permanence. Nevertheless a number of ponds had to be filled in and made into flower beds, since humidity proved too high and caused condensation to drip from the ceiling.

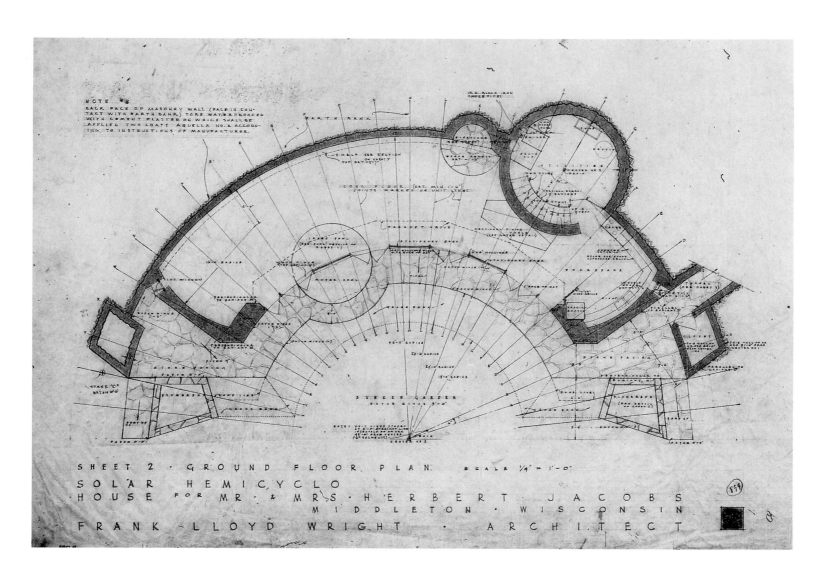

Plan of the ground floor
The Frank Lloyd Wright Foundation

View from the inner courtyard
United States Information Service, Bonn

Bruce Goff
House for Eugene and Nancy Bavinger near Norman, Oklahoma, 1950–1955
Photo Julius Shulman
The sculptor Eugene Bavinger, who, like Goff, taught at the University of Oklahoma, and his wife Nancy, who had studied art there, loathed conventional spatial boxes. Instead they wanted an undivided, open space in which they could live freely and practise their hobby, plant breeding. They wanted to keep building costs below 5,000 dollars, which they succeeded in doing by performing much of the work themselves and by utilizing ready-made parts, in particular airplane scrap. The central mast is, for example, the pipe of an oil drill, while the roof hangs from biplane struts.

Section

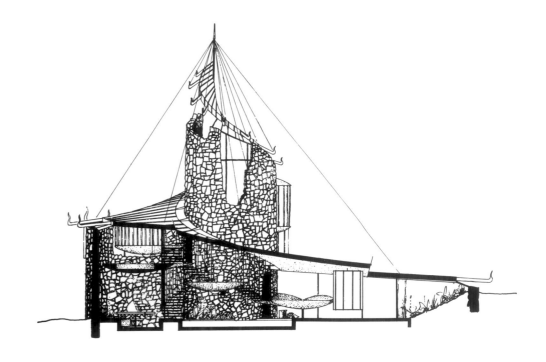

Bruce Goff
House for Glen and Luetta Harder near
Mountain Lake, Minnesota, 1970–1971
Photo Julius Shulman

Three massive chimneys made from boulders seem to anchor the wood-frame house. The roof, covered with bright orange weather-proof carpeting, has the tautness of a tent awning. The outer walls are hung with cedar-wood shingles. The interior, for which Goff was also responsible, is distinctly kitschy. The centre of the living room, for example, is a circular, fabric-covered flower bed with fountain. Bright-coloured glass and mirror mosaics are inserted within the visible wood construction. The Harders had a turkey farm, and thus even insemination tubes found a place in the decor.

Plan

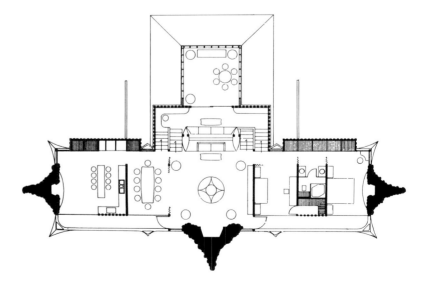

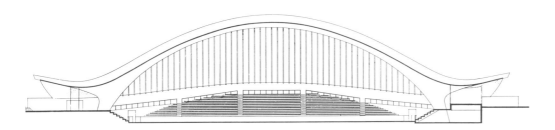

The Flying Roof

Eero Saarinen (arch.), Fred Severud (eng.)
David S. Ingalls Hockey Rink, Yale University, New Haven, Connecticut, 1953–1959
Photo Ezra Stoller / Esto
The roof of the ice hockey stadium with seating for 2800 spectators is suspended on both sides from the central concrete arch. The surface consists only of a wooden shell over supporting steel cables. Despite the nterplay of concave and convex forms, the static principle is simple and comprehensible and is only dramatized through the upward-curving ends of the support.

Longitudinal section of the stadium

Harley Earl's 1959 Cadillac, the queen of all tail-fin street cruisers, marks the notable high point of an era of opulent, neo-baroque fiction. The glittering, gross trim of the technical appliance had outlived itself; reality caught up with the designer dream. The gruffly charming Lockheed "Constellation" propeller plane, with its three round horizontal tail units, was now succeeded by the sleek, jet-propelled Boeing 707 as the embodiment of modern mobility. The new ideal form was streamlined and functional.

In architecture, dynamic, upswinging roofs in every imaginable curving form expressed culturally optimistic statements in coolly objective shapes. The necessary technology had already been developed by Dischinger, Finsterwalder and Bauersfeld in the thirties, although initially employed almost exclusively for single-arched shells, and in particular barrel vaulting. Statics were further improved by more complex forms, such as the double-arched saddle. There is an undoubted expressiveness about such structures, and it is surely no coincidence that the achievements of civil engineering in this field were taken up in the fifties. In his General Motors Technical Center, Eero Saarinen had already placed the auditorium of the Design Department under a flat, silver calotte shell. He continued this line in his design for the Massachusetts Institute of Technology auditorium with a cupola roof resting on only three points. The results were not, however, entirely satisfying. It lacked an obvious front, and above all it lacked dynamism. Therefore a completely different approach was adopted for the Yale University Ice Hockey Stadium, which he built just a short time later. From a standing central arch spanning the entire length of the building, the roof panes swing out to lateral concrete frames of identical radii. Saarinen thought this hanging roof still looked too apathetic from the outside; it reminded him of a turtle. He therefore extended the ends of the arch beyond their bases and curved them skywards. The long, craning tip above the entrance ends in a lamp sculpture by Oliver Andrews, whereby this visual manipulation re-acquired functional justification. The comment of one hockey player – that the stadium vault shouted "Go, go, go" at him as he chased the puck – confirmed precisely the impression of dynamism intended by this architecture. Unlike the M.I.T., however, this sculptural building is not prominently placed on an empty plot of land, but stands in a crowded urban environment to which its form bears no real relation.

Function and experimental form also found outstanding fusion in a new terminal for Trans World Airlines in New York. On the one hand, the very concept of a passenger terminal for air travellers invited a futuristic approach; on the other hand, competition between private airlines made a striking architectural statement particularly desirable. Above a curving low building facing the approach ramp rises the daring roof of the passenger area. It is in principle composed of four arched shells of spectacular cut. They each stand on two feet, their tips meeting above the centre of the hall. Narrow overhead windows along this interface emphasize the autonomy of the different

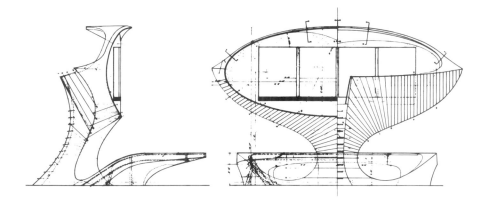

Eero Saarinen
Trans World Airlines Terminal at the
International Airport in Idlewild, New York,
1956–1962
Terminal hall
Photo Ezra Stoller / Esto
"All the curves, all the spaces and elements
right down to the shape of the signs, display
boards, railings and check-in desks were to
be of a matching nature. We wanted passengers passing through the building to experience a fully-designed environment, in which
each part arises from another and everything belongs to the same formal world."
(Eero Saarinen 1959)

Constructional drawing of the Information
desk (above); plan

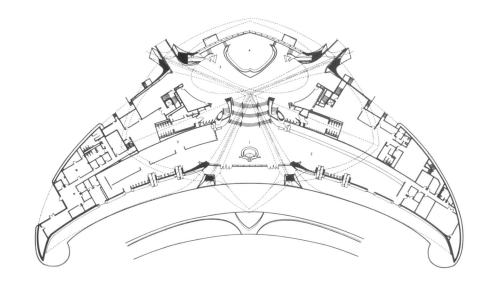

segments. The thickened shell rims, echoing the lines of force in reinforced concrete, add to the organic character of the building. An overall image of a bird with spreading wings is confirmed in the beak-like projection of the roof. The interior is characterized by powerful curves which carry the dramatic style of the roof into even the smallest details.

A – not insignificant – problem accompanying large ferroconcrete shells are the large wooden frames required for their casting, which can account for more than half of total construction costs. It was for this reason that Pier Luigi Nervi worked largely with prefabricated parts in the Palazzetto dello Sport, his "small" stadium for the Olympics in Rome. Its shallow calotte shell is composed of 1620 polygonal prefabricated parts which form a textured diamond pattern on the inside, created by the webs in which the connecting steel reinforcements were laid. Their progression was organic in effect, but did not describe the actual lines of force. The development of the rim zones was thereby of particular note. Since unequal load could cause substantial static problems in these areas, Nervi found a new solution: triangular

Overall view from the approach ramp
Photo Ezra Stoller/Esto
Four Y-shaped supports carry the four arched roof shells of the Terminal Building. The form was fundamentally influenced by Saarinen's idea of creating the impression of a rising roof.

252

Pier Luigi Nervi and Annibale Vitellozzi
Palazzetto dello Sport in Rome, 1956–1957
One of the eight spectator entrances
Photo Giovanni Gherardi
The stadium was built for the 1960 Olympic
Games and can accommodate 4,000–5,000
spectators. The load of the dome roof, with
its 60-metre diameter, is transferred via 36
slanted, Y-shaped pillars to a reinforced-con-
crete ring in the ground.

Opposite page:
Eero Saarinen (arch.), Amman and
Whitney (eng.)
Dulles International Airport of Washington
D.C. in Chantilly, Virginia, 1958–1962
Narrow end of the Terminal Building
Photo Ezra Stoller/Esto
32 angled pillars carry the sagging roof of
the Terminal Building, which introduced a
number of new solutions as regards the organization of passenger flow. The paths of
the arriving and departing passengers were
strictly separated; shuttle buses operating between the planes and the terminal had
height-adjustable cabins and could dock directly onto the planes. A short film by Charles Eames rationalized promotion work vis-à-
vis the airline companies.

concrete elements transfer the load to sloping piers, angled in the exact direction
of vault pressure. The concrete surface of the roof is continued between these piers
and ends in an undulating border. The roof skin is thus drawn optically lower than
the load-bearing shell actually extends.

Dulles International Airport in Washington D.C. was also built with prefabricated
parts. Saarinen here designed a huge hanging roof, held by arms which raise its
broad surface to the sky like the flag bearers at the Olympic Parade of Nations.
Concrete slabs were hung between the supporting steel cables and, as in Nervi's
stadium, covered above with a reinforced closed concrete ceiling.

Saarinen's hanging roof in Washington and Nervi's cupola in Rome both represent
very simple geometric forms. More complicated, however, are the so-called "ruled
surfaces" created via the movement of a generating straight line along two directrices.
At any rate the volumetric figures which result can be manufactured in a mould with
straight boards. In the case of the hyperbolic paraboloid there are even two systems
of generating straight lines; the covering boards can thus also be joined straight,
making the wooden framework simpler and cheaper to build. Such surfaces can be
built both as normal shell roofs and as hanging roofs. Their transformation into an
architecture which is economical as well as constructionally illuminating is not without
its difficulties, however, as the story of the Benjamin Franklin Hall in Berlin reveals.
Presented to the city as a gift by the USA on the occasion of the 1957 Interbau
Exhibition, it was to offer a visual illustration of its function as a congress hall, a
forum for free speech. Architect Hugh Stubbins planned a hanging roof which was
held by two arched supports on each side and which, spectacularly, rested on only
two points. It only actually roofed the central auditorium; the large complex was
otherwise covered with a flat, quadratic cement slab. Since a roof which rests on
only two points is statically almost impossible, a solution was adopted which provoked
much criticism at the time: the walls of the auditorium assumed the load of the roof
section suspended between them, while the clearly-visible wings only supported the
oversailing "hat brim", creating a contradiction between the seeming and the actual
load distribution.

Hugh A. Stubbins with Werner Düttmann and
Franz Mocken (arch.), Fred Severud (eng.)
Benjamin Franklin Hall in Berlin, 1957
Landesbildstelle Berlin

In 1980 the front wing collapsed, following the corrosion of its steel members. In its reconstruction over the next few years it proved possible to execute the original plan, and to indeed base a wide-span roof on only two points. The roof is now raised fully clear of the separate auditorium roof below. Its dimensions are slightly modified as a result of its new structural calculation bases. From an aesthetic point of view, however, the building can still be criticized. In the mad ride of its architecture, the communicative element is left far behind. The interior is both unclear and awkward; the foyer is disfigured by the strange pot-belly of the auditorium above. The – in places very low – ceilings produce a cramped atmosphere, and the lecture hall itself is too much oriented towards purely one-sided communication. Possibilities for meaningful long-term usage are limited by the lack of flexibility of the rooms. This huge architectural gesture today represents little more than a memorial to a past epoch, and the hall was perhaps rebuilt for that very reason.

Cross-section of the 1987 rebuilt version of
the Congress Hall

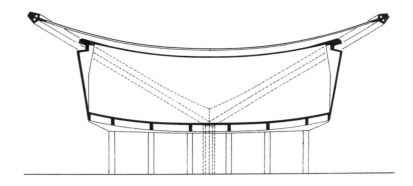

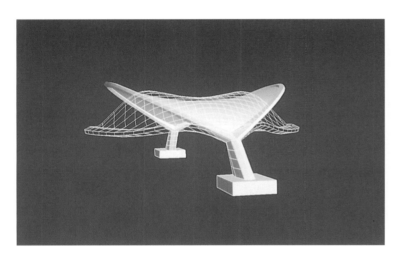

Simulations of roof deformation in the rebuilt
Congress Hall; on the left, load scenario own
weight multiplied by 200, on the right load
scenario wind pressure and wind suction
multiplied by 200. The pictures were gener-
ated with a computer program developed by
Peter Jan Pahl, Rudolf Damrath and Wilhelm
Cattes.
Institut für Allgemeine Bauingenieurmethoden
der TU Berlin

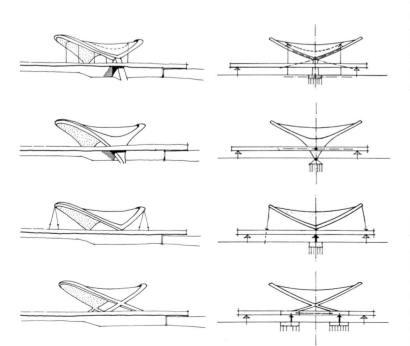

Diagram of alternative possible supporting
frameworks: above, the executed version; second, stabilization via joints in the platform
and the foundation zone; third, bracing of the
arches at the crown; below, crossover of the
rim arches and anchoring on four feet after
the example of the Trade Fair Hall in Raleigh.
From: Karl Heinz Schelling: Ein Nachwort;
Baukunst und Werkform, 1958

255

Paul Rudolph
Yale University Art and Architecture Building
in New Haven, Connecticut, 1958–1964
Photo Ezra Stoller/Esto

Concrete Containers

With the development of the "glass box" architecture entered the era of its technical reproducibility, and the role of the architect threatened – as Vincent Scully wrote – to become that of the packaging designer. The rejection of exterior glamour and fashionable flourishes produced an architecture concerned with the "honest" use of materials, with the clear delineation of functional areas and with gestural "expression". In particular Le Corbusier, who developed sculptural objects – his pilotis, for example – from elements with purely functional origins and then combined them in symbolic ways, intensified the search for expressive construction solutions which reacted individually to their respective functional assignments. For this work Le Corbusier preferred coarse exposed concrete, rough from the mould, which he awarded the dignity of "a face covered with wrinkles".

Louis Kahn also built almost exclusively in concrete. According to his cryptically-esoteric theory of architecture, steel construction permitted no "real" walls and no "real" supports, since during building the actual supporting structures always disappeared behind the obligatory fireproof covering. He only sporadically concealed exposed concrete with brick. His plans, developed from the functional programme, were to reflect the difference between "servant" and "served" spaces; their rhythm appears outside in the alternation of closed towers and open fenestration. In a clear allusion to Le Corbusier, Kahn spoke of the floor plan as a harmony of rooms – rather than volumes – in light, and he consequently sought to deny individual elements their independence. The design of his buildings reflected the duality of access route and workplace, public space and intimacy. That the principles so plausible on paper did not always function as planned in practice in no way reduces the quality of his institute and laboratory buildings.

The design of such low-detail, large-scale architecture demanded particular sensibility. Conflicts arose above all where egoistic architectural self-assertion irritated sensitive innercity nerves. Paul Rudolph's Art and Architecture Building for Yale University in New Haven thereby treads a thin line. Many more floors than at first suspected lie hidden behind a solid and, at the same time, irritatingly fragmented street front. The broad crossbar of the sixth storey is forced against the upward thrust of the windowless towers. The building's Cyclopean overtones apparently rub off on its users, nurturing aggression – there seems little other explanation for the vandalism which reduced the building to a desolate state. In the following years Rudolph placed such "urban construction accents" with much less subtlety: his Parking Garage in New Haven, only a few blocks away from the Institute, is nothing more than a brutal concrete container.

Concrete also proved the easiest solution to the structural, constructional and economic requirements of mass housing. Le Corbusier was given an opportunity to implement his concept of a "vertical housing city" in his "Unité d'Habitation" in Marseilles. This wide concrete complex – a huge "bottle-rack", as Le Corbusier

Louis I. Kahn
Jonas Salk Institute of Biological Studies in
La Jolla, California, 1959–1965
Stairs between the offices and the
laboratory building
Photo Julius Shulman

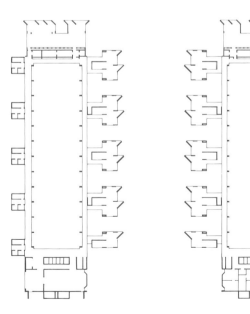

Plan of the laboratory building
The laboratories in both wings are free of
supports and undivided. Stairs, offices and
secondary rooms are attached in front in
separated sections.

called it – forms a frame into which apartments are slotted like drawers. These apartments extend the full depth of the building and include a second floor of half the depth. This made it possible to create a living area double the normal room height. Two rows of cleverly interlocked apartments border on a common central corridor, a dark, windowless passageway which passes through the building like a "road". Yardstick and generator of architectural proportions was the Modulor which Le Corbusier developed at this time, and which combined the Continental metric and English anthropomorphic measurement systems and ordered them in an ascending numerical sequence. The ultima ratio of room height thereby emerged as a humble 226 centimetres, or 7 feet 5 inches.

Two storeys of shops on the seventh and eighth floors were to be the centre of the internal road network and heart of the self-sufficient unit. But even assuming that all the families living here would also shop here, 340 parties were simply too few to keep in business a whole range of stores with attractive selections. The arcade soon became a wasteland with only one store remaining. Further mistakes can be

Entrance to the laboratory building from the visitor's car-park
Photo Julius Shulman
The overall complex provided for a concentration of the three function areas of work, living and community life in three differently-designed building sections. The hermetic impression of the laboratory building thereby corresponds to the secluded, self-absorbed world of scientific research.

Le Corbusier
"Unité d'Habitation" in Marseille,
1945–1952
Roof terrace
Photo private collection
The apartment block's two ventilation shafts
end in powerful, sculpturally-moulded superstructures which dominate the varied roofscape. To the rear on the left is the child day-
care centre with swimming pool, on the right
the running track and, in the foreground, the
steps leading up to the bar and sun terrace.

Opposite page: Le Corbusier print with
Modulor figure
Fondation Le Corbusier, Paris

View from the road
Photo private collection
56 metres high, 137 metres long and 24 metres deep, this "vertical housing city" provides room for 337 apartments. Each apartment has a loggia and a two-storey section with a gallery, and extends the full depth of the building. The room heights are 226 cm (7' 5") and 480 cm (15' 9"). These – in cross-section L-shaped – units slot over each other in such a way that space for the access corridor is left in the centre. The shopping and communication centres on the seventh and eighth floors are identified by a change in the façade structure. The entire building surface is bare concrete; only the balcony and window niches are painted a clear red, blue, yellow and green.

Kenzo Tange
Kagawa Prefectural Office Building in
Takamatsu, 1956–1958
Roof terrace of the main building
Photo Ezra Stoller/Esto

Overall view
Photo Ezra Stoller/Esto
Two new buildings were built onto two already existing administration buildings. A raised wing with conference rooms rests on an open storey of stilts. Sitting on top of the nine-storey office building behind is a cube with a tea room and observation platform.

Kenzo Tange
Yamanashi Press & Broadcasting Centre in
Kofu, 1964–1966
Burkhard Verlag Ernst Heyer Archives
Sixteen concrete pipes each with a diameter
of five metres serve as the supporting structure for the inserted office spaces and contain service and access installations. The
building structure is part of the city structure
designed by Tange; both are viewed as
coherent, freely-expandable systems.

seen in the design of its access areas which posed major obstacles to the practical transformation of the social premise underlying the complex. The indecisive territoriality of the neither private nor public corridor system, plus its darkness, made leaving the apartment seem an excursion into "enemy" territory and created insecurity and fear. There is simply no development of the sense of home which should ultimately accompany the communal ideal behind the "Unité". The architectural pose of this house on stilts primarily allowed an all-round view of the large parking lot: what passes under the house is not "landscape" but strong winds and the noise of car engines.

Lewis Mumford's verdict in the "New Yorker" magazine in 1957 was devastating: "With the 'Unité' Le Corbusier betrays human needs for the sake of a monumental aesthetic effect. The result is an egocentric extravagance, as imposing as an Egyptian pyramid meant to give a corpse immortality and, humanely speaking, just as bleak."

Le Corbusier's experiment, repeated and modified in numerous subsequent variations, nonetheless exercised a strong influence over a whole generation of architects, and the impressive modelling of the façade relief, as well as the decisive identity of the main body of the building, indeed earned respect. The price for all this was, however, unusually high construction costs.

The structuring of large masses by means of plastically-developed individual elements

Moshe Safdie
"Habitat 67" Apartment Block at Expo '67,
Montreal, 1966–1967
Bavaria Verlag Archives
Of the 900 apartments planned for this gigantic building block, 158 were completec.
354 prefabricated individual containers are
stacked in a confused order and connected
by steel cables. Projections and recesses are
organized in such a way that each apartment has a balcony on the roof of the apartment immediately below.

was also the aim of Japanese architect Kenzo Tange. As already in his Peace Centre
in Hiroshima, he sought to communicate classical Japanese architectural language
using Western ideas. He thereby found his way to modular systems which – even
in only partially realized forms, such as the Communications Centre in Kofu –
permitted the flexible organization of spatial programmes. He met demands for
more densely-populated development with a container architecture which related
aspects of urban planning to the inner functional logic of the building. The image
of the hive suggested by Le Corbusier's "Unité" was reflected in the cell structure
of all these models.

Enrico Castiglioni and Carlo Fontana
Technical College in Busto Arsizio,
1963–1964
End view of the northern wing
Burkhard Verlag Ernst Heyer Archives
The school was conceived as a symmetrical
two-winged complex. The members of the
two halves stand back to back; classrooms
and workshops are staggered towards the
light. In the middle axis lies a flat access
wing which seems to bend open the building. The dynamic curve in the verticals of the
longitudinal façades is also shared by the
horizontals of the main façade.

Plan

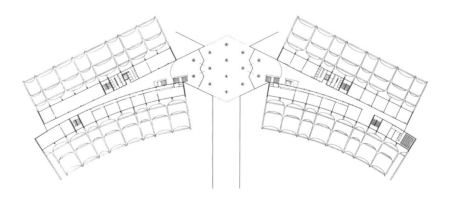

Oscar Niemeyer
Congress Building and Administration Block
on the Plaza dos tres Poderes in Brasilia,
1958
Photo C.W. Schmidt-Luchs / G+J Fotoservice

The planning of the new test-tube Brazilian
capital lay in the hands of architect Lucio
Costà. The designs with which he won the re-
stricted-entry competition proposed two
main axes crossing at right angles – one
gently curved, with residential developments.
and one completely straight, running six kilo-
metres from the "Square of the Three
Powers" via an entertainment and services
centre at the intersection and up to the railway station. The Congress Building stands
as vanishing point at one end of this
monumental axis.

Section and plan of the Congress Building
The Senate Chamber lies beneath the come
on the left, the Chamber of Representatives
in the bowl on the right.

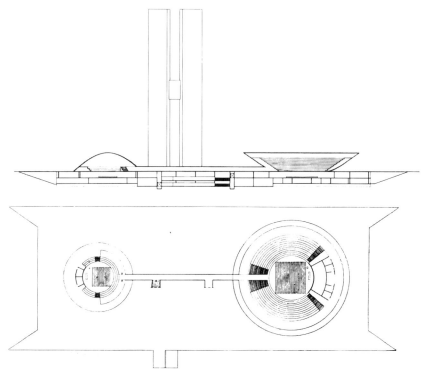

1956–1990

Learning from Las Vegas

It was Robert Venturi and Denise Scott Brown who redefined the tasks of architecture from a sociological understanding of visual communication. Subject of their analysis were the typical characteristics of the radically-commercialized American "Main Street". In their search for new maxims for the design of urban spaces, they oriented themselves towards the subjective daily perceptions of pedestrians and car drivers. Accordingly, in their book "Learning from Las Vegas", they related the flood of image-laden advertising and neon signs on the Las Vegas Strip to architectural symbols. The chaotic state of innercity organization demands more than the "simple" and "clean" solutions of the functional school. For unlike a work of art in a museum, architecture is always perceived in an urban setting. It cannot escape direct confrontation and competition with the signals of consumerism and traffic.

The pictorial and commercial-strip qualities of architecture now became increasingly important. The symbolic character of the façade was analytically separated from the constructive and functional elements of the building. From this Venturi and Scott Brown deduced the existence of two basic architectural manifestations. "Where the architectural systems of space, structure, and program are submerged and distorted by an overall symbolic form", they speak of a "duck" — in honour of a small drive-in diner whose exterior indeed had the shape of a duck. The opposite of this is the "decorated shed", in which "systems of space and structure are directly at the service of program, and ornament is applied independently of them." They thus negate the "classical" understanding of Modernism, whereby the value of a building arises from its successful fusion of construction and programme.

The interplay between façade and form is made apparent in the Guild House Retirement Home in Philadelphia. The strongly axial central projection with its white base, the granite pillar before the entrance, the flat arched window at the top and the symmetrical wings with fine ribboning at the level of the penultimate floor articulate the front with a variety of historical echoes. These are clearly contradicted by the perforated plates of the balcony parapets, the ferroconcrete supports revealed behind the glazed arch and the "Guild House" sign, which could just as well stand above a shop door. The reverse perspective of the graduation of window size and the delicate slits in the centre bay which openly acknowledge the superficial nature of the brick façade represent the essential architectural vernacular of the Venturi, Rauch & Scott Brown partnership. Single elements are extracted from their usual surroundings and integrated into the composition in such a way that they function like quotes, alluding to conventional perspectives without taking them any further. Thus, in the Guild House, any hint of actual representation and monumentality is repressed by countermeasures of a disillusioning nature. Against compulsively uniform building design, devoted to the fetish that "even less is even more", Venturi set an "architecture of complexity and contradiction", which "is not, however, to be confused with a picturesque architecture or an architecture of the subjectively expressive will

Charles W. Moore Associates and Urban Innovations Group with August Perez Associates
Piazza d'Italia in New Orleans, Louisiana, 1974–1978
Plan
The pattern of cobbles circles around Sicily as the central point. An island in the fountain resembles the boot of Italy.

Opposite page: View of the Triumphal Arch
Photo Norman McGrath
Set in the spandrels of the implied serliana are water-spouting masks in the likeness of the architect; Moore calls them "wetopens". The slightly higher background arch, in un-classical "Deli Order", was to be the entrance to a restaurant.

Robert Venturi with Cope and Lippincott
Guild House Retirement Home in Philadel-
phia, Pennsylvania, 1960–1963
View from the south
Photo VRSB

Shadows emphasize the angled cut of the
entrance doorcasing. The ax ally-symmetric
façade is crowned by a stylized television antenna: an ironic reference to the main preoc-
cupation of its residents which was, however,
soon removed.

Plan of the ground floor
Analogous to the staggered façade, the design of the interior access cores was able to
avoid the dismal feature of endless corridors.

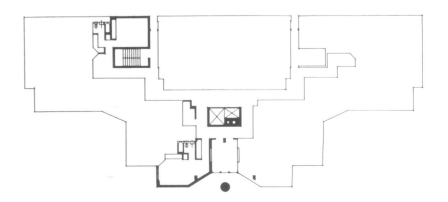

Robert Venturi with Arthur Jones
Vanna Venturi House in Chestnut Hill,
Pennsylvania, 1962–1964
Plans of the ground and upper floors
Similar to the Guild House, an indent leads
to the front door, here positioned at right
angles to the façade. The diagonal walls of
the ground floor can be mentally expanded
into an ellipse. A stairway squeezes itself behind the chimney and up to the next floor,
where a door reveals another flight of steps,
too steep to walk up and leading nowhere
anyway – except perhaps to jars of jam and
preserves.

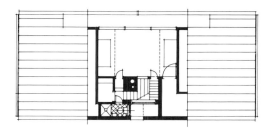

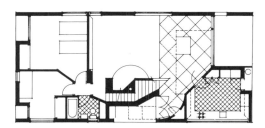

View of the entrance
Photo VRSB
Robert Venturi calls the house, which he built
for his mother, "a small house on a large
scale. . . The signs of the 'large' scale in the
exterior are the projecting elements: large,
few in number, in central or even symmetrical positions, together with the simplicity and
tangibility of the silhouette as a whole." Venturi's first important book, "Complexity and
Contradiction in Architecture" (published in
1966), was written during the construction of
this house.

View of the rear with its balcony incision
Photo George Pohl/VRSB

Robert A.M. Stern and John Hagmann
Ehrman House in Armonk, New York,
1975–1976
Garden front
Photo Edmund Stocklein
Robert Stern here sought to realize his interpretation of an associative and perceptional
architecture by means of confusing collages
and overlappings. By freeing surfaces from
the façade and placing them like scenery before his rooms, he blurs distinctions between
inside and outside and leaves actual volume
unclear. Changing room heights and shifted
axes organize the extensive spatial programme, whose hierarchy remains open in
complex interrelationships. What distinguishes this house from others of Stern's
works is the avoidance of overly-obtrusive
architectural quotations and excessive façade rhetoric.

Axonometric projection
The main entrance must be imagined behind
the chimney in the top right of the drawing. It
leads to the central living area and from
there, via a long corridor leading to the
other end of the house, to the bedrooms. A
striking palisade is situated in front of the
curving glazed front of the last room.

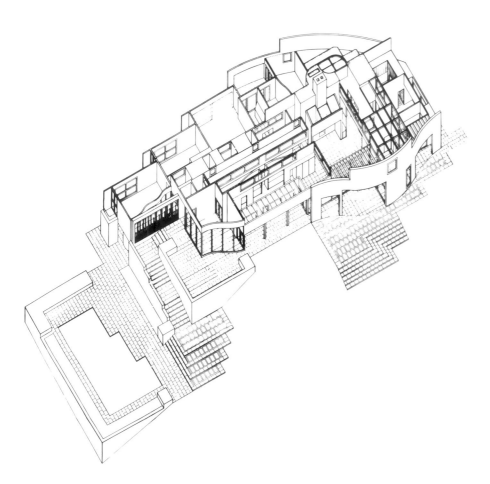

Robert Venturi, John Rauch and Denise Scctt
Brown
Brant House in Greenwich, Connecticut,
1970–1973
View from the driveway
Photo VRSB
This complex building is distinguished by a
number of special features: the bulging
axially-symmetric façade with its green-
glazed blocks, whose diagonal texture
breaks the symmetry; the entrance at the
level of the sunken garage; the central position of the kitchen and the spread of the living room – its plan recalling art deco motifs –
which provides the room with indirect light.
The split levels of the spatial programme
point to the influence of Adolf Loos, Venturi's
declared model.

Plan of the ground floor

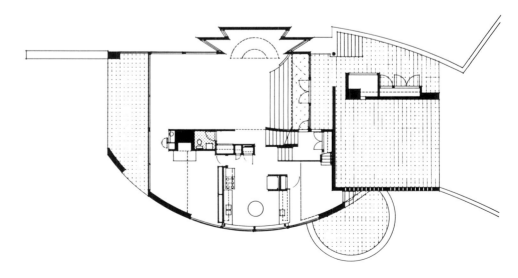

Robert Venturi and John Rauch
Dixwell Fire Station, New Haven,
Connecticut, 1967–1974
Photo VRSB

The simple building gives an otherwise amorphous road junction a dominant vanishing point. Its narrow window band, functional garage doors and spaced lettering recall architecture of the 1930s.

Steven Izenour with John Case and Robert Venturi
BASCO Showroom in the Oxford Valley Mall, Bristol Township, Pennsylvania, 1979
The O of the sign
Photo VRSB
"What can you do with a 5-metre-high and 350-metre-long building which has only one door and not a single window? We were commissioned to 'beautify' this run-down and long-unused fifties shopping mall. . . The wide open space of the parking lot, further underlined by the unredeemed banality of the architecture, suggested a design aiming at summary communication rather than subtle expression." (Venturi and Rauch)

Opposite page, below:
Denise Scott Brown
City Edges Planning Study, 1973
Welcoming billboards showing the city skyline and William Penn on the Schuykill River Parkway in Philadelphia, Pennsylvania
Photomontage VRSB
Object of the Planning Study was the recording and revision of the existing visual signals on two of Philadelphia's large arterial roads. This was to form the subsequent basis of "refurbishment" with significant symbols, which would communicate to passing motorists the special social and historical attractions of the region – a function given particular emphasis within the framework of preparations for America's bicentennial celebrations – and at the same time improve orientation and thus safety on the roads.

to create". The pictorial "building blocks" should correspond – objectively – to task and situation. Site is thereby made significant: historical set pieces and the respect for local forms and materials lead to the recovery of identificatory characteristics of architecture, perhaps even of home. This also seems to apply to the work of Charles Moore, whose very personal style is won from a wealth of traditional motifs. He works with superimposed, often disproportioned false façades and interrupted walls developed from a playful "house within a house" concept. His pleasure in architecture is clearly evident.

Moore's Piazza d'Italia in New Orleans is a climax of such an understanding of design. The arrangement is accompanied by a stage setting of wittily-manipulated orders of classical columns: fine water jets trace Doric fluting, Tuscan-order columns are made of slit steel, capitals are crowned with neon tubes. Reproduction is determined by elision; that which is omitted is just as symbolic as that which is included. It was this that made the Piazza a typical Post-Modern subject for architecture critic Charles Jencks: "A Post-Modern building speaks, to give a brief definition, to at least two groups at once: architects and an interested minority who concern themselves with specific architectural problems, and the general public or local visitors who are concerned with questions of comfort, traditional construction methods and their style of living." This "double coding" can only be successful, however, where symbolic references resist overstatement and remain open in their interpretation.

Supermarket renovations carried out by the SITE (Sculpture in the Environment) group for BEST Products combine paradox with destruction; the architects themselves spoke of "De-architecture": "Architecture is regarded, in the Houston project, as a matrix for art ideas and as a "found object" – or the "subject matter" for art, rather than

SITE Projects Inc. with Maples-Jones Associates
Indeterminate Façade Showroom
in the Almeda-Genoa Shopping Center,
Houston, Texas, 1975
View of the artificial ruin from the south-west
Photo SITE

SITE Projects Inc.
Cutler Ridge Showroom in Miami, Florida,
1979
Perspective drawing of the main façade

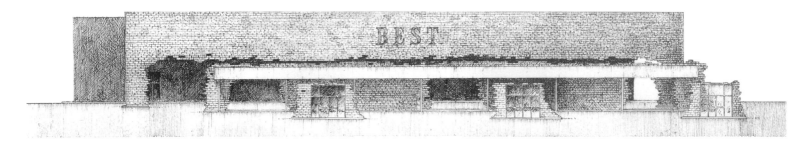

SITE Projects Inc. with Simpson/Stratta Associates
Notch Showroom in the Arden Fair Shopping Center, Sacramento, California, 1977
Photo SITE
The notch of the corner slides open on rails to allow access to the main entrance.

SITE Projects Inc.
Peeling Project in Richmond, Virginia, 1972
Entrance façade
Photo SITE
The brick wall – the old trademark of BEST supermarkets – seems to be peeling away from the main concrete body. It in fact represents a complex work of craftsmanship using a special adhesive mortar.

the objective of design. The building also uses architecture as a means of social and psychological commentary, as opposed to an exploration of form, space, and structure." Peeling, crumbling and seemingly pointlessly disintegrating façades pose an obvious contradiction to the lavish, precise execution of the brickwork. Chaos is mastered. In these "take-another-look" designs, the customer remains safe – a subtle promise within the chaotic environment of the American suburb. The secular box behind the façade is not affected by the transformation, and neither is the sign, smallest common denominator of this provocative corporate identity.

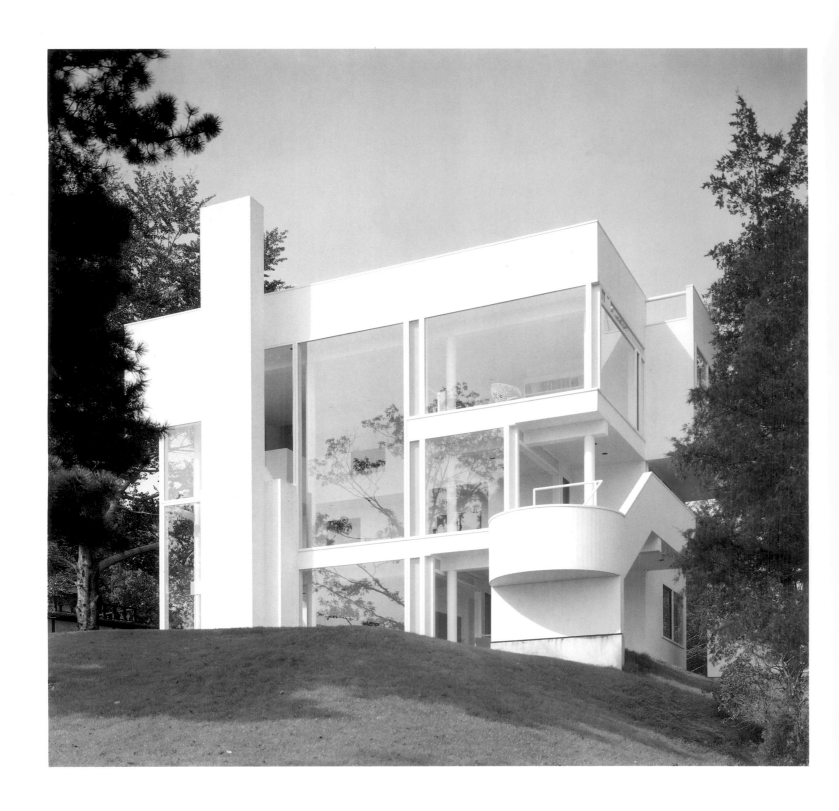

Richard Meier
Smith House in Darien, Connecticut,
1965–1967
View from the south-east
Photo Ezra Stoller/Esto
This white solitaire on Long Island Sound
was Meier's first publicized house. It is a
wooden construction with individual steel
supports; brickwork was only employed for
the chimney. The axis is oriented along the
path from the end of the drive to the coast-
line.

The Whites

On the occasion of a CASE (Conference of Architects for the Study of the Environment) symposium in 1969, an exhibition in the Museum of Modern Art in New York introduced five previously barely-known architects. These were Peter Eisenman, Michael Graves, Charles Gwathmey, John Hejduk and Richard Meier, called The New York Five after the title of the accompanying publication, "Five Architects". The press, in an allusion to the sparkling white façades of their houses, soon had their own name for the group: the Whites. For Richard Meier it was a question not of reduction but simply of the best choice. "It is against a white surface that one best appreciates the play of light and shadow, solids and voids. For this reason white has traditionally been taken as a symbol of purity and clarity, of perfection. . . Goethe said, 'Color is the paint of light'. Whiteness, perhaps, is the memory and the anticipation of color. . . Whiteness is one of the characteristic qualities of my work; I use it to clarify architectural concepts and heighten the power of visual form."

The attention attracted by the rigidly black-and-white drawings and first buildings by the Five arose from a combination of their mathematical play of ideas with an artistic handwriting. They were unmistakably oriented towards the classics of Modernism, above all Le Corbusier's villas of the twenties, but also towards the buildings of Italian Rationalism, such as by Giuseppe Terragni; they thus fell within the traditions of architectural history. Their published theories were rather more difficult to follow, however, and remote from everyday building practice.

The theoretical excursions of Peter Eisenman in particular – for the most part expressed in a series of analytical transformation drawings – represent a radical confession of faith in an autonomous architecture which entirely frees itself from criteria of habitability. The rejection of the positivistic character of form and function finds its correlation in "anastrophic manipulation", the conscious inversion of the terms of architectural language. Modernism – as he sees it – mirrors man's displacement from the centre of the world and can thus by no means be considered complete. The architectural object becomes the vehicle of contradictions to which its design reacts with the strategies of intersection, rotation and omission. Line, plane and volume appear as geometric variables in competition with support, wall and space. The design concept takes pride of place: the house actually built is ultimately just a more complex form of its representation. It therefore looks – according to Eisenman – like "a cardboard model and demands to be read in a conceptual manner. . ., whereby you turn it around in your mind as you would a model."

John Hejduk is considered, alongside Eisenman, the leading theoretician of the Five. Designs such as his Diamond Houses remained drawing-board experiments. Their construction in storey slabs, reminiscent of Le Corbusier's Dom-ino system, their support grid and their in-built elements turned through an angle of 45 degrees within the cube are the apparent motifs of his research on architectural syntax. "The

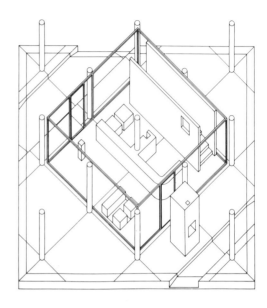

John Hejduk
Diamond House A, Project, 1967
Isometric drawing of the ground floor
The four-storey house is structured throughout by supports and wall planes in a 45° grid. While the fully-glazed, rotated lounge on the ground floor does not fully exploit the dimensions of the construction, the glass walls on the upper floors, with their angled sunshades in front, extend to the boundary line shown.

Richard Meier
Weinstein House in Old Westbury, New York, 1969–1971
Walkway between the annex and main building
Photo Ezra Stoller/Esto
The longitudinal axis of the house lies – with a deviation of 15° – in a north-south direction; the bedrooms face east and the communal rooms west. The comprehensive spatial programme included eleven bedrooms and accompanying bathrooms, whereby the accessibility and simultaneous separation of personal retreats and family areas became a central theme.

Entrance front
Photo Ezra Stoller/Esto
A free-standing steel pillar extends the support grid up to the gate house and marks the beginning of the footpath. The tall glazed recess above the entrance offers a view through the entire building, past the central ramp to the walkway connecting it with the annex.

West front
Photo Ezra Stoller/Esto
The two extended cubes of the main building flank the glazed ramp building, not visible in this picture.

Plan of the first floor and section

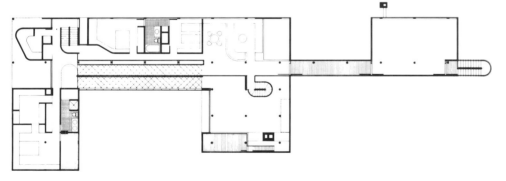

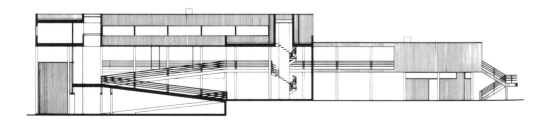

Gwathmey Siegel & Associates
Haupt Villa, Amagansett, New York,
1977–1978
View from the west
Photo Norman McGrath

North front with entrance and garage
Photo Norman McGrath
Behind the north wall lies the access ramp;
its lower incline is shown as c cut-away section in the façade. Clearly visible in the glanc-
ing light are the narrow groove and tongue
boards of the white-stained cedarwood facing.

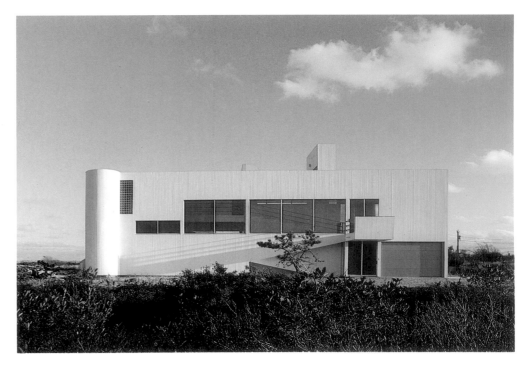

284

South front with pool
Photo Norman McGrath
The level of the living area had to be raised in line with building regulations governing this high-water area. The pool terrace continues this level, whereby the pool was sunk into a shallow box construction. The bedroom, linked to this open space via a small flight of steps, lies at a different height to the living area, since it falls directly above the garage.

Axonometric projection

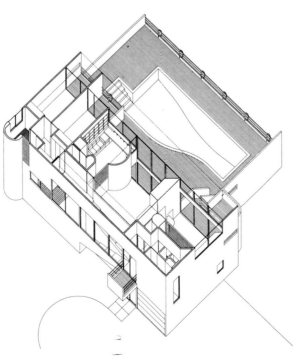

Michael Graves
Hanselmann House in Fort Wayne, Indiana,
1967
Entrance front
Photo Tom Yee

Plan of the second floor
A second cube, suggested by a false façade, was originally intended to sit in front of
the main cuboid house. It was to be made
of gas pipes but – like the small studio
sketched on its right – was never actually
built. Graves speaks of a house with three façades. The second is the strongly-articulated
actual house front and the third is the rear
wall of the living room, featuring a large
mural.

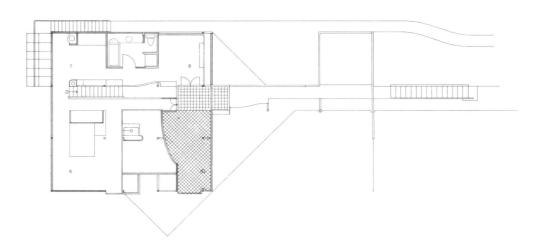

Interior view
Photo Tom Yee
The balcony on the second floor is reached
via a small walkway; the window wall curves
into the open hall.

286

Peter Eisenman
House III (Miller House), Lakeville,
Connecticut, 1970
Eisenman assigns this house to his formalist
phase: having oriented himself towards Le
Corbusier and Terragni, he sought here to
find a form of architectonic expression which
"did not thematize function".

Axonometric projection
Numerous "unclear" overlapping situations
result from the penetration of a cube by two
smaller squares of which one is rotated
through 45°.

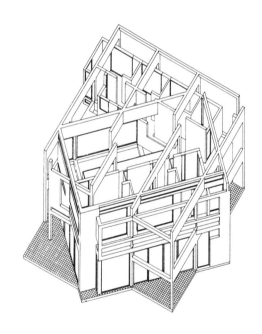

mysteries of central-peripheral-frontal-diagonal-concave-convex,. . . the arguments
of two-dimensional and one-dimensional space,. . . the concepts of configurations,
the static and the dynamic: everything begins to take on the form of a vocabulary."
Charles Gwathmey and Richard Meier, on the other hand, have not only built in
considerable quantity but have also retained a high degree of lucidity in their play
of rotating, intersecting wall planes and volumes. Meier bases his designs on three
pairs of reference criteria: program and site, entry and circulation, structure and
enclosure. The environment dictates axes and vanishing points to which the building
reacts. This can be seen particularly clearly in Meier's Atheneum, an information
centre for visitors to the history-laden town of New Harmony. In reaction to the
accompanying course of the river and the city grid, wall slabs break through the
cube at angles of 5 and 45 degrees. Views through and beyond its structures make
interrelationships the subject of this architecture.

External relationships cannot become such central themes in residential housing,
where inner organization forms the leitmotif. It is derived from the development of
the spatial program, whereby ramps, vistas and graduated levels are employed to
deliberate effect. Charles Gwathmey exploits the possibilities offered by overlapping
layers of space to arrive at buildings with very clear lines. The core of the design is
often a "joint" at which vertically or horizontally-offset bodies meet. Gwathmey
progressed from strictly cubic and cylindrical forms to increasingly dynamic, complex
spatial constructions animated by a wealth of inner moments of tension.

Michael Graves was rather more loosely related to the group and soon distanced
himself in his work from the crystalline clarity of his colleagues. With his cultivation
of "constructed decoration", single quotational elements thrust themselves to the
fore. Although his early Hanselmann House, with its positive-negative interplay of
two house cubes and its "layered" façade, pays conceptual homage to the design
programme of the Whites, the latters' disciplined boundaries are quickly violated
by murals suggesting Pop mutations of Cubist or Purist art of the twenties.

Peter Eisenman
House VI (Frank House), Cornwall,
Connecticut, 1972–1973
View from the north-west
Photo Norman McGrath
This house became something of a celebrity
thanks to its "upside-down" staircase.

Right: View from the south-east
Photo Norman McGrath

Opposite page: Interior view
Photo Norman McGrath
Stairs lead from the entrance to the upper
floor, while a shallow sequence of landings
leads down to the living area. The colour
scheme indicates to which system each building component – or even just one of its sides
– belongs.

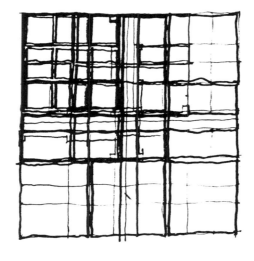

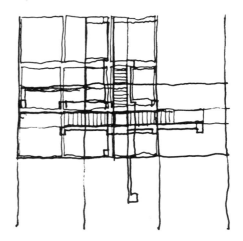

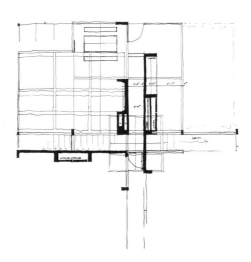

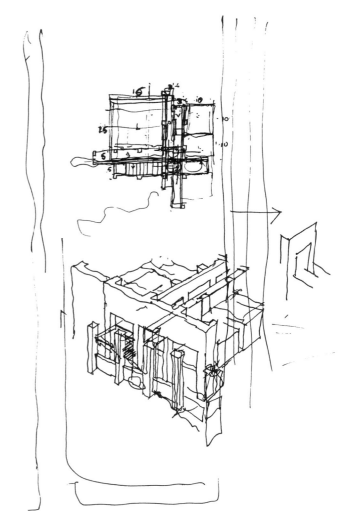

Design sketches
The plan develops from a number of geometric transformations and omissions which increasingly destroy the regularity of the original structure.

Richard Meier
The Atheneum, New Harmony, Indicna,
1975–1979
View of the west front with main entrance
from the Wabash river plain
Photo Ezra Stoller/Esto

East front with stair ramp
Photo Ezra Stoller/Esto

The building displays clearly accentuated lines of reference to the river moorings, the town and the parking lot. Its basic grid lies parallel to the town plan and is cut at an angle of 5° by the long stair ramp, which leads towards the historical buildings. This axial rotation is continued in the interior as the overlapping of two reference systems. A large wall segment above the entrance in the west side flexes through 45° to stand perpendicular to the footpath from the parking lot. The curve of another section echoes the course of the river. Numerous ramps and stairways emphasize the passage-type character of the building and give access to various observation points. Their railings, along with the white-enamelled façade panels cladding the steel-skeleton construction, recall ocean liners. The complex as a whole does not, however, support this association; the building is too crystalline and, in its dynamics, open in too many directions.

The Atheneum serves as a Tourist Information centre for New Harmony, whose history was determined by Georg Rapp's pietistic religious communion of Harmonists and the social Utopian co-operative of Robert Owen. Tours of the historical town start here. The Atheneum lies outside New Harmony's rigid grid plan and represents the continuation of a series of buildings created within a programme of urban revival and situated freely on the town periphery. The Atheneum lies closest to the Wabash River, whose extreme fluctuations in water level necessitated the building of embankments along its sides. Of the originally more extensive building programme, only one section – containing auditorium and model exhibition – was realized.

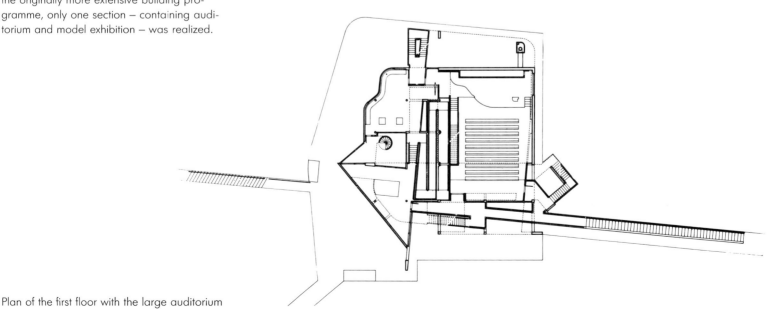

Plan of the first floor with the large auditorium

Work on Modernism

15 July 1972 saw the memorable dynamiting of the Pruitt-Igoe Estate in St. Louis, Missouri. Its monotonous, eleven-storey slab skyscrapers, built twenty years earlier by Minoru Yamasaki, had been an award-winning model settlement by all the standards then held to be progressive. It represented the successful creation of inexpensive housing for many, surrounded by public parks and in disciplined rows of housing units. But in the long corridors between its anonymous apartment doors, chaos reigned. Vandalism and crime could no longer be controlled. Critic and architect Charles Jencks took the demolition of the block as the occasion to declare Modernism dead, only to be promptly contradicted. According to Jencks, James Stirling and Philip Johnson insisted "that they were still modern architects – and still alive". It was true that no funeral could as yet be announced for the "decline in authority of the Holy Trinity of function, material and construction", as Wolfgang Pehnt described it. Uninspired lumps of cement cast dubious light on the claims of functional architecture, but for this reason many architects were by no means ready to be classified as Late or even Post-Modern.

Modern architecture had meanwhile been developed in very different directions, whereby narrative and commercial-strip tendencies came to the fore. But there was – and is – a tradition which carefully employed and cautiously expanded the vocabulary already established. Its representatives sought neither exaggerated effects nor defensive, half-hearted integration within the changing urban environment. Egon Eiermann was one such architect resisting the adoption of both sculpturally-fissured façades and conventional architecture in neo-romantic gesture. "Modern architecture", as he observed in 1964, "can be seen to be throwing itself at concrete with a wasteful, baroque intensity of form reminiscent of sculpture rather than architecture. As a lover of steel, I would like to say that, for me, the steel building represents the aristocratic principle of architecture. It has nothing in common with that mushy moss which, poured into moulds, can be bent and turned, hardens slowly and is only given its backbone by steel. . ."

The attempt to make new buildings forcibly conform to historical cityscapes seemed to Eiermann a betrayal of Modernism, especially since official objections were often only directed at appearances. Buildings such as the Johns-Manville headquarters at the foot of the Rocky Mountains, and the University of Lethbridge in Canada, sit like giant foreign bodies in the middle of nature, and yet the simultaneous clarity of their magnificent statements may – for all their apparent brutality – be interpreted as an expression of respect. The same may be said of the buildings of Cesar Pelli, of Kevin Roche John Dinkeloo and Associates and others besides. Their sealed bodies are like the spaceships of science fiction epics which – confidently self-contained – appear to have landed on their powerful supporting structures only briefly, and might fly away at any time. The attempt to unite all functional areas under the same skin leads to a loss of scale, since the uniform façade grid of the

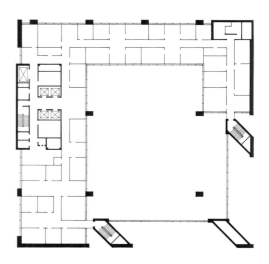

Kevin Roche John Dinkeloo and Associates
Ford Foundation Building in New York,
1963–1968
Interior view
Photo Norman McGrath
The volume of the building requisitions the whole of the square site. Two twelve-storey office wings are wrapped around a fully-glazed inner courtyard with abundant plants. Galleries at dizzying heights cling to the massive vertical pillars and close the frame on the street side.

Plan

Egon Eiermann
Josef Neckermann KG Distribution Centre in
Frankfurt am Main, 1958–1961
Photo Horstheinz Neuendorff / Institut für
Baugeschichte der Universität Karlsruhe

Inner courtyard on the fourth floor
Photo Horstheinz Neuendorff / Institut für
Baugeschichte der Universität Karlsruhe
At 257 metres long and 65 metres wide, the
Distribution Centre occupies a volume of approximately 400,000 cubic metres. Its reinforced-concrete supports form a grid of 6 x 6
metres. The perimeter escape balconies also
serve the maintainance and shading of the
glazed areas. Colour helps articulate the
long façades: thus concrete is light grey, railings white or blue and awnings and emer-
gency exits yellow or red.

Egon Eiermann
Headquarters of Olivetti Deutschland in
Frankfurt am Main, 1968–1972
View of the towers
Photo Berengo Gardin / Institut für Baugeschichte der Universität Karlsruhe
Two towers of administrative offices and
guest apartments are linked to a low building housing the sales, computer and training
centre. Their goblet form – whereby the
floors only reach full size at the sixth level –
allowed the buildings to be placed close
together. As in the Neckermann Distribution
Centre, escape balconies and awnings were
supported by a lightweight steel frame, giving the façades a technical open-work delicacy.

Section

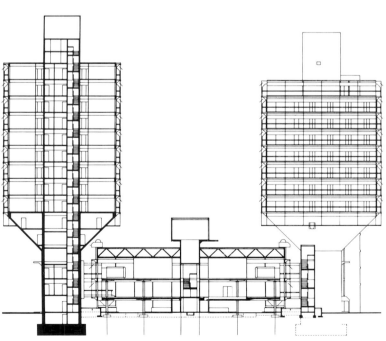

James Stirling and James Gowan with
Michael Wilford and Malcolm Higgs
University of Leicester Engineering
Department, 1959–1963
Axonometric projection
Attached to a tower of offices and laboratories is a large hall of workshops. Many of
the angular volumes are cut at 45°; the shed
roof of the workshop building is also rotated
through 45° to the façades. Terracotta tiles
face the concrete surfaces of the – otherwise
steel-supported – building.

Opposite page: View from the park
Photo Richard Einzig/Arcaid

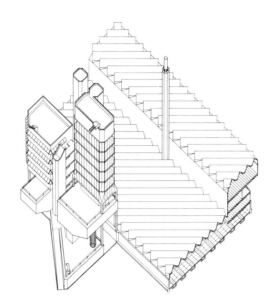

James Stirling with Michael Wilford, Briar
Frost and David Bartlett
Cambridge University History Faculty,
1964–1967
Main entrance
Photo Richard Einzig/Arcaid
Seminar and office rooms are contained within
two seven-storey wings. They lie at right angles
to the glass-roofed library reading room, which
in turn borders the low building in which the
books are housed.

Axonometric projection

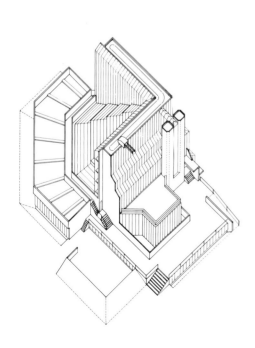

Vittorio Gregotti
University of Calabria near Cosenza, 1973
Gregotti Archives

Perspective drawing

Adolfo Natalini
Bank in Alzate Brianza, 1985
Photos Gabriele Basilico
The reinforced-concrete construction is clcd
completely with panels of granite. The
striped pattern arises from the alternating
use of light-coloured variegated stone and
dark grey polished stone.

Adolfo Natalini
Bank in Alzate Brianza, 1985
Photos Gabriele Basilico

Philip Johnson and Richard Foster
Laboratory Tower of the Yale University
Biology Institute, New Haven, Connecticut,
1964–1966
The load-bearing concrete structure remains
hidden behind brick cylinders; the column
motif is continued in the covered walkway in
the front courtyard. Its elevated hillside location places the Institute in an exciting urban-
architectural relationship with the Knights of
Columbus tower on the far side of Common
Green in the middle of the city.

curtain wall and the size of the volume offer almost no points of orientation. Some architects now prefer to give their buildings a self-created scale by means of outsize constructional elements, as can be seen in the large buildings of Kevin Roche and John Dinkeloo. Others do away with all surface structure and make the building disappear under a reflective or opaque glass cover wrapped around the building like foil, as in the deep blue Pacific Design Center by Cesar Pelli.

Such buildings, grandiose and impressive, nevertheless have about them an indefinable quality which leads the observer to wonder what it is they remind him of. Distortions of scale and reflecting surfaces ultimately suggest very small objects which have grown to a gigantic size and have thus become building blocks from Gulliver's box of toys. In a college project, students were asked what associations Cesar Pelli's Pacific Design Center in Los Angeles provoked in them. Amongst the numerous and very varied replies, the image of a decorative strip of moulding stood out in particular.

As mentioned above, the common characteristics of such architecture included the desire to house all functional areas in a single building, the emphasis upon its technical skin and the rejection of narrow-minded conformity to the surrounding urban or natural landscape. Many saw these as the sine qua non of Modernism, but it can be seen in the works of such as James Stirling that the rejection of the

Opposite page:
Kevin Roche John Dinkeloo and Associates
New Haven Veterans Memorial Coliseum
and Headquarters of the Knights of Columbus in New Haven, Connecticut, 1965–1969
Photo Yukio Futagawa/Retoria
The four corner cylinders of this office fortress
are brick-faced concrete pipes; the ceiling
joists are brown, weatherproof steel. The
elevators operate within a central core, while
escape stairs and sanitary facilities are
housed inside the pipes. The Coliseum with
its ice hockey stadium and multi-purpose hall
occupies the neighbouring site beside the
city expressway. A car-park for 2400 vehicles
was created inside the huge, four-storey roof
section and accessed via two spiral ramps.

Cross-section

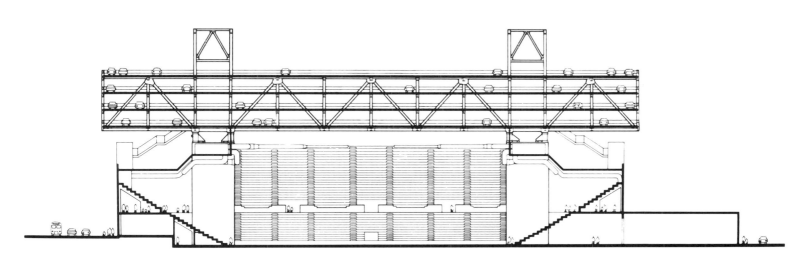

Victor Gruen Associates and Cescr Pelli &
Associates
Pacific Design Center in Los Angeles,
California, 1975
Photo Joe C. Aker/Aker-Burnette Inc.

The steel construction covered with opaque
blue glass offers companies in the interior
decoration and furnishings sector a sales
and display area totalling 67,000 square metres. Extension buildings were planned in the
eighties. The first was completed in 1988; a
green glass cube lying slightly angled behind
the original building. It is to be followed by a
red building whose plan is based on an elliptical section. Linked to the new extension
was the design of the square on San Vicente
Boulevard, a welcome zone of tranquillity
containing a fountain, small amphitheatre
and exhibition pavilion.

Site plan

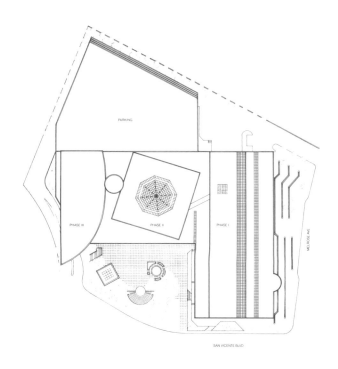

Kevin Roche John Dinkeloo and Associates
Headquarters of the College Life Insurance
Company of America, Indianapolis,
Indiana, 1967
Photo Yukio Futagawa/Retoria
The usual specification of in-built expansion
options here led to the conception of nine office towers, three of which were completed
during the first construction phase. They
stand as autonomous bodies in slightly offset
alignment, connected via bridges and tunnels. Their deep blue glass façades "lean"
against solid-looking concrete slabs containing utility and service rooms.

Plan

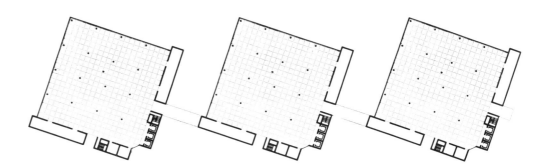

The Architects Collaborative Inc.
Johns-Manville Headquarters in
Jefferson County, Colorado, 1973–1976
Photo Nick Wheeler
The materials employed in the façade of this
330-metre-long building at the foot of the
Rocky Mountains are aluminium panels and
metallized glass. The design won the competition from amongst the more or less freely-ar-
ranged detached-building solutions submitted in other entries because – as the jury
argued – it convincingly symbolized the
standards of an international corporation
while nevertheless showing respect for the
landscape in its clear lines.

Axonometric projection
The vast number of parking spaces required
were in part created on the roof and are
reached via ramp towers.

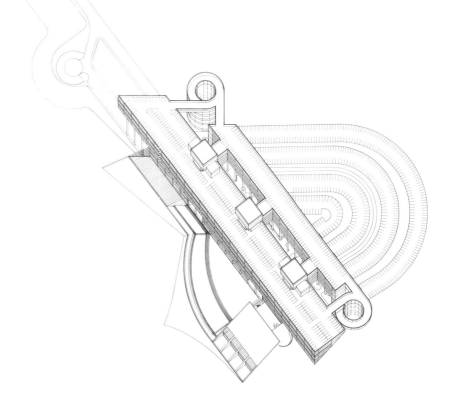

technically-smooth uniform body should not be equated with an abandonment of the classic vocabulary of Modernism. Stirling showed this in his Engineering Building for Leicester Universty: in the graduation and separation of the offices and workshops, the variety of activities performed inside are reflected and translated into formal objectivity. He extends the brick cladding into far-oversailing areas, whereby it is given the appearance of a purely "protective layer" and is thus placed in the same functional context as the other glass and metal façades.

Philip Johnson, who also returned to natural stone façades, said in a speech on the "Seven Shibboleths of Architecture": "We have spoken about material progress and about the fact that we should employ the latest techniques and the latest materials — but are not granite and bronze still the most beautiful materials?" They were not cheap either, of course, but it was necessary to get away from the view that good architecture could be had for little money. No one could close their eyes to the fact that "great buildings are always very expensive".

Arthur Erickson Architects Inc.
Lethbridge University in Alberta, 1972
Photo Simon Scott
All the university theory and research facilities were incorporated together with student apartments under one roof; a self-sufficient scientific space ship.

Cross-section

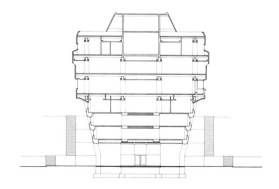

Alberto Campo Baeza
School in San Sebastián de los Reyes,
Madrid, 1983
Baeza Archives
Sealed cylinders of secondary rooms are ar-
ranged in strict stereometry around the class-
room block with its flat gable roof.

The Rational South

"With almost endless rows of arches and façades, with long straight lines, with enormous masses, simple colours, with almost ominous chiaroscuro, he succeeds…in creating the impression of distance, loneliness, motionlessness and rigidity, brought forth by many a drama in the memory of our sleeping souls." These were the words with which, in 1914, Guillaume Apollinaire introduced the painter Giorgio de Chirico, in whose pictures the public square, filled with ghostly emptiness and the dream image of a disappearing train, shows the communal stage in an unaccountable light. The arcades casting their hard shadows evoke a metaphysical city within whose sets people are abandoned alone. Architecture appears as part of the "collective dream consciousness" (Walter Benjamin); its significance arises from the invocation of eternally-valid symbols, which in their association form the city — arcade and square, gable and house, column and temple, arch and bridge, tree and grove.

Aldo Rossi starts from such interpretations of architecture. For him, the geometric elements, the non-reducible basic forms of cube, cylinder, pyramid and prism, have gained a "precise meaning" through history. The designer — according to Rossi — combines the building blocks of the task in hand in accordance with the logical rules of order, as if from a building set of memories. The location for this event is the historical city; this is the theatrical set within which people play merely walk-on parts. They appear, travel a short distance and then exit. Thus Rossi's memorials have no inscriptions, for it is not language but geometry which has durability. Similarities with theatre are apparent; as a window onto another reality, it gives visual expression to metaphysical excursions. The stage is the public square, where the poetry of community life is concentrated. Rossi therefore seeks to create urban space; he rejects the construction of autonomous solitaires such as those produced by Le Corbusier. In place of arbitrarily-justified design, which he sees as too bound by current rigid preconditions and superimposed ideologies, he turns to the art of architectural composition. It creates a new unity out of existing fragments and added symbols, "by alternately reducing or increasing formal possibilities". Its worth arises solely from the context and the choice of the symbols built. Rossi made this clear in citing his declared mentor Adolf Loos: "When we find a mound in the forest which is six feet long and three feet wide, built in a pyramid shape with a shovel, we grow serious, and something says to us: someone lies buried here. That is architecture." Works such as the Monument to the Resistance in Segrate and the design for the San Cataldo cemetery in Modena are prototypical for Rossi, even if only finally realized in curtailed form. The interplay of light and shadow on their raw stereometries becomes a catalyst for impressions which lead beyond the simple organization of the architectural elements. This aim is often more apparent in his drawings than in the finished buildings, which for him only represent the other side of the same reality on paper. Without the hard southern light, the buildings would lose much of

Aldo Rossi with Gianni Braghieri
School in Broni, 1979–1982
Exit to the playing fields
Photo Roberto Schezen / Agenzia Fotografica
Luisa Ricciarini

Plan
The classrooms form a square within which
the autonomous octagonal of the assembly
hall rises from a round base. Covered walkways lead from here in all four directions,
dividing the inner courtyard.

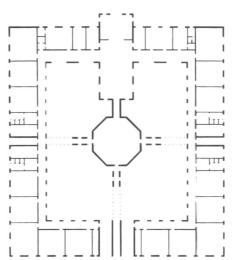

Aldo Rossi with Gianni Braghieri
San Cataldo Cemetery in Modena,
1971–1984
Photo Maria Ida Biggi
The columbaria-lined courtyard of an existing
cemetery dating from the 19th century was
joined by a second courtyard with further
room for cinerary urns. At the heart of this extension lies the cube of a house; in contrast
to Rossi's original plan, in which it was left a
shell, this was later made an ossuary. Its
empty, square window recesses symbolize
the resting place of the dead. The colonnade
shown here, with its niches for the reception
of urns in the upper storey, crosses the central axis of both cemetery complexes.

their vitality. For this is "an architecture of shadows. . . The shadows mark time and
the passing of the seasons." But the shadows in the empty window recesses of the
ossuary at the Modena cemetery also evoke the melancholy of de Chirico; silence
reigns where the dead are laid to rest.

In the Gallaratese 2 balcony-access complex in the Monte Amiata Estate in Milan,
Rossi aligned the small apartments in rows and packed them into an unusually long
cuboid on stilts, sliced – abruptly and sharply – only at one point, namely where
the ground level changed. The radically-reduced façades – from whose formal
asceticism he has meanwhile explicitly distanced himself – were endless, monotonous
rows of concrete slabs and uniform, quadratic openings. With the tenants came
clothes lines and improvised awnings, which brought life to the monolith. Rossi saw
such interventions and modifications, however small, as significant further developments of the architecture, and not as disturbances to a single and binding final form.

Other architects followed Aldo Rossi along the path of formal reduction, among them Giorgio Grassi, who avoids fictional elements in his work with almost greater conviction than Rossi. Architecture – as he says – must represent nothing more than architecture, left behind as "collective trail marks for the future". Thus, in his Student's Residence in Chieti, tall colonnades of pilasters fall into rank before the three-storey room layers in a silent parade of unnerving coldness. The relinquishment of all individualistic design elements also characterizes the Stadtvilla which Grassi created for the Internationale Bauausstellung in the Rauchstrasse in Berlin. The villa offers a soothing, compensatory counterpoint to the overblown opulence of the buildings around it; it does not seek to conceal the prespecified smallness of its apartments behind an excess of design, but admits in its very exterior the unambitious nature of the contractor's programme. Such honesty may seem out of date, but nevertheless appears far less synthetic than the decorative excesses to be seen around it.

The traditions of a rational, stereometrically clear architecture were successfully taken up in other southern countries besides Italy. In Spain, for example, Alberto Campo Baeza moved from white, cubic structural shapes with ramps and rails to more self-confident forms. His school buildings in Madrid successfully assert themselves within incoherent surroundings as self-contained, unimposing objects, serious and yet not without a certain sense of humour. In Mexico, old master Luis Barragán deserves particular mention. His themes are wall and colour, structure and light. Raw-stuccoed, pigmented walls enclose courtyards and clear-cut spaces. Elementary forms and simple, lucid geometries characterize the composition, which draws upon the vernacular of traditional Mexican village architecture, pre-Columbian houses and churches from the Spanish colonial era. Although building large-scale projects for a wealthy clientèle, he retains a poetry of sparseness. This is probably most forceful in the motif of the empty courtyard, which lives from the contrast of luminous colours and the hard contours of light and shadow. It was – he believes – a mistake on the part of Modernism "to give up the protection of walls in favour of the transparency of glass. . . Any architecture which does not express security fails in its spiritual mission." Barragán's architecture, like Aldo Rossi's, carries history. His figurations are, however, more vital and emotional.

Compared to the poetry of Barragán, the works of Swiss architect Mario Botta appear abstract products of the drawing-board. In Botta, too, reigns the archaism

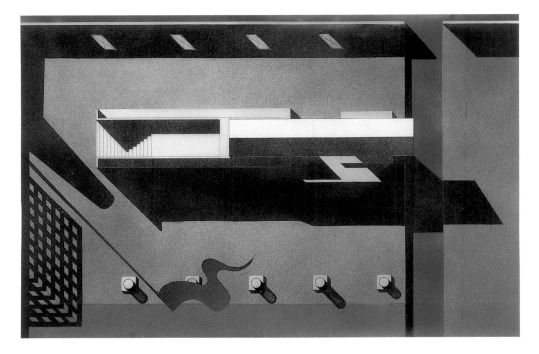

Aldo Rossi
Town Hall Square with Monument in Segrate, 1965
Design drawing
Bildarchiv Foto Marburg
Of a comprehensive design for the square in front of the town hall in Segrate, which planned a broad, shallow flight of steps, perimeter wall slabs with arch openings, a row of low, truncated pillars and a Monument to the Members of Resistance in World War II, only this last was realized: circle, triangle and rectangle are the geometric forms from which its seemingly loosely-superimposed bodies are developed.

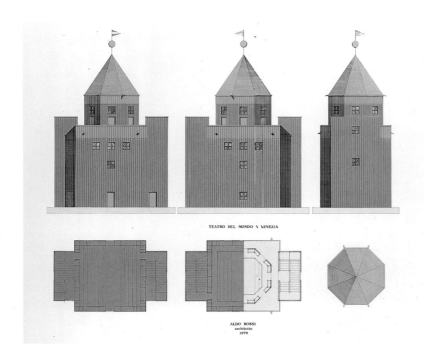

TEATRO DEL MONDO A VENEZIA

ALDO ROSSI
architetto
1979

Aldo Rossi
Teatro del Mondo for the Venice Biennale, 1979–1980
Views and plans
Bildarchiv Foto Marburg
The former Venetian tradition of the floating theatre, which would moor in the city for the Carnival, was to be revived for the 1980 Biennale. Rossi modified the traditional form, orientating himself more towards Shakespeare's central stage. The raft theatre sat at the Punta della Dogana like a Noah's Ark of culture until being towed to Dubrovnik and finally broken up.

Giorgio Grassi and Edoardo Guazzoni
"Stadtvilla" in the Rauchstrasse in Berlin, 1982–1984
Design drawing
Deutsches Architekturmuseum, Frankfurt am Main

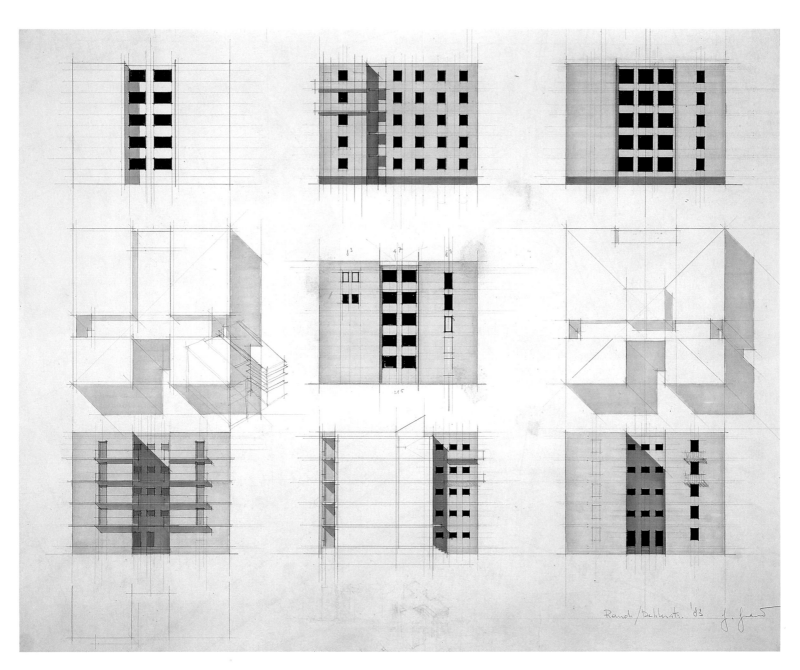

Mario Botta
"Casa Rotonda", Medici House in Stabio,
1980–1982
Photo Roberto Sellito

Mario Botta
Bianchi House in Riva San Vitale, 1971–1973
Photo Alo Zanetta
As a four-storey tower, accessible via an
open-work steel bridge, this detached house
on Lake Lugano appears closed and introspective. Hidden behind its cut-away surfaces and slits, however, are terraces which
convey a hermetic intimacy with the expanse
of the landscape.

Axonometric projections of the floors

Alberto Campo Baeza
School in San Fermin, Madrid, 1985
Opposite page: Stairwell. Below: Courtyard
Baeza Archives

Axonometric projection

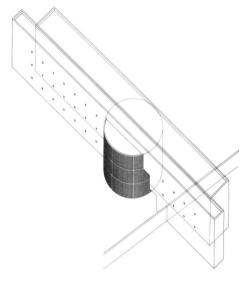

Luis Barragán with Andrés Casillas
"San Cristobal" Stud Farm for Folke
Egerstrom in Los Clubes, Mexico City,
1967–1968
Photo Tim Street-Porter

The Egerstrom couple breed thoroughbreds
which are trained as racehorses. Generous
stables were thus built next to the house,
around a shallow pool fed by a powerful
water jet. The courtyard is screened from the
neighbouring training track by the long wall
slab with wide openings shown here. Pink,
purple and russet are the colours chosen for
the rough-stuccoed walls, whose harmonious
proportions and archaic tranquillity provide
the background for the protagonists of the
scene, the horses.

Overall plan

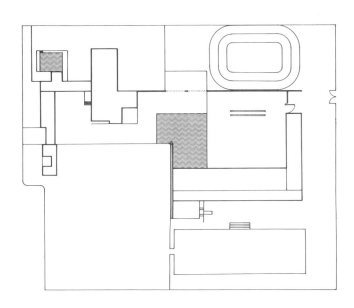

Ricardo Legoretta
Hotel Camino Real in Mexico City, 1968
Photo Armando Salas Portugal

of the wall and the pure stereometric form. Large cut-away areas rob his massive, often prismatic and cylindrical façades of clear statics, however. Conventional windows are extensively avoided; instead, rooms open to the exterior from behind punched rectangles, slits and circles via conciliatory intermediate zones. The geometry is dispersed, the continuum deliberately fractured. There is emphatic craftsmanship in the handling of materials. Dazzling effects of detail are achieved via the skilful rotation of stones in exposed masonry, changes in brickwork patterns, and gloss coatings. The formal force of large surfaces strengthens the block-like character which makes Botta's houses so autarkic and erratic; he himself ikes to call them "caverne magiche". For Botta, architecture must be "a counterpoint to Nature, a dialogue with Nature. Architecture is an artificial factor. The only means of paying tribute to Nature is to be in exact opposition to her, in confrontaticn. . . Architecture is a violation of landscape; it cannot simply be integrated, it must create a new equilibrium." To the accusation of his critics – that his buildings dispense with all consideration and any conciliatory reference to their setting –, Botta's reply is blunt and unrepentant: "I believe that it is wrong to submit to the existing surroundings. If values are there, I include them. But I cannot relate to the stupidity all around."

G. Lippsmeier and F. Reiser
Hall at the German Industrial Exhibition in
Khartoum, 1961
Mero-Raumstruktur Archives

Open Structures

"The futuristic house must be like a giant machine. The elevator should no longer hide itself like a tapeworm in the shaft of the stairwell; the now superfluous stairs must disappear and the lifts should rise like snakes of iron and glass." This declaration in the 1914 manifesto "L'archittetura futurista" was a clear renouncement of artificial disguise of any kind. Antonio Sant'Elia wrote "that the decorative value of futuristic architecture depends solely on the use and imaginative application of the raw, naked or gaudy material." Technology as the vehicle of Utopia supplied the building blocks of a new machine aesthetic which was at once a source of hope and an ideal. Engineering, with its concern to reduce constructive elements and simplify calculations, takes the opposite stance. Common to both is their definition of the house as a technically-organized artefact.

Actual progress was the domain of the practitioners. During World War II engineer Max Mengeringhausen had already developed a system allowing the rapid assembly of lightweight spatial trussed structures with the aid of standardized joints and bars. Its modular concept – distinguished by the reuseability of its industrially-produced parts – was being employed in scaffolding, temporary bridges, pylons and cranes soon after the War. This MERO system, as it was abbreviated, celebrated its first large success at the 1957 Interbau exhibition in Berlin. Under the title "City of Tomorrow", a luminous hall introduced the new system in an architectural form designed by the architect Karl Otto.

Simple constructions from MERO components employ standardized rod elements, their lengths in a ratio of $\sqrt{2}$, thus permitting the formation of squares with reinforcing diagonals. With computer-assisted calculations, however, even complex, non-cubic forms remain economical, despite the numerous special variations required. The results are particularly lightweight constructions – to a certain degree, bicycles in the third dimension.

A second variation of this lightweight building principle uses membrane and hanging constructions which can span large areas with minimal costs. For Frei Otto, diatoms, spiders' webs and soap bubbles served as perfect examples of optimized spatial structures, for Nature always achieves her ends with the most economical means. Thus the equalization facilitated through their flowing skin enables soap bubbles of even the smallest surface area to achieve uniform membrane tension. The application of these characteristics to large buildings is not without its problems. Natural constructs actually only function statistically, in that a majority in the total number of creations ensures the survival of the species despite constant destruction. In 1914 Antonio Sant'Elia had even declared this – albeit in aesthetic terms – his programme: "Houses will be shorter-lived than we. Each generation will have to build its own city."

Although Frei Otto's "mushrooms", "moths" and "four-point tents" of highly-soph-isticated textile webs received much praise, they were not considered Architecture. There was no air of eternity about them. Even the roof of the Olympic Stadium in

Frei Otto and Rolf Gutbrod
German Pavilion at Expo '67 in
Montreal, 1965–1967
The supporting net before the fitting of the
membrane skin
Institut für leichte Flächentragwerke,
Stuttgart
The German Pavilion interpreted the exhibition motto "Man and His World" with "a
landscape built by human hands".

The completed Pavilion
Institut für leichte Flächentragwerke,
Stuttgart
Eight conical sheet-steel masts of up to 37
metres in height carry the pre-stressed cablenet roof. It is sealed by a suspended skin of
translucent polyester textile and supplemented by a shallow dome of latticed wood.
It covers a total area of some 7,700 square
metres. Compared to Otto's earlier tent constructions, the German Pavilion achieved the
definitive separation of supporting cable net
and purely protective membrane, a concept
which was reused in the roofs of Munich's
Olympiapark.

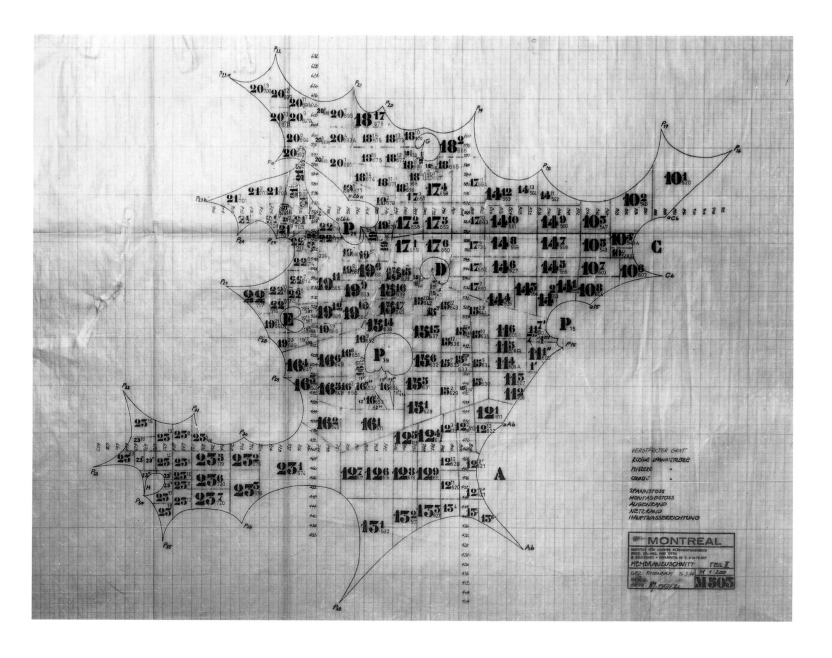

Membrane pattern, Part II
Institut für leichte Flächentragwerke, Stuttgart

Munich was to be covered with heavy concrete slabs. The further development of membrane constructions was sooner possible in temporary buildings, such as those for the Bundesgartenschau exhibitions and, later, for Expo '67 in Montreal. A cable-net construction was substituted for the older style of self-supporting membrane skin which was simply hung below the net. At the same time, the symmetrical basic arrangement of the earlier tents was replaced by a free combination of high and low points. Thus, for the first time, a "roofscape" was created which, in its creation of seemingly arbitrary forms from simple and lucid basic patterns, in fact follows Nature's own methods of construction. The basic tenor of Frei Otto's work is the peaceful appropriation of the world, and thus his sensitive, filigree works spread a sense of optimism. "Architecture is suspected future", as he said in 1976.

Renzo Piano and Richard Rogers' Centre Pompidou in Paris demonstrated that the train of progress was actually heading in another direction. The architectural design of the technical elements is given particular emphasis in this gigantic, muscle-flexing cultural machine. Utopia becomes concretum. Helmut Jahn's State of Illinois Center similarly sits in the Chicago Loop like an object from outer space. Its form results from the overlapping of a sphere with a cube developed from the site square. Upon entering the building, its impression changes entirely: a cylinder is punched out of the main form and projects as an obliquely-cut positive element from the level roof.

Günter Behnisch & Partner, Frei Otto,
Leonhardt and Andrä
Olympia Tent in Munich, 1968–1972
Photo Christian Kandzia
Planning for the Munich Olympics made pro-
vision not only for the necessary stadium
buildings but also for an urban recreation
area integrating architecture, traffic and natural vegetation. The television tower and a
rubble hill were incorporated within this landscape architecture concept.

Roofing in the northern entrance zone
Bildarchiv Foto Marburg
The tent roof is carried by braced masts. It serves as a "shield over the landscape", its panes of transparent plexiglass providing optimal lighting.

Renzo Piano and Richard Rogers
Centre Pompidou in Paris, 1971–1977
Photo Antonio Martinelli
The externalized skeleton of the supporting
construction dominates the building. Krupp-
manufactured brackets are attached to the
vertical supports. The reinforcing cross
braces lie six metres in front of these supports. Truss girders at intervals of 13 metres
each span 48 metres without supports and
give the interior rooms extreme flexibility. The
French national colours are used to accentuate depth gradations.

View of the rear
While the glazed escalator tubes of the front
façade emphasize building access, the rear
is dominated by supply pipes.

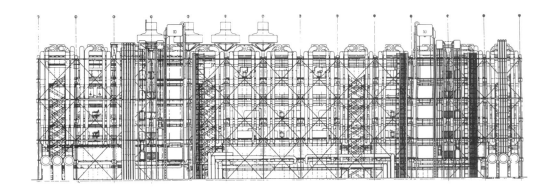

The offices converge via peripheral galleries into this spectacular inner hall, whose contours are frustratingly confused by the strong colours of the exposed steel construction and the alternation of clear and reflecting glass. The complete opening of the inner space to the atrium underlines the democratic philosophy of the administrative bodies it houses, but must also – from the point of view of the employees – occasion a sense of unease. The use of the stairways – hung free in the spacious interior – is something, in the upper floors at least, for those who are not afraid of heights.

In such forms of self-portrayal by public institutions and industrial companies, the attraction of a Modernism qua Modernism, as it appears in such technical displays, entered the service of affirmative strategies. Thus the Renault company considered the publicity value of its English distribution centre in Swindon to be so high that it was the only plant used in advertising. Even the otherwise compulsory mounting of the Renault emblem was foregone. Both Rogers and Norman Foster developed their technical building machines into increasingly monumentalized forms. Their offices produced such sensational and massively-publicized wonders as the new Lloyd's building in London and the headquarters of the Hongkong and Shanghai Banking Corporation in Hong Kong. These are basically simple, rectilinear forms which are accentuated through central halls and technical entrails fed to the exterior. The

Richard Rogers & Partners
Lloyd's Building in London, 1979–1986
Stair towers on the street
Photo Norman McGrath
At Lloyd's, contracts are distributed through brokers amongst a large number of insurers assuming partial risks. This system requires a vast underwriting hall in which up to 10,000 persons may be employed at any one time. The new building was to take into consideration the company's continuing expansion and to allow step-by-step extensions. The solution was found in a high glass-roofed courtyard into which the floors converge. The storeys not yet required for use contain offices which if necessary can be easily transformed into open galleries for insurer's "boxes".

exposed construction is deployed like a style element, though naturally considered no such thing in the mind of the architect. The ambivalence of construction and style continues in the interior: although the overly-slender halls may resemble Gothic churches, any such further reference, anyway unintended, is undermined by the numerous horizontal floor levels. The comparison is nevertheless still argued by many critics. But if they are cathedrals, then they are cathedrals of capitalism, as Gert Kähler wrote in the magazine "Werk, Bauen + Wohnen": "No one builds for society anymore, but for a client, and this is precisely what their programmes express." Here lies the decisive difference to the Constructivism of the twenties. Social utopia is replaced by corporate image.

The "most beautiful bank in the world" was to be built in Hong Kong; certainly it was the most expensive. According to the client himself, it cost five billion Hong Kong dollars. The bank wanted a symbol of the "fertility of the company", in other

words of their power, and at all events a statement of optimism in view of the approaching end of the British administration of Hong Kong in 1997. Norman Foster addressed very concrete problems: the lighting of the large atrium by sunlight, the flexibility of the plan, the expandability of the surface area, the full opening of the ground floor and the access to the spaces for public use via escalators. Even the smallest details were embraced within the overall plan, including covers for the air conditioning vents, taps and toilet-paper holders. What distinguishes Foster are his pleasing moments, ingratiatingly-rounded corners and perfect surfaces. But in the Hongkong and Shanghai Bank, the scale of the constructive elements at times proves overpowering compared to the — rather lost-looking — workplaces below. The structures of the surfaces can easily turn into endless grids, whereby a conscious awareness of the themes of prefabrication, of the controlled world of industry, is transferred into everyday life.

View of the Hall
Photo Klaus Frahm
The glass construction of the twelve-storey hall, with its externalized supporting structure, towers over the stepped sequence of office wings. On the periphery lie the stair towers, wrapped in steel panels. Permanently-installed cranes are used for the maintenance of these complex façades.

Murphy/Jahn Associates
State of Illinois Center in Chicago, Illinois,
1979–1984
Interior view
Photo Peter Gössel

On the other hand in the buildings of Gustav Peichl, and in recent works by Ove Arup and Santiago Calatrava, technical constructions are given a more human face. In the interplay of humour and carefully-considered form, they arrive at harmonious solutions which carry the awareness that technology should serve humankind. Despite functional arrangements, they use gentle hints in design to convey a meaning which goes far beyond the building itself. Even if their plans were not based on the ships, pagodas and glass palaces of the nineteenth century, the associations they never-theless provoke lends them a charm which can turn even an encounter with a sewage treatment plant into an experience.

328

Foster Associates (arch.), Ove Arup and
Partners (eng.)
Renault Sales Headquarters in Swindon,
Wiltshire, 1981–1983
Partial view of the side façade
Photo Richard Davies
The elongated hall is composed of 42 identical construction units. Their roofs are hung
from 16-metre-high steel supports in Renault
yellow. The functional areas of sales headquarters, computer centre, display area, technical training centre and restaurant, together
covering a total of 10,000 square metres,
are all united under one roof. The design
originally planned serial shield elements with
constrained central supports; the façade simply represented a spatial conclusion. It was
not until the construction was changed to a
framework with exterior walls situated behind
the edge supports that the dynamic nature
of the design was properly communicated.
The building now appears as an addition of
screens, although statical questions were
otherwise resolved.

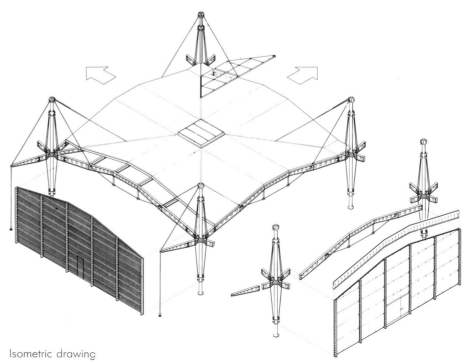

Isometric drawing

329

Foster Associates (arch.), Ove Arup and
Partners (eng.)
Headquarters of the Hong Kong and Shanghai Banking Corporation, Hong Kong,
1979–1986
Plan of Level 30
The new design abandons the classic model
of a central core and surrounding façade
skin. The building is supported by eight
masts, each of four tubes. Reinforcing struts
at levels 11, 20, 28, 35 and 41 divide the
building. The floors are hung from these. 139
modules for toilets and technical installations
as well as stairs and elevators are located at
the sides of the building.

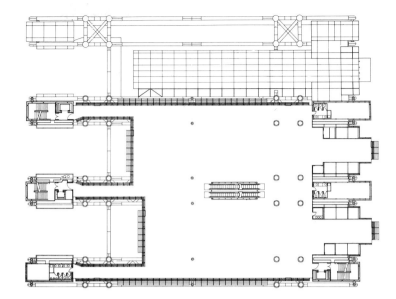

Interior view
Photo John Nye
A computer-controlled mirror and reflector system supplies the slender hall with daylight. A
suspended glass ceiling forms a climatic barrier
to the open ground floor. Huge diagonal
braces "brake" the over-emphatic verticality of
the interior. Where they intersect office and relaxation areas, they appear to threaten and
dwarf the people beneath them.

Opposite page: Overall view
Photo Richard Davies

331

Gustav Peichl
Regional Studio for Austrian State Radio
(ORF) in Graz, 1979–1981
Gallery in the round entrance foyer
Photo Ali Schafler
Pillars of polished aluminium exhaust pipes
flank the stairs of this central hall. Both the
studio annexes, shaped like the segments of
a circle, and the administrative block composed of stacked cubic elements can be
reached from here. Four ORF studios had already been completed in Salzburg, Innsbruck, Linz and Dornbirn by 1972, and the
two new buildings in Graz and Eisenstadt
were built on the same basic plan. They are
all constructions of prefabricated concrete
elements. The radially-segmented organization of the plan allows each functional area
to be separately expanded outwards.

View of the Eisenstadt Studio

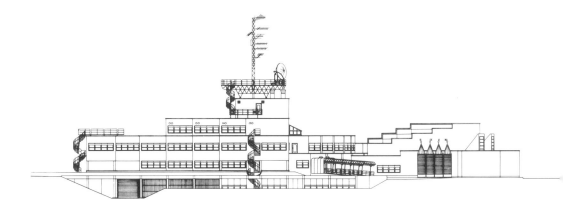

Gustav Peichl
Regional Studio for Austrian State Radio
(ORF) in Eisenstadt, 1980–1982
Entrance area; basement
Photos Ali Schafler
With their pointed caps and vanes, the fat
ventilation pipes are transformed into mini-
ature towers – an architectural joke in the
two newer studios.

Sketch illustrating the building-block principle

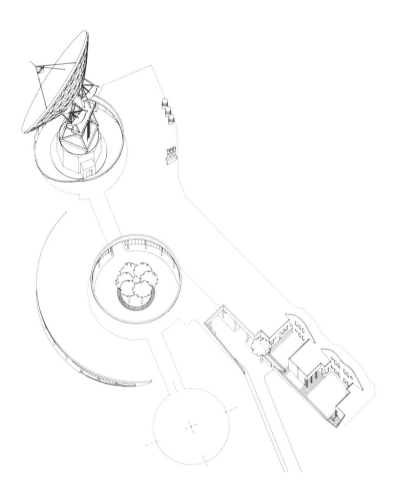

Gustav Peichl
Ground Signal Station in Aflenz,
1976–1980
Axonometric projection
The optimal location for this satellite signal re-
ceiver was found to lie in – of all places – a
nature reserve. As a consequence, technical
facilities as well as employee apartments
were concealed underground in order to mi-
nimize the intrusion upon the environment.
Only the large parabolic antenna is visible
from afar.

Exposed façade section cf the grassed-over
ring building
Photo Ali Schafler

Gustav Peichl
Phosphate Elimination Plant in Berlin,
1979–1985
Peichl Archives
This purification plant, which treats sewage
flowing into Lake Tegel, was one of the most
prominent buildings on show at Berlin's Internationale Bauausstellung. The prespecified
technical spatial programme was incorporated into a ship-like body complete with
"bridge". This offered a view over the three
large purification tanks, called "flockers".

Axonometric projection

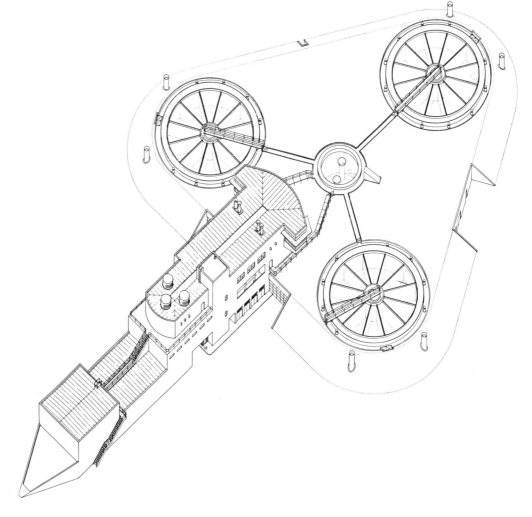

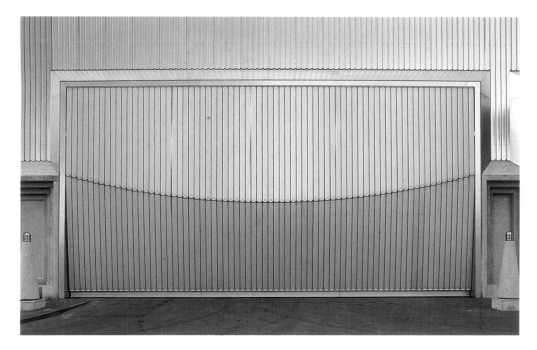

Santiago Calatrava, Bruno Reichlin and
Fabio Reinhart
**Factory Building for the Ernsting Company
in Coesfeld / Lette, 1980–1986**
Gates in the west façade
Photos Paolo Rosselli
Each of the factory's façades was differently
designed. The south front, for example, is
characterized by a wavy outer skin, while the
attraction of the west façade is derived from
three large aluminium gates, each measuring
13 x 5 metres. The curved positioning of their
hinges produces unusually-shaped canopies
when the gates are opened.

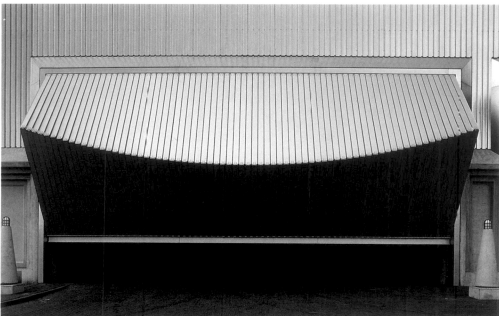

Opposite page:
Arup Associates
**International Garden Festival Hall in
Liverpool, 1984**
Arup Associates Archives
This horticultural exhibition hall was designed
for subsequent simple transformation into a
sports centre with swimming pool. The overall form is given by the two halves of a
spherical dome separated by flat barrel
arches. The domes at each end are faced
with aluminium, the central barrel with
translucent plastic panels.

View

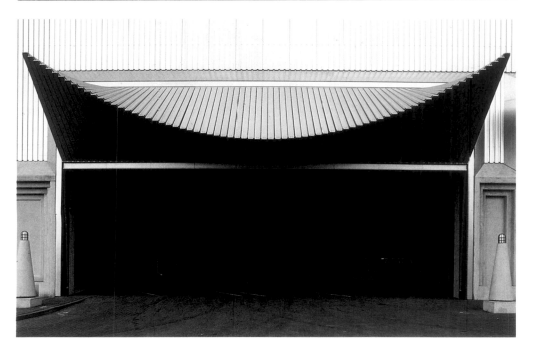

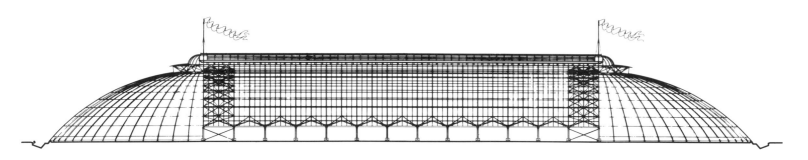

337

The Post-Modern City

"Now they're decorating the box." Such or similar words opened many of the articles written after the completion of the new office tower of American telephone company AT&T in New York. Architect Philip Johnson employed 132,000 metric tons of pink granite to give the 195-metre-high building a magnificent, individual façade. Above the publicly-accessible ground floor, behind whose huge arched portal reigns the gilded genius of electricity, rise 28 identical floors of offices, fused by slim, profiled pillars into a dynamic, soaring gesture. But the climax is a rounded notch in the pointed roof, a self-confident departure from the convention of the flat roof. After many long and lean years the New York skyline was thereby given a striking new landmark, in which Johnson revived Louis Sullivan's idea of an articulated skyscraper featuring "base, shaft and capital".

Thus the lobby of the AT&T Building corresponds to the two massive bottom floors of the Guaranty Building built by Adler and Sullivan in Buffalo in 1894 to 1896. Similar, too, is the "office pile", the stack of identical office floors above, although here three times as high. The Guaranty Building concluded with a crowning wreath of oculi, behind which were hidden a variety of technical systems. The exploded gable contours of the AT&T Building further served to promote corporate identity by making an unmistakable contribution to the skyline. In their analysis of buildings by the Johnson and Burgee partnership, Marc Angélil and Sarah Graham described the characteristic division of technical and formal specifications: "Building volume, supporting structure, elevator shafts, installations, ceiling heights and other matters are determined on the basis of economic factors. Articulating volume at a formal level in an interesting manner and defining the design of the outer covering is the architect's role."

In the public area at street level, Philip Johnson – like Edward Larrabee Barnes in his almost contemporaneous IBM Building, and the Trump Tower by the Swanke, Hayden, Connell partnership – adopted the new building regulations for midtown Manhattan which came into force in 1982. For installations serving the public interest, owners are thereby permitted to increase floor surface area and thus their usable office space. In order to preserve unbroken the continuity of avenue walls, plazas such as that in front of the Seagram Building are no longer approved. Buildings must extend as far as the development limit but are thereby required to incorporate subway station entrances. Covered squares, inner courtyards and passages bring bonuses in terms of site use. Complicated calculation procedures are designed to guarantee adequate lighting in the narrow streets, since schematic regulations have, in the past, led to undesirable ziggurat solutions. By exploiting all their options, clients can now obtain a total commercial area which is approximately 22 times the surface area of the property. Meanwhile, provisions for pedestrian precincts in Manhattan are out of the question; against the background of increasing competition between motorized traffic and pedestrians, however, increasing importance is being assigned

Richard Meier & Partners
Bridgeport Center in Bridgeport, Connecticut, 1984–1988
View from the highway
Photo Jeff Goldberg/Esto
The complex presents itself as a grouping of angular, seamlessly-integrated and smoothly-taut volumes clad in white and grey-enamelled steel panels and granite of irridescent shades of red and brown. The approaches from the road and car park converge in a five-storey atrium from where the entire building can be centrally accessed.

Opposite page:
Johnson/Burgee Architects
AT&T Building in New York, 1978–1982
View from Fifth Avenue
Photo Peter Mauss/Esto
Its cladding of pink granite, strong vertical emphasis, exploded gable and entrance hall with gilt, outsize Genius of Electricity behind a monumental, 24-metre-high semicircular arch are the trademarks of this flagship of modern highrise architecture.

Chicago skyline with the John Hancock Center by Skidmore, Owings & Merrill (1970) on the right-hand edge of the picture and the Leo Burnett Company Headquarters (1989) by Kevin Roche John Dinkeloo and Associates rising prominently on the left
Photo Peter Gössel

The windows of the Burnett Building are cut deep into the green granite of the façade; their uprights of stainless steel glitter before their dark, reflecting glass. Like other Chicago skyscrapers built at the same time, it adopts the basic principles of the AT&T Building in New York. But what distinguishes the buildings of Chicago is their reference to local highrise tradition, as illustrated in the steep gables of 190

South Lasalle Street by John Burgee and Philip Johnson, which recall the Burnham & Root Masonic Temple. Other examples include 900 North Michigan Avenue by Kohn Pedersen Fox Associates, with four corner turrets on its pinnacle, and the new AT&T Corporate Center by Skidmore, Owings & Merrill with a particularly lavish façade in twenties style.

Michael Graves
Public Services Building in Portland, Oregon,
1980–1982
View from the park
Photo Peter Aaron/Esto
The cube-shaped main volume is raised on a
pedestal and crowned by two flat, stepped
storeys. The municipal administration depart-
ments are housed in 15 office floors. The
plans had proposed considerably richer façade decoration. A statue of "Portlandia"
adorned the entrance, and the ribbon strips
on the sides had greater animation and volume. An assembly of small individual bodies
was originally intended to conclude the summit.

Façade view from Madison Avenue

Opposite page:
Michael Graves
Humana Building in Louisville, Kentucky,
1982–1986
View from the west
Photo Peter Aaron/Esto

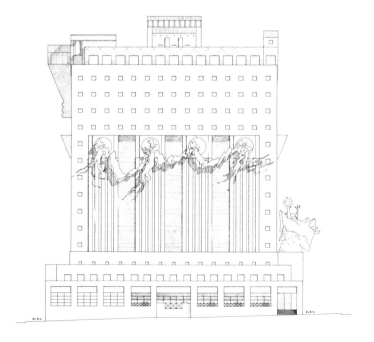

Arquitectonica
"The Atlantis" Apartment Block in Miami,
Florida, 1979–1982
View of the south front
Photo Norman McGrath
The eighteen-storey building on Biscayne
Bay is – as dictated by building regulations –
a narrow slab. The further development of
this clear stereometric body is typical for Arquitectonica architecture: the east front is
rounded, a four-storey-high square is
"punched" out of the longitudinal façades,
and geometric symbols in bright colours
are placed on the façade and roof. They
turn an economically-planned building into
a residence with southern charm. The
name underlines the emphasis on identity.

The pool on the ninth floor
Photo Norman McGrath

344

Overall view of "The Atlantis"
Photo Norman McGrath

to freedom of movement for people on foot. Public space is incorporated into buildings as winter gardens, shopping malls and covered walkways. Architects respond with arcades, generous portals and advancing base zones.

One of the buildings approaching the new concept of urban space is the headquarters of the Humana Corporation. Michael Graves designed an eight-storey loggia combining areas of private and public use, with its frontal arcades forming a "part of the city". Their height is matched to that of neighbouring houses, while the line of the street is continued in three upper floors. Behind these soars the office block proper. The distinctive helmet of the roof, with its projecting bay and gable, offers an interesting response to the axes determined by Main Street and the avenues crossing it. The scale of the elements employed gives the façade an almost anthropomorphic appearance, without denying its classical borrowings. Many comparable buildings share the preference here revealed for expensive materials, in particular granite, for the emphasis upon windows recesses instead of their concealment in continuous grids and glazed surfaces, and for clear structural articulation.

Unattractive cities in economic decline have become the particular object of attempts to synthesize city culture with elaborate building projects, not least in order to attract further investment. The competition for capital between America's communities allows for many a successful experiment, as demonstrated in Richard Meier's Bridgeport Center, for example. The town now imprints itself upon the memory with a striking piece of architecture, turned with its "best side" to the highway, which passes through

Rob Krier
Schinkelplatz in Berlin, 1977–1987
Plan and ideas for the design of the square

Rob Krier
Gate House, Ritterstraße Süd, Berlin,
1977–1980
Developed façade views
This block development scheme was a co-
operative effort by several architecture firms.
The Gate House with its significant central pillar opens an axis which links several courts
in the southern Friedrichstadt district.

Bridgeport on stilts. The site is filled not by a single body but by a complex addition
of volumes subtly differentiated by colour, which intersect and overlap each other
and incorporate a small historical museum building with tower and onion dome.
From the welcoming forecourt in front of the semicircular, concave main façade
facing downtown, the visitor enters a brightly-lit atrium, whose ramps and vistas
invite exploration. Sadly, they reveal only a bank.

With European cities generally governed by different conditions, American solutions
cannot simply be adopted without intruding on mature urban structures. Nor have
they yet addressed adequate attention to the design of housing, an area in which
deficiencies in urban planning emerge particularly clearly. Blatant errors of mass
housing were manifested especially in the standardized construction of monotonous
satellite towns. Apartments were built as densely as if they had been in the city, but
the identificatory and social structures of the "city" as residence had disappeared.
Change needed to be initiated above all by communal institutions, and the technocratic
regulations which reduced human beings to an abstract planning variable and which
stood in the way of possible new solutions, had to be corrected.

It is in this context that mention should be made of probably the most important
architecture exhibition of recent times, whose own history illustrates in a nutshell the
problems of modern architecture – namely the Internationale Bauausstellung held
in Berlin in 1987. Its achievements lay above all in the field of "urban repair", a term
which arose during the planning period. The extensive projects carried out within
the framework of new development, which was structured under the aegis of architect
Josef Paul Kleihues, are of interest in so far as the planning phase coincided with
the discussion on Post-Modernism and the return of visible historical references. In
view of the restrictions governing ground-plan solutions, there was a surprising

general willingness on the part of "star" international architects to adapt themselves to the Berlin landscape, or rather its ruins, whereby dialogues were rapidly branded as using all too bald an architectural language. Thus, shortly after the completion of Alvaro Siza's Kreuzberg apartment block, the comment "Bonjour tristesse" was sprayed conspicuously – and not entirely without justification – on its walls. A convincing alternative is argued by the block of flats on the Schinkelplatz, which continues northwards the axis of the Gate House on the south side of the Ritterstraße. The controversy between back-to-back block building and row housing seems here to have been overcome. Behind the entrance arches is a courtyard of almost Italian character, which in its combination of natural stone façades, trees and vehicles awards equal status to both private and public life. More intimate courtyards with individual garden designs are reached via corner buildings, whose generous stairwells echo the cheerful, unforced mood of the complex as a whole. They show Rob Krier overcoming the danger of merely picturesque design.

The complex between the Alte Jakobstraße and the Lindenstraße, financed from public housing funds, was the joint achievement of seven architectural offices. The street sides are integrated into their surroundings with five-storey brick fronts and four-storey stucco surfaces. Inside the block, their scale matches that of the reconstructed façade of Schinkel's Feilnerhaus. Once a distinguished private residence, the rebuilt section serves as an identificatory centre: memory of the past and human dimension instead of alienation and anonymity.

Rob Krier
Schinkelplatz in Berlin, 1977–1987
Photo Rob Krier
After the "hypertrophication of personal artistic design" in the Ritterstraße Süd, Krier speaks of a conscious reduction and tightening of the designs for the project on the north side of the Ritterstraße, leading to a logical climax in the inner courtyard design.

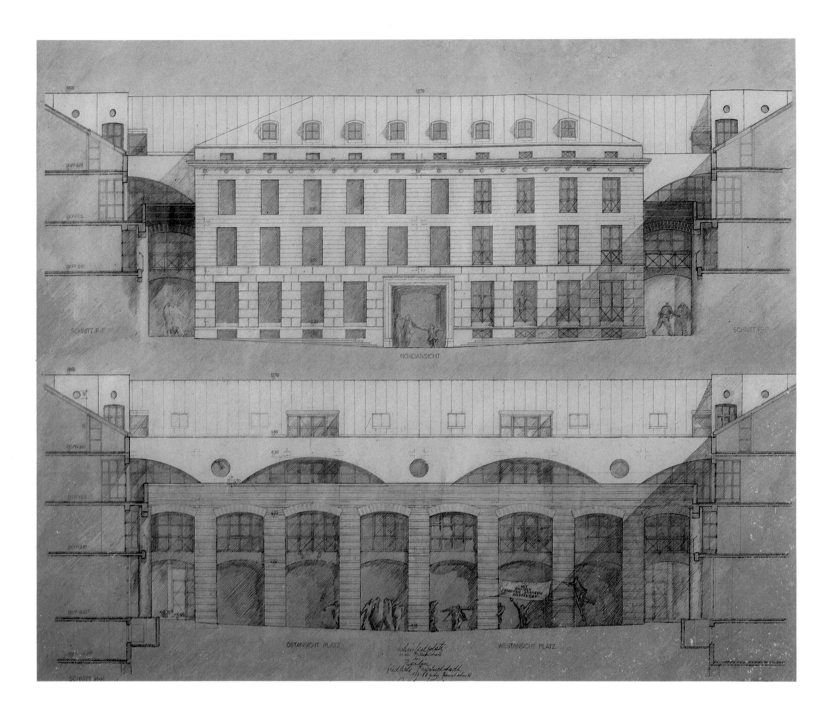

Façade drawings
The new complex takes as its point of reference the reconstructed façade of Schinkel's Feilner House. Its saddle roof and symmetry are adapted in the residential buildings strung between the octagonal towers of the block. The arcades aligned in front of the ground and first floors recall Schinkel's similarly destroyed Academy of Architecture.

Myron Goldfinger
House for Norman McGrath in Patterson,
New York, 1979
Photo Norman McGrath

Plans of the first and second floors
Between circular segments on the entrance
side and triangular components on the south
side a walkway spans the ground floor, featuring kitchen, guest room and living room,
and leads to the bedrooms. Above the
bridge crossing the living room as far as the
fireplace, a semispherical skylight is set into
the roof terrace with its extensive panaroma.

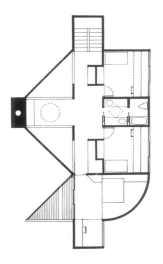 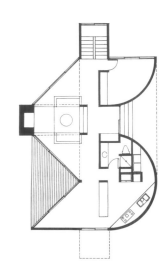

350

Bellevue

A beautiful view of a virgin landscape, of unimproved or domesticated Nature, or simply of naked concrete walls taken out of their shells: within a framework uninhibited by neighbourly considerations or bureaucratic regulations, the seemingly humble detached house can offer unexpected architectural challenges. Where all starting-points for conformity and subordination are lacking, the alignment of a building requires new systems of reference. The decisive factors now become topography, wind direction and the position of the sun, together with the customer's preferences and, of course, expectations as regards spatial programme.

The confrontation with environment thereby often takes place at a very abstract, almost philosophical level. Japanese architect Tadao Ando bases his extremely ascetic forms on man's alienation from nature, which conventional gardens in his opinion only reinforce. He admits sun and cold, wind and rain as alone authentic. "Things like light and wind only have meaning when they are introduced into a house in the form of extracts from the outer world. The isolated fragments of light and air illustrate the whole of Nature." For this reason, his houses – often fully fortified against the outside world – open onto bare inner courtyards, oases of quiet, which relate to the rhythm of the passing days and seasons. Tadao Ando prefers – inside as well as out – exposed concrete, whose contours appear as cold, sharp incisions or soft undulations, depending on the position of the sun. While elementary Nature is defined as a direct component of living, there is a graduated retreat from the street in firmly defined semi-public and public zones.

Demarcation within the indefinite is also a theme of American country houses: the house appears as a fortress within the landscape. Although access roads, coast lines and other landmarks are incorporated, the actual location is purely coincidental. Tod Williams said of his house for William Tarlo in Eastern Long Island: "The site, like many in America, is one with little apparent context. The road is parallel to a distant ocean view. The fields are treeless but change with planting. The sun has its set of changing coordinates, and the winds change with the seasons. The architecture takes its cues from these simple realities . . . At the center is the self-contained microcosm. It might be duplicated inside a loft in Soho; and is precisely a house within a 'house'. Although in this case the container did not pre-exist. The road and ocean pre-exist; and a precedent of farm land into urban fabric. Vehicular access . . . the movement of sun and wind, and urban precedent generate the envelope or superenclosure. This in turn provides a formal field of reference, related to the external world, for the enclosure proper which then can interact indirectly with these elements."

What at first reads as a purely formal concept reveals itself upon closer inspection as a newly-defined Functionalism. The logically-composed spatial programme is assigned exciting orientations via multiple axes. When symbolic façade designs such as David Connor's Lundstrom House further visualize the extrovert wishes of their clients, the spectrum of possibilities is demonstrated.

Tod Williams
**House for William Tarlo in Sagoponack,
New York, 1978**
Above: View from the north
Below: South front
Photos Norman McGrath

View from the south-east
Photo Norman McGrath

Plan of the ground floor
Within a frame on a square floor plan, which
lies parallel to the road and coast, the house
is rotated in an east-west direction. While the
high north wall offers privacy and protection
from the wind, the screen on the south side
shades the tall glazed surfaces. A roof over
the car port relates the two staggered north
façades and creates a covered outdoor seating area. The building thus finds orientation
in its featureless surroundings within a self-
created reference system.

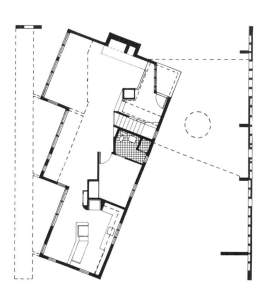

Tadao Ando
"Wall House", Matsumoto House in Ashiya,
Hyogo, Japan, 1976–1977
Street front
Photo Yoshio Takase/Retoria

Plan
A heavy concrete framework – with barrel
vaulting – structures the house, which is fully
concealed from the road behind a hermetic
wall.

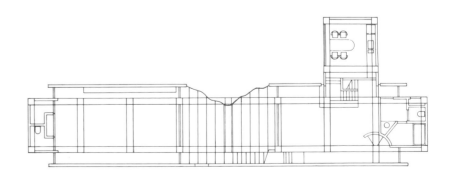

354

Tadao Ando
Koshino House in Ashiya, Hyogo, Japan,
1979–1981
Living room
Photo Yoshio Takase/Retoria
A narrow slit in the ceiling provides the corner seating area with contoured light. The
windows on the opposite side of the room
look into an inner courtyard. The mood is
typical of Ando's reserved and introspective
architecture.

Plan
Six children's bedrooms and a tatami room
line the second wing which, like the main
wing with its living room, parents' bedroom
and kitchen, is recessed deep into the
ground. The connecting corridor runs underground.

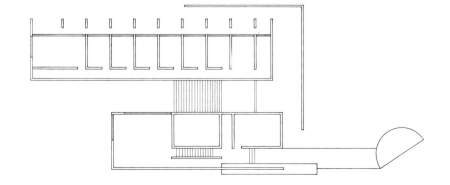

David Connor with Julian Powell-Tuck and
Gunnar Orefelt
"Villa Zapu", House for Thomas Lundstrom
in the Napa Valley, California, 1984
View from the south
Photo Tim Street-Porter

Plan of the ground floor

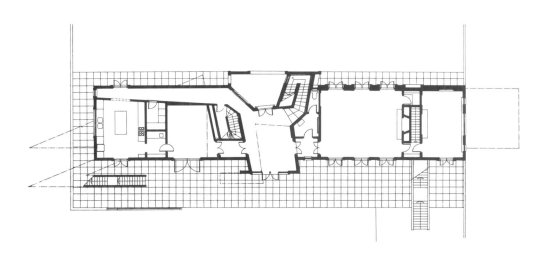

View from the east towards the pointed
master bedroom
Photo Tim Street-Porter

Plan of the upper floor
The bedrooms lie like an arrow along a
quiver above the ground floor, with its living
and utility rooms. In the lateral axis the entrance leads to the central hall through a
symbolically-designed portal. The seignorial
gesture was both calculated and commer-
cially exploitable for the owner's wine label.

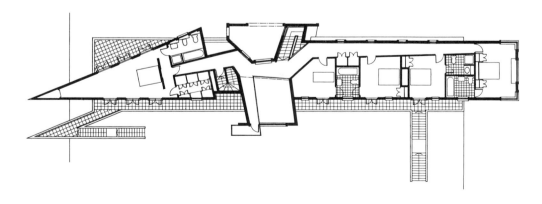

Concrete Poems

The history of ideas has shifted its emphasis since the 1920's from a Utopian world view to a self-absorbed hermeneutics which, in its criticism of "cynical reason", knew of no argument which could itself not be criticized. Frenchman Jacques Derrida seems to stand at the point of intersection of philosophy and architecture; starting from works of literary criticism, he discovered his interest in architecture when Bernard Tschumi invited him to a discussion on the Park La Villette in Paris.

Following the conversion of the never-completed livestock market halls for the new Paris abattoir into the "Cité des Sciences et de l'Industrie", an international competition was held for a "Park of the 21st Century" in the surrounding 136 acres of unused land. Architect Bernard Tschumi won the competition with his strategy of "a discontinued building, a whole which is split into a number of landmarks distributed over the entire site". Covered galleries along the main axes and serpentine paths link the main attractions of the site, whose focal points are red pavilions, its "folies". Avenues trace the geometric plan and enclose open areas of lawn. Not only the buildings are considered objects here, but also the space between them, fully in the spirit of concrete poems, which similarly determines the reading of words by means of spatial caesura and omission. And poetic is indeed the word for those parts of the park already completed.

Derrida formulated his thoughts in an essay entitled "Point de folie — maintenant l'architecture", whose ambiguous meaning might be as variously translated as "No madness at all—maintaining architecture" and "Point of madness—now architecture". For him, architecture becomes a significant event, but to questions on its content "an answer will not be provided by gaining access to a meaning whose fulfilment would ultimately be promised us. No, it is precisely a question of what happens to that meaning." Tschumi's "folies", which are actually only playful pavilions for various leisure activities, can be seen in this context as contributions to the discussion on the possible transformations of architecture within a self-created reference system of points, lines and planes.

Derrida describes the red point in his "structure as open to combinatorial substitutions or permutations, which relate it as much to other frivolities as to its own parts". These "folies", recalling the "follies" of English garden architecture, "primarily, but not solely, deconstruct the semantics belonging to architecture". Derrida also defines architecture itself as "an inhabited construct, a heritage which embraces us even before we have attempted to think it". This naturally means that manipulations performed by architects can only be understood as such in so far as the viewer also shares the heritage in question. In order to develop critical significance, therefore, deconstruction would have to refer to a socially-established language of form, a general understanding of architecture. Many critics, however, see Tschumi's concept of heritage above all in Russian Constructivism, and in the works of Leonidov and Tschernikov in particular. James Wines from the SITE office noted by way of contrast

Behnisch & Partner; F. Stepper, A. Ehrhardt
University of Stuttgart Hysolar Research Institute, 1987
Photo Klaus Frahm

Frank O. Gehry
The Architect's House in Santa Monica,
California, 1978
Photo Tim Street-Porter

"A boring but charming old house" was the
starting-point for Gehry's manipulations. The
kitchen, dining room and terrace were
added in such a way that they open up and
partly surround the original building while
nevertheless preserving its independence.
Corrugated iron, wire netting and plywood
boarding create the external impression of
an imaginative provisional solution. while
generous spaces arose inside.

Design sketch

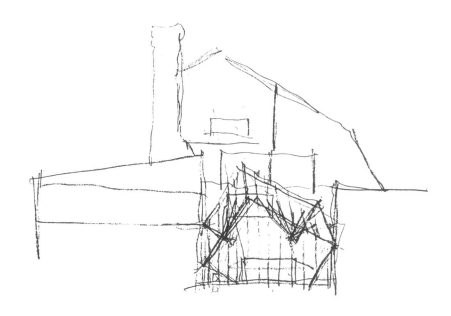

Coop Himmelblau
Roof Conversion for a Lawyer's Office in
Vienna, 1983–1988
Corner solution with conference room
Photo Gerald Zugmann
"No oriels or turrets" were to be placed on
the roof; a "context of proportions, material
or colours" was not desired, but rather "a
visualized energy line which, coming from
the street, overarches the project and shat-
ters and thereby opens the existing roof. During the drafting phase we had thought of an
inverted flash of lightning and a drawn bow.
This space-creating bow. . .is the steel backbone of the project. And the posture."

Design sketch

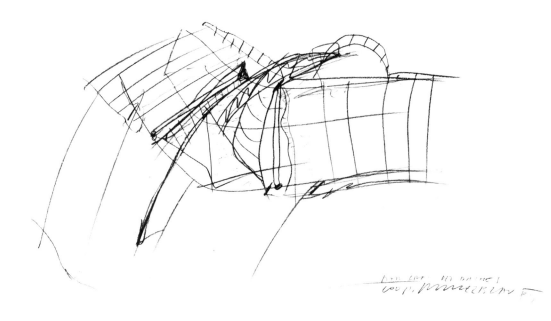

Frank O. Gehry
Loyola Law School in Los Angeles,
California, 1981–1984
View from the street
Photo Michael Moran

Steps between the main building and the
courtyard
Photo Tim Street-Porter
The building programme included offices,
seminar rooms, lecture theatres and a chapel. Gehry chose not to compress them all
into a single compact body, but to combine
only the administration and smaller teaching
rooms into a building block, which seals off
a courtyard from a car-park opposite. The
lecture theatres and chapel are carefully distributed as detached bodies within the courtyard. Their layout creates a campus with exciting visual axes and pleasant relaxation
areas. A limited budget necessitated extremely cheap construction methods which, as
visible structural damage suggests, seem
hardly justified even in Californ a's dry cli-
mate.

Opposite page: Plan
"This is not a plan. I took trouble to disor-
ganize it; I didn't want the design to be recognizable", Gehry declared.

Frank O. Gehry
California Aerospace Museum in Los
Angeles, 1983–1984
Photo Michael Moran
The Aerospace Museum was added to the
existing museums complex in Exposition Park
in time for the 1984 Olympics. Angular volumes were stacked in front of an older building to which they bore no clear relationship;
the hidden entrance lies at their interface. An
F-104 mounted on the outside hallmarks the
sealed main façade.

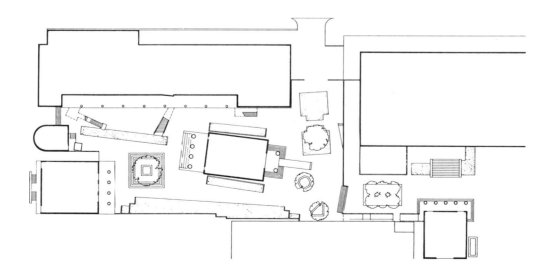

Frank O. Gehry
Edgemar Center in Santa Monica,
California, 1987–1988
Opposite page: Tower superstructures
Photo Peter Gössel
A former dairy was converted into a small-
scale shopping centre with car-park, offices,
restaurant and the Santa Monica Museum of
Art. Surviving constructional components
were thereby carefully restored and their set-
tings developed. The buildings create a
friendly, inviting inner courtyard in typical
Gehry manner.

Stair tower with elevator
Photo Peter Gössel
The wire mesh surround creates a striking,
ambiguous space in which the definition of
interior and exterior remains ambivalent.

that the cut and slashed house ruins of sculptor Gordon Matta-Clark indeed embody the concept of the dismembered archetype and thereby encourage critical consideration of the unquestioning daily perception of architecture.

Frank Gehry's buildings, which make strong reference to concrete urban chaos and local traditions, can be interpreted along similar lines. Widely-employed as a skeletal structure in Los Angeles is the stucco box with a wooden lath frame, concealed within simple and cheap industrial parts in such a way that associations with improvised architecture cannot be altogether dismissed. But Gehry employs his means with such sophistication and subtle colouring that the artistic intention is immediately apparent. Where he fills the inner courtyard of a law school with borrowings from the classical vocabulary of a Roman forum, it is both understandable and fully in the spirit of his client. At the same time, these "quotations" – not truly such since they remind rather than quote – are robbed of their original components and their monumentality in such a way that the final result develops congenially out of the surrounding urban space. Plywood panels intended as lining boards are combined with ridiculously weak aluminum struts and inlaid plexiglass strips into a small chapel. Columns lose their bases and capitals to become nothing more than cylinders of concrete or galvanized iron; their significance is revealed only by their positioning within the site. Gehry also plays – as in the Edgemar Center in Santa Monica – with

Behnisch & Partner; F. Stepper, A. Ehrhardt
University of Stuttgart Hysolar Research
Institute, 1987
Photo Klaus Frahm
The Institute is dedicated to research into
new energy technology based on hydrogen
produced with solar power. The character of
the building was to reflect the experimental,
innovative nature of this work. The end product indeed suggests something of an "architectonic test arrangement", and improvisa-
tion accounted for a large portion of the
planning which accompanied construction.

Section

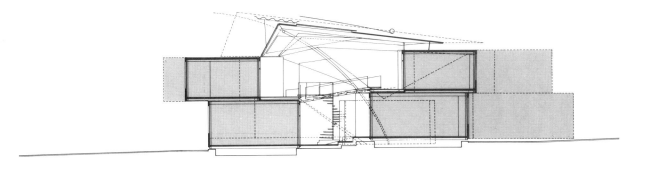

Hall between the laboratory wings
Photo Klaus Frahm
The funnelling interior space between the industrial containers was not originally planned. It was developed by the architects as a point of communication, illustrating interactive relationships in its linking walkways. The collage complex satirizes the supposed perfection of technology: the gremlins of architecture show humour.

purely constructive alienation effects, creating a crown from a distorted cube of steel framing, for example. Originally subordinate architectural elements begin to lead a life of their own: stairwells, chimneys and porches are clearly overemphasized.

These gestures might all too easily be interpreted as pure, superficial style elements. Philip Johnson was probably aiming to launch a new style when, in 1988, he organized an exhibition at the Museum of Modern Art in New York entitled "Deconstructivist Architecture" and thereby made the new wave marketable.

The diversification of cultural identity patterns finds its architectural equivalent. But should the entertaining game in which insiders decode its messages take on a life of its own, architecture is drowned by mere "Look! No hands!" sensationalism.

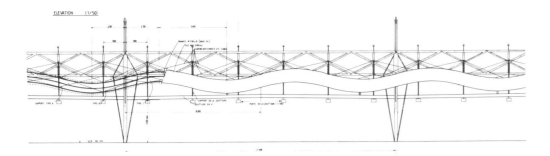

ELEVATION (1/50)

Bernard Tschumi
Parc de la Villette in Paris, 1982–1990
(still unfinished)
Folie No. L5 at the intersection of the
north-south axis and the Canal de l'Ourc,
and Folie No. P7
Photos Peter Gössel
Of the cultural activities which are supposed
to develop in the "folies", as these pavilons
are called, there still remains little trace. L5 is
run as a restaurant, P7 as a café. Well-
known designers were invited to supply a
number of the details. Thus Philippe Starck
designed the aluminium swivel chairs secured to the ground in small groups – a convincing alternative to the traditional park
bench.

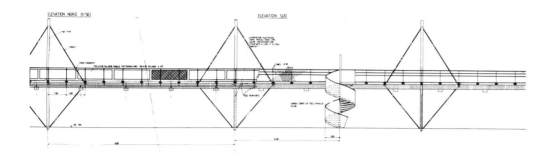

Folie No. N7, a stylized mill with a Red
Cross post, and No. P6, a viewing tower
Photos Peter Gössel

Axonometric projection
The park is developed from the superimposi-
tion of planes (site structure), points (folies)
and lines (path network). Since each system
has its own geometric order, there arise overlappings and thereby "conflicts", which
Tschumi interprets as "dynamic moments".
The bright red "folies", modifications of a
basic cube with edges 10 metres long, are
spaced at intervals of 120 metres. Each con-
ceptually complete form is composed of 27
cube parts; the realized units play upon
omission and addition.

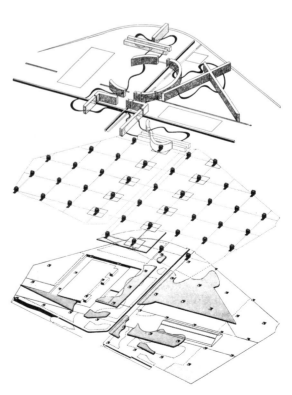

Coop Himmelblau
Funder Factory Works 3 in St. Veit/Glan,
1988–1989
Overall view
Photo Gerald Zugmann
The power-station with its "dancing stacks"
is set back from the production hall of the
paper-coating factory, and connected to it
via a "media bridge". Below, the approach
road for heavy-goods traffic is sheltered by
a roof with upward-bending wings.

Opposite page: Personnel entrance with
"red comb"
Photo Gerald Zugmann

Axonometric projection of the overall complex

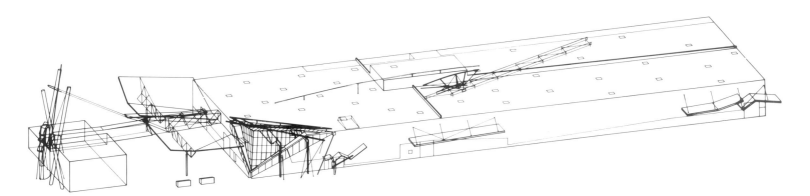

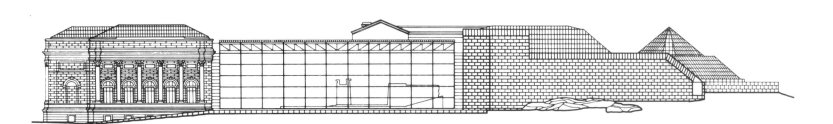

Architecture for the Arts

Kevin Roche John Dinkeloo and Associates
North Wing of the Metropolitan Museum
of Art in New York, 1967–1979
Interior view with the Temple of Dendera
Photo Norman McGrath
This cult site was a gift from Egypt to the
USA by way of thanks for American ar-
chaeological aid during the Aswan Dam
project.

View of the north front

Like Boullée's Cenotaph glorifying the scientific empiricism, the museum as a public, civic institution is a product of the Enlightenment. It conveys knowledge and is a centre of education, and is thus a part of the leading "of man out of his self-incurred nonage", as postulated by Immanuel Kant. But it is also a place of secularized edification where "one can admire the great artists, the highest among mortals, in still and silent humility and edifying solitude, and with the long and steadfast con-templation of their works can warm oneself in the sunlight of their charming thoughts and impressions" – as expressed in the "Heartfelt Outpourings of an Art-loving Monk" of 1797. Such institutions not least raised the reputation and standing of their patrons and sponsors, who thereby wanted to take their place in western cultural tradition.

Museum architecture took as its model the eighteenth-century palace, with its noble entrance and awe-inspiring galleries. Examples here include the Fridericianum in Kassel and the old Stuttgart Staatsgalerie. "The sight of a beautiful and sublime room" should, as Karl Friedrich Schinkel wrote in 1830 in conjunction with the building of the Altes Museum in Berlin, "encourage receptiveness and create an atmosphere for the enjoyment and appreciation of that which the building contains". Thus the muses took their seats in temples of "Greek raiment", inspired by Winckelmann's ideal of "noble simplicity and quiet grandeur" – even if not all exhibits were as literally interpreted as in Leo von Klenze's Glyptothek in Munich.

The declarations of intent made at the founding of the New York Metropolitan Museum of Art in 1870 seem sober and pragmatic in comparison: "It is important", according to poet William Cullen Bryant, "that we counter the temptations of vice in this large and too rapidly-growing city with attractive entertainments of an innocent and educative nature." Art, thus functionalized, subsequently found itself much abused; in its early years in particular the museum formed the setting for some positively bucolic scenes. If the weather in Central Park was bad, the Sunday picnic was promptly relocated to the museum, where gnawed chicken legs were thrown into the nearest amphora and afternoon naps were taken in the niches between Egyptian sarcophagi.

The advent of Modernism brought the museum new roles and responsibilities. Whereas it had originally been sought to bring the aura of works of art and the aura of museum architecture to congruence by giving them a "classical blessing", this was bound to fail in the case of works which took issue with the very nature of art. Deliberately or not, the immediate effect of a ready-made exhibit in the traditional galleries of the Louvre will be to irritate, to appear foreign and alienating and even to spark uncontrollable confrontation with the architecture around it. A background as neutral and non-committal as possible was therefore sought against which to set interchangeable, temporary exhibitions – a tabula rasa for a calculable sceno-graphic effect. The exhibition concept includes the consumability of art, a fact which

373

Carlo Scarpa
Museo Castelvecchio in Verona, 1956–1964
Exhibition room with view towards the
basement
Photo Antonio Martinelli

Opposite page:
Passage between the museum wing and the
old city wall
Photo Antonio Martinelli
Scarpa's museum project is distinguished by
its love of detail, sensitive use of precious
materials and delight in formal experimentation. In Verona every staircase is differently
designed, each room has its own character.
In the 1920s the Napoleonic building underwent neo-gothicizing modifications. Scarpa
left the main façade, but destroyed its sense-
less central symmetry through a variety of in-
cursions and emphasized its nature as a separate "display wall".

Plan

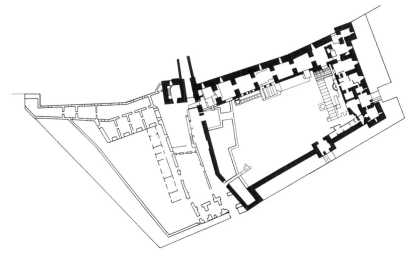

José Rafael Moneo
Museum of Roman Art in Mérida,
Spain, 1980–1985
Gallery in the side aisle (above). Main hall
(below)
Photos Klaus Frahm
Moneo sees the lively colour play of the
bricks in a "dialectic relationship" to the light-
coloured marble treasures: sculptures, reliefs,
columns and other fragments of antiquity.
Natural lighting is supplied via glazed bands
in the ceiling and overhead windows in the
side walls.

Street front with main entrance
Photo Klaus Frahm

From the entrance building, to which offices, workshops and store-rooms are connected, a catwalk leads across a small inner court-yard to the exhibition building proper (left). The basement contains an archaeological site with the remains of a Roman settlement; pillars at axial intervals of six metres carry the ceiling of this "crypt". The main hall above, in which the region's finest treasures are on display, consists of a tall central nave, a row of small niches on the road side and two low ambulatories towards the rear. The Roman method of building is quoted in the construction: the space between the wall slabs of flat bricks is filled with concrete. Although it lacks the decorative dimension of Roman buildings, the museum nevertheless pays homage to the monumentality of the buried architecture of the Roman Empire.

Plan of the basement

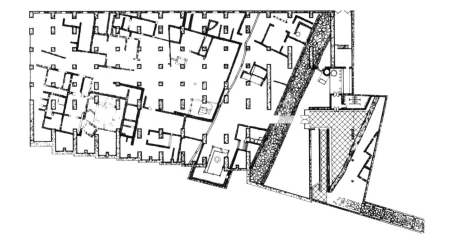

James Stirling, Michael Wilford & Associates
Extension to the Staatsgalerie in Stuttgart,
1977–1984
Terrace with the undulating glass front of the
entrance hall
Photo Klaus Frahm

Peter Beye, Staatsgalerie director, did not
want to see this difficult urban site filled with
the "structure of a container architecture
which applies the principle of total flexibility
to the whole museum complex without reflection". Instead, a consciously "public building" of almost polemic character was created. The handrails of the outdoor ramps
have swollen into colourful guides of bright
blue and pink which also house the lighting
system. Like the glazed sweep of the entrance, they undermine the monumental pos-
turing of the stone-clad, U-shaped building
with its classicizing overtones, and thematize
access to the building. The climax of this
highly-allusive architectural collage is the sunken rotunda in the courtyard.

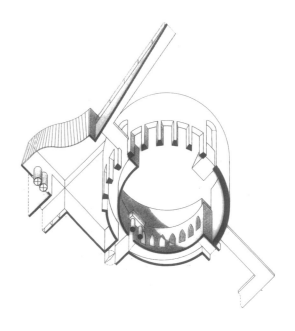

378

Exhibition room with figures from Oskar
Schlemmer's "Triadic Ballet"
Photo Klaus Frahm
Indirect light is provided by wall lights in the
form of cornice fragments held by thin steel
consoles – one of the few mannerisms which
Stirling permitted himself in these generally
more severe, traditional galleries.

Axonometric projection with the public footpath leading through the building

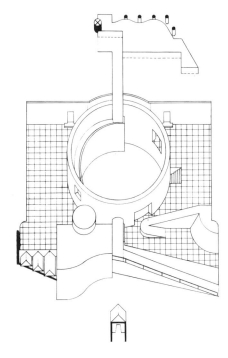

Sequence of exhibition rooms with works by
Sol Le Witt and Mario Merz
Photo Klaus Frahm
As in the museums of the 19th century – such
as the prototypical "Altes Museum" by Karl
Friedrich Schinkel in Berlin, for example – the
exhibition galleries are here laid out as an
enfilade, an easily comprehensive alignment
of rooms in sequence. The numbers
"stamped" into the pediments above the
doorways emphasize the one-way track.

Opposite page:
Axonometric projection of the entrance area
and rotunda

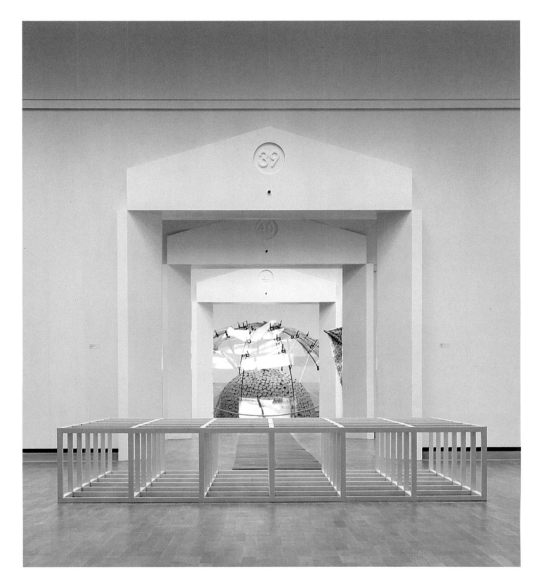

Barry Gasson
Burrell Collection in Glasgow, 1972–1983
View from Pollok Park
Photo Burrell Collection
The collection which shipowner Sir William
Burrell bequeathed the City of Glasgow, on
condition that an appropriate museum was
built to house it, contained not only paint-
ings, drawings and sculptures but also artistic window glazing, stone portals and complete wood ceilings from old buildings. The
central rooms of the donor's private residence were also to be incorporated into the
new building. Medieval portals were installed in doorways and also in the main entrance; joists and rafters of wood moderate
between the old and the new. Long window
strips and glazed roofs let generous quantities of daylight into the galleries.

Axonometric projection

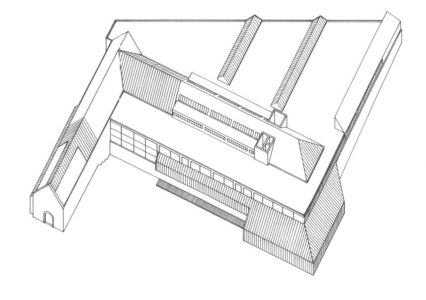

380

Ambulatory on the entrance floor with
Auguste Rodin's "Thinker"
Photo Burrell Collection

has provoked unkind references to the "supermarket of art". Japanese museums often directly adopt advertising slogans from the consumer world, when they advertise their latest acquisitions or the highlights of their collections on huge billboards like special offers.

Re-establishing the museum as a place of calculated cultural unity means acknowledging that the impact of the modern work of art reaches far beyond its frame and hence responding with spaces which are directly tailored to the works to be exhibited. Architecture does not take a subordinate role in such a dialogue situation, but rather discusses art in the full awareness of its content, as is extensively the case in Hans Hollein's Museum Abteiberg in Mönchengladbach. The museums of the 21st century will no doubt have to go even further and present not just the actual work of art but also the social environment. Otherwise the museum with its educational aims will find itself under threat of domination by the art market and its superlatives. Every historical period will thus express its understanding of and relations with art in the architecture of its museums, which shall hence serve as a sensitive barometer of the state of culture.

Renzo Piano
De Menil Collection in Houston, Texas
1981–1986
Exhibition room and exterior view
Photos Paul Hester

Art collector Dominique de Menil was thinking not simply of a new home for her grow-
ing collection, but also of a centre for music,
literature, theatre and cultural educational activities when she planned this new building in
a small park surrounded by low residential
housing. It was to be free of all stylistic borrowings, flexible and open, and above all
was to be illuminated with natural light, a
specification to which Piano subordinated all
other design stages. The solution was a roof
of "leaves" of thin ferro-cement which would
span both the free areas as well as the display rooms of the flat building, and to which
additional lights could be easily attached.
Above this, a sealed superstructure contains
the "treasury" – an air-conditioned storage
space for works of art not on display. The
traditional timbering of the outside walls is a
reference to the surrounding houses: "De-
monumentalization" was the motto.

Section of an exhibition room showing ceiling
and floor construction

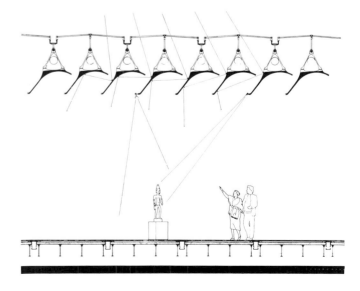

Richard Meier
High Museum of Art in Atlanta, Georgia,
1980–1983
Entrance and interior
Photos Ezra Stoller/Esto
Similar to that of the Frankfurt Museum für
Kunsthandwerk, the design for Atlanta is
based on three cubes occupying the corners
of a square. The building concludes towards
the fourth corner in a generously-glazed
quarter circle. A long, diagonal ramp links
road and entrance and thus optically enlarges the limited space in front of the building.
The design of the interior, featuring window-
like breaches, cabinets in the form of houses
and displays on small "stages", corresponds
extensively to the Frankfurt concept.

Richard Meier
Museum für Kunsthandwerk in Frankfurt am Main, 1979–1984
View from the embankment into the inner courtyard
Photo Ezra Stoller/Esto

Starting-point of the design was the old home of the museum, the Metzler Villa, which was to be appropriately integrated into the new complex. Meier left it free-standing, leading only a bridge to its rear side. Three cubic building volumes, which are oriented towards the dimensions of the villa but avoid any other similarity, now house the arts and crafts collection. A narrow, glazed hall containing the access ramps is rotated 3.5° out of the cube arrangement, whereby it relates to the axes of the neighbouring park and thus introduces a dynamic moment into the construction. Meier's office also planned the entire interiors on the basis of detailed lists of exhibits.

Axonometric projection

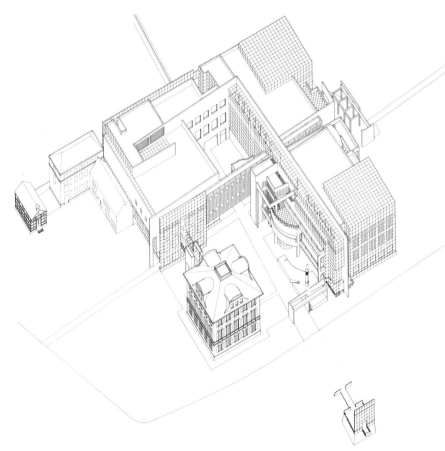

385

Arata Isozaki
Okanoyama Graphic Art Museum in
Nishiwaki, Hyogo, Japan, 1982–1984
Left the entrance portico, right the ramp
entrance and meditation room
Photo Yukio Futagawa/Retoria

This location, at the very heart of Japan, was
originally planned as a park, to be designed
by artist Tadanori Yokoo for his home town
of Nishiwaki. In the end, however, a museum for his works was built instead, its form
inspired by a nearby railway line. The rooms
are coupled together like the waggons of a
train and exhibit in chronological succession
the artist's works from the sixties, seventies
and eighties. Isozaki left the three exhibition
rooms neutral in pure white, lit by overhead
lighting. Small halls linking these main rooms
reflect the themes of the respective decade
in metaphors: thus a palm tree on a blue mosaic floor stands for South Sea paradise, a
tilted square pattern on the walls for the radi-
calization of artistic means.

Plan of the exhibition level

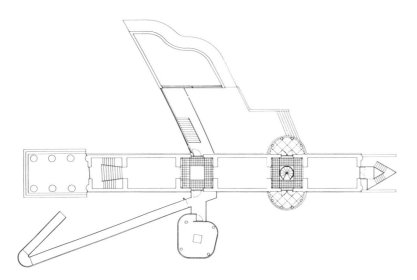

Arata Isozaki
Art Museum in Takasaki, Gunma, Japan,
1970–1974
Overall view
Photo Yukio Futagawa/Retoria
Isozaki's museum design in Takasaki builds
upon a cube module with edges 12 metres
in length, and thereby replaces considerations of content by a geometric scheme.
The rectangular order of the main body is diagonally pierced by an extension, whose
upper floor contains the gallery of Ancient
Japanese art. The open-air area below,
screened by pools, can also be used for exhibitions.

Hans Hollein
Städtisches Museum Abteiberg in
Mönchengladbach, 1972–1982
Exterior view of the exhibition rooms from
the level of the roof terrace
Hollein Archives
The halls of the "clover-leaf" exhibition rooms –
as Hollein calls them – are lit from north-facing
shed windows; the metal cladding appears
spartan and industrial. The square individual
rooms are accessed via opened corners, leading to exciting diagonal vistas and extensively
uninterrupted wall planes.

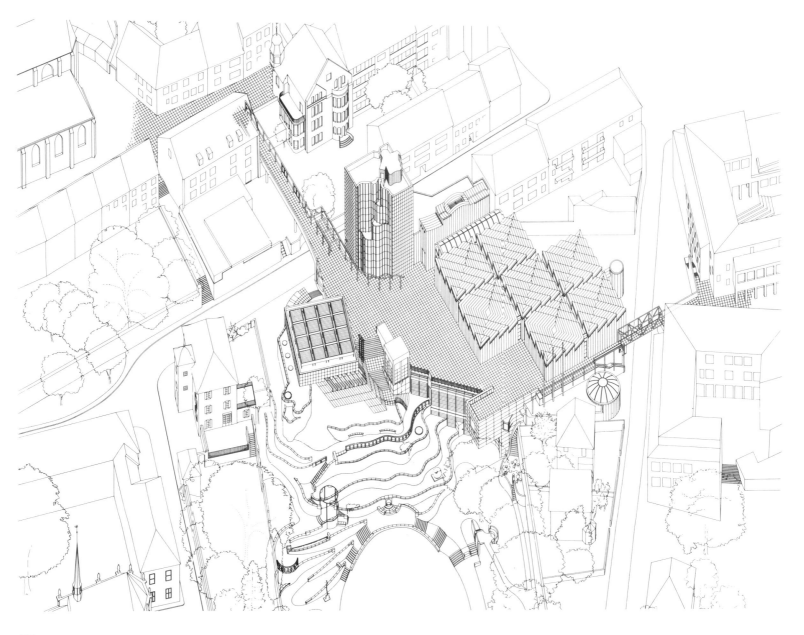

Opposite page:
Axonometric projection of the overall complex
The museum is reached via either the monastery garden, a walkway from the town centre, the Abteistrasse or the passage over Am Spatzenberg. On the roof-terrace level lie, on the left, the pavilion for temporary exhibitions, on the right, the "clover-leaf" shed halls and behind, the tall administration building with workshops and store-rooms. Facing the park, the bay of the cafeteria, with its panorama window, projects from this multi-membered complex.

Entrance pavilion
Hollein Archives
The division of the museum into variously-designed bodies convincingly integrates the complex into its small-scale urban environment and is orientated towards the incline of the former monastery garden, whose gently curving terraces rise above the underground sections of the building. Visitors walk across the roof to reach the prominent glass pavilion. White marble and glittering chrome pillars transform this small building into a powerful point of attraction.

Hans Hollein
Städtisches Museum Abteiberg in
Mönchengladbach, 1972–1982
Interior views: above, sculptures by Giulio
Paolino and Giuseppe Penone; right, a group
by George Segal
Photos Marliese Darsow
The architect was able to start in his planning from a clearly limited inventory of exhibits, and was thus able to create spatial
situations directly related to the art they
house. Close collaboration between Hollein
and museum director Johannes Cladders
produced the final concept: richly-varied sequences of rooms group themselves around
a spacious central area with ticket counter
and cleverly-integrated cafeteria.

Biographies

First CIAM Congress, 1928
Group photo in front of the Chapel
of Castle La Sarraz
From l., standing: Mart Stam, Pierre
Chareau, Victor Bourgeois, Max Haefeli,
Pierre Jeanneret, Gerrit Rietveld, Rudolf
Steiger, Ernst May, Alberto Sartoris, Gabriel
Guevrékian, Hans Schmidt, Hugo Häring, Za-
vala, Florentin, Le Corbusier, Paul Artaria,
Hélène de Mandrot, Friedrich Gubler, Ro-
chat, André Lurçat, Robert von der Mühll,
Maggioni, Huib Hoste, Sigfried Giedion,
Werner Moser, Josef Frank
From l., seated: Garcia Mercadal, Molly
Weber, Tadevossian

Alvar Aalto

Hugo Alvar Henrik Aalto 1898–1976

Aalto studied architecture from 1916–1921 under Armas Lindgren at the Polytechnic of Helsinki. On graduation, he travelled around Europe, acquiring knowledge and experience with various architects until, in 1923, he founded his own practice, in Jyväskylä where his wife Aino joined him in 1925. Aalto's early works, which he produced here, are the Workers' Club (1923–25) and the Patriots' Associations Building, completed in 1929. In 1927, he moved his office to Turku and designed and built the "Turun Sanomat" newspaper offices (1927–1929), the tuberculosis sanatorium Paimio (1928–1933), and the Municipal Library in Viipuri (1930–1935), whose glass-walled outside staircase was frequently imitated. In 1928, Aalto became a member of the CIAM. In 1933, he moved to Helsinki and in 1935 with his wife Aino, Harry and Maire Gullichson, and Nils Gustav Hahl he founded the Artek furniture company. Aalto won the competition for the Finnish Pavilion at the World's Fair in Paris in 1937, a building constructed entirely of wood. On the occasion of an exhibition of his work, he travelled to the USA for the first time in 1938. At the New York World's Fair of 1939, he designed the Finnish Pavilion, which featured an ingenious tilted display wall stretching the entire length of the interior. At the same time, he completed the first section of the Cellulose Factory in Sunila. In 1940 Aalto taught as professor of architecture at the Institute of Technology in Cambridge, Massachusetts. His only project for an American client was the 1947–48 Baker House Dormitory for the students of the Institute of Technology in Cambridge. The extensive list of his projects numbers 200, of which about half were actually built, predominantly public buildings like the Town Hall in Säynätsalo

(1949–1952), the House of Culture in Helsinki (1955–1958), the Institute of Technology in Otaniemi (1955–1964), and the parish centre and church in Seinäjoki (1958–1965). In Germany he built a housing complex for the Interbau in Berlin (1957) and the "Neue Vahr" apartment complex in Bremen (1959–1962) with its fan-shaped ground plan. It was some time after his death before the opera house in Essen was finally completed.

Arquitectonica

The group of architects Arquitectonica International was formed in 1977 in Miami by husband and wife Bernardo Fort-Brescia and Laurinda Spear, the present owners of the firm, Hervin A.R. Romney, who remained with them until 1984, and Andres Duany and Elisabet Plater Zyberk, who both left the office in 1979. One of their first projects was the house of Laurinda Spear's parents in Miami, Florida (1977–1979), with its clear geometric form built around a courtyard and painted pink. Pastel shades were also used for the Mulder House in Lima, Peru (1983–1984), in which two high walls intersect at right angles to form four differently styled rooms. This organisatory principle of overlap and inter-penetration is also employed in their larger apartment buildings; for the Helmsley Palace Hotel in Miami, Florida (1978–1980), a slender high-rise block is intercepted at a right angle by a staircase building. On Biscayne Bay, Miami, appropriate names such as "Atlantis" (1979–1981) and "Babylon" were given to underline the concept of the buildings. For the Banco de Credito in Lima, Arquitectonica designed a four-storey complex around a central courtyard in which there appears to have been a landslide. The colourful details of the designs give the impression of being works of art in their own right. One of their most recent projects is the Bank of Luxemburg. Arquitectonica regularly receives commissions from all over the world, notably London, Paris, and Milan, and has branches in Houston and New York.

Erik Gunnar Asplund 1885–1940

Asplund studied architecture at the Technical College (1905–1909) and the Free Architectural Academy in Stockholm. After working for two years as Assistant Lecturer at the Technical College (1912–1913), he travelled in Italy and France. With Sigurd Lewerentz, one of the founder members of the Free Architectural Academy, he won a competition in 1915 to design the South Cemetery in Stockholm. His first independent projects include the Snellmann Villa in Djursholm (1917–1918) and the Forest Chapel in Stockholm (1918–1920). Asplund went on to design the County Court in Sölvesburg (1917–1921), the Carl Johan School in Gothenburg (1915–1924), and the Municipal Library in Stockholm (1920–1928), a central cylinder flanked by three low, cube-shaped wings which form a horseshoe. From the imaginatively interpreted neo-classicism of these buildings Asplund switched to uncompromising modernity. For the 1930 Stockholm Exhibition, he designed a series of pavilions with glass walls, light steel frames, and coloured sun-screens. With their thematically varying accentuation, these pavilions are high points of the new "1930 Style". From 1931 to 1940, Asplund was professor of Architecture at the Technical College in Stockholm. During this period, he designed and executed the extension to the Town Hall in Gothenburg (1934–1937), and the forest crematorium of the South Cemetery, Stockholm (1935–1940), consisting of a crematorium and three chapels. The main entrance is characterised by a portico, its flat roof supported by square pillars.

Peter Behrens 1868–1940

Behrens studied painting in Karlsruhe and Düsseldorf before moving to Munich in 1890. As graphic artist, painter and designer he was a founder member of the Munich Sezession in 1892 and in 1897 also joined the "Vereinigte Werkstätten für Kunst im Handwerk" (United Workshops for Arts and Crafts). In 1899 he was invited by Grand Duke Ernst Ludwig of Hesse to join the newly-formed Artists' Colony in Darmstadt, where he taught until 1903. Behrens built his first house for the Colony's exhibition on the Mathildenhöhe, "Ein Dokument deutscher Kunst" (A Document of German Art), in 1901. Subsequently, he worked from 1903 to 1907 as Director of the Kunstgewerbeschule (School of Applied Arts) in Düsseldorf. During this period he executed the Obenauer House in Saarbrücken (1905–1906). In 1907 he was commissioned by Emil Rathenau as artistic adviser to the AEG (General Electric Company) in Berlin. Here he was responsible for everything from letterheads and industrial design to architecture. Behrens not only produced a "Festschrift", an arc-lamp and a water-boiler but also important AEG factory buildings such as the turbine factory (1908–1909), the high tension plant with production hall and two further wings for storehouse and workshops (1909–1910), and the small motors factory (1910–1913). From 1910 to 1911 he executed a whole housing complex in Henningsdorf for the AEG workers. At this time, Le Corbusier, Walter Gropius and Mies van der Rohe were also employed in Behrens' office. In 1911 and 1912 Behrens executed his designs for the office building of the Mannesmann-Röhrenwerke in Düsseldorf and the German Embassy in St. Petersburg. In the post-war years he designed and built the head office of the IG-Farben chemical factory in Höchst (1920–1924), a complex 150 metres long with a high cathedral-like entrance-hall decorated n all the colours of the rainbow and with a prismatic glass dome. From 1922 to 1927, while retaining his architect's office in Berlin, he was successor to Otto Wagner as head of architecture at the Vienna Academy of Arts. In 1927 he presented a terrace house as his contribution to the "Werkbund" exhibition at the Weißenhof in Stuttgart and in 1929 took part in the competition for the urban renewal of the Alexanderplatz in Berlin; two eight-storey office buildings were built of reinforced concrete (1930–1931). In 1936 he became head of the department of architecture at the Prussian Academy of Arts in Berlin.

Hendrik Petrus Berlage 1856–1934

Berlage studied from 1875 to 1878 at the Polytechnikum in Zurich; he then travelled in Italy, Germany and Austria and returned to his home town of Amsterdam in 1882. With Theodorus Sanders as partner he worked on such projects as the Focke & Melzer Building in Amsterdam in the neo-renaissance style (1885). In 1889 he established his own practice. With the office building for the insurance company "De Algemeene" in Amsterdam (1893) he freed himself from stylistic borrowings. Through Carel Henny, the director of the insurance company "De Nederlanden van 1845", Berlage was able to develop his architectural ideas further. The result was two office buildings, both in unrendered brick, in Amsterdam (1893–1895) and The Hague (1895). This connection brought him further commissions in the course of his artistic career, including a house for Henny himself in The Hague (1898). From 1896 Berlage worked on his plan for the Amsterdam Beurs (Stock Exchange), a design originally entered for a competition. The building was completed in 1903. It is generally considered to be the high point of his career as an architect and provoked great criticism among his contemporaries because of its austere façade. Among other important works is the Diamond Workers' House in Amsterdam (1899–1900). In addition, Berlage worked on city development plans for Amsterdam (1902,1925), The Hague (1908,1924), Rotterdam (1922), Utrecht (1924) and Groningen (1927–1928), although these projects were only partly completed. On a trip to America in 1911, he was particularly impressed by the buildings of Louis Sullivan and Frank Lloyd Wright. From 1913 he was commissioned by the Kröller-Müllers and consequently moved to The Hague. Among these commissions was a design for a villa, in fact never built, an office building in London (1914–1916), and the Sint Hubertus Hunting Lodge in Otterlo (1915). Berlage was also active as author; his most important publications include "Gedanken über den Stil in der Baukunst" (Thoughts on Style in Architecture, 1905) and "Grundlagen und Entwicklung der Architektur" (Principles and Development of Architecture, 1908). From 1924 Berlage taught at the Technical University in Delft.

Mario Botta

Mario Botta *1943

Born in Switzerland, Botta began his training as a draftsman in 1958 at the office of Luigi Carmenisch and Tita Carloni in Lugano. From 1961 to 1964 he attended the Liceo Artistico in Milan. Botta was only eighteen when he designed and built his first house, the rectory in Genestrerio (1961–1963). From 1964 he studied under Carlo Scarpa and the art historian Giuseppe Mazzariol at the Istituto Universitario di Architettura in Venice. In 1965 he worked beside Julian de la Fuente and José Oubrerie in the office of Le Corbusier on the latter's last project, the new hospital in Venice. Towards the end of his university studies he met Louis Kahn. The meeting led to collaborative work on an exhibition in the Palazzo Ducale in connection with a project for the new congress building in Venice. In 1970 Botta went into private practice in Lugano. Two years later he planned his most ambitious project to date, the Secondary School in Morbio Inferiore (1972–1977). His numerous designs for detached residences are based on basic geometric forms, for instance the square house in Cadenazzo (1970–1971), the rectangular tower with access bridge in Riva San Vitale (1971–1973) and the cylindrical house in Stabio (1980–1982). Also worthy of note is the library of the Capuchin monastery in Lugano (1976–1979). Although built underground, it receives generous quantities of daylight through a glass roof like that of a greenhouse. For later major projects such as the extension of the Staatsbank in Fribourg (1977–1982), Botta attempted to apply his clear geometry in the context of the city. In 1983 he became Honorary Professor at the University of Lausanne and Honorary Fellow of the "Bund Deutscher Architekten" (League of German Architects).

Coop Himmelblau. Wolf D. Prix *1942, Helmut Swiczinsky *1944

The group of architects Coop Himmelblau was founded in Vienna in 1968 by Wolf D. Prix, Helmut Swiczinsky and Rainer Michael Holzer, who left the group in 1971. Initially the three worked on ideas and projects in experimental architecture, often based on pneumatic constructions of space, for instance a movable, inflatable and inhabitable cloud (1968–1972), and the cloud as backdrop for the "Wiener Supersommer" (1976). The switch to aggressive language came in 1977 with the "Reiss Bar" in Vienna. A telescopic steel tube spanned between the walls gives the visitor the optical illusion that the room has been stretched apart and that a 49 centimetre wide rip has appeared which extends along the floor and up the wall to the ceiling. This deep black crevasse is in stark contrast to the brightness of the walls. For a town residence project, appropriately named "Hot Flat", the group designed a glass roof in the form of a naked flame. This was installed as a fragment in the Technische Universität in Vienna (1978–1979). "Architektur muß brennen" (Architecture must burn) is also the title of a publication in Graz in 1980. The next step in this concept of architecture determined by violation and distortion can be seen in the HUMANIC branch offices in Mistelbach (1979) and Vienna (1980–1981). At about the same time the group began with the Viennese "Liederbar" "Roter Engel" (1980–1981), a wine bar with attached concert-hall seating 120. Between 1983 and 1988, besides numerous unfinished projects like the "First Media Tower" for Hamburg, the group built a lawyer's office in Vienna, a roof extension whose new elements protrude over the traditional façade, making the act of conversion clearly visible. A new phase began in 1988–1989 with a large industrial commission to build the Funder Chipboard Factory in Carinthia. Here dancing chimneys and jagged roofs form a tumultous covering to a functional building complex. A recent construction is a video pavilion in Groningen which has screens which open and close as a reaction to the film being shown – architecture in motion.

John Gerard Dinkeloo 1918–1981

Dinkeloo studied architectural engineering at the University of Michigan in Ann Arbor until 1942 and subsequently worked as a designer with Skidmore, Owings and Merrill in Chicago. After his military service, he became Chief of Production there in 1946. In 1950 Dinkeloo moved to the office of Eero Saarinen in Bloomfield Hills, Michigan, and in 1956 became his partner. After Saarinen's death he was joined by Kevin Roche and moved the office to Hamden, Connecticut, where he worked to complete Saarinen's projects. In 1966 the firm was renamed "Kevin Roche John Dinkeloo and Associates". They collaborated on many projects,

Egon Eiermann

where Dinkeloo frequently employed unusual materials such as weathering steel and sprayed metal glass. Their most important works include the Oakland Museum, California (1961–1968), the Ford Foundation Building in New York (1963–1968), the high-rise building "Knights of Columbus" in New Haven, Connecticut (1965–1969), and the extension to the Metropolitan Museum of Art in New York (1967–1985). After Dinkeloo's death in 1981, the work of the office was continued by his partner Kevin Roche.

Willem Marinus Dudok 1884–1974

Trained as an engineer at the Royal Military Academy in Breda, Holland, Dudok opened his first office in Leiden in 1913. In 1915 he accepted a post as Director of the Municipal Works in Hilversum, where in 1927 he was appointed Municipal Architect and also worked on city development plans. One of Dudok's early works in Hilversum is the school on the Geraniumstraat (1917–1918), a brick building with a tall central tower and white window frames. In the twenties he designed and built the Public Baths (1920), the Dr. Bavinck School (1921), the Minchelers School (1925), the Fabritius School (1926), the Vondel School (1928–1929) and the Valeris School (1930). The town hall (1928–1931) is a milestone in Dudok's career. Structured on different levels, it is dominated by a high tower reflected in the water of a garden pool below. It shows his development from a style oriented towards the Amsterdam School to an expressive modernity. Noteworthy buildings not executed in Hilversum are the Dutch Student Residence at the Cité Universitaire in Paris (1927–1928), the department store in Rotterdam (1929–1930), which has not survived, and the Municipal Theatre in Utrecht (1939–1941). From 1934 Dudok worked as town planner for The Hague.

Egon Eiermann 1904–1970

After studying architecture at the Technische Hochschule in Berlin under Hans Poelzig from 1923 to 1927, Eiermann joined the architectural office of the Karstadt Company in Hamburg and thereafter the BEWAG (Berlin Electric Company). Although he designed many buildings in the thirties in collaboration with Fritz Jaenecke (from 1931), the most influential period of his career came after the War. In 1947 he accepted the Chair of Architecture at the Technische Hochschule in Karlsruhe. In the post-war years of reconstruction his industrial buildings with their characteristic steel skeleton structure were regarded as exemplary. From 1949 to 1951 he built the handkerchief weaving Mill at Blumberg and won the Hugo Häring Prize for the clear layout of its factory complex. On study trips to the USA he met Walter Gropius, Marcel Breuer and Konrad Wachsmann in 1950 and Ludwig Mies van der Rohe in 1956. For the Brussels World's Fair in 1958 he designed with Sep Ruf a group of pavilions consisting of eight elegant, transparent glass cubes. For the Nekkermann firm in Frankfurt he designed a 300 metre long, six-storeyd Distribution Centre (1958–1961). In Berlin he won the competition for the reconstruction of the Kaiser-Wilhelm-Gedächtniskirche (1959–1963). On a platform clearly defined by steps an octagonal main building and a narrow, octagonal tower flank the old ruined church tower in the middle. For the German Embassy in Washington (1959–1964) Eiermann conceived with E. Brandl a terrace structure for 140 employees which is tailored to fit its surroundings. Like the Members' Building for the Bundestag in Bonn (1965–1969), the embassy has the characteristic filigree structure, a kind of secondary envelope of horizontal sun-screens and vertical supports. Striking office buildings of the latter period of Eiermann's career are the IBM Administration Building in Stuttgart (1967–1972) and the funnel-shaped concrete bases of the high-rise towers for the firm Olivetti in Frankfurt (1968–1972), which were only completed two years after his death.

Peter Eisenman *1932

Eisenman was educated at the universities of Cornell in Ithaca, Columbia in New York, and Cambridge in England. From 1957 to 1958 he worked for the group founded by Gropius, The Architects Collaborative (TAC). In 1967 in New York, he founded the Institute for Architecture and Urban Studies, where he remained as director until 1982. Eisenman conceived a series of houses based on square plans, but modified in various ways, and numbered consecutively. Those actually built were House I, the Barenholtz Pavilion in Princeton, New Jersey (1967–1968), House II, Falk House in Hardwick, Connecticut (1969–1970), House III, the Miller

Norman Foster

House in Lakeville, Connecticut (1970), and House IV, the Frank Residence in Cornwall, Connecticut (1972) with a non-usable inverted red staircase. Among more recent projects by Eisenman are an apartment block at Checkpoint Charlie in Berlin (1982–1986), and the Wexner Centre for the Visual Arts at Ohio State University in Columbus. With Michael Graves, Charles Gwathmey, John Hejduk and Richard Meier, Eisenman belongs to the group, the New York Five, that drew on ideas from the twenties but increasingly developed them into his own esoteric theory of architecture, which led in due course to his participation in the exhibition "deconstructive architecture" in 1988 at the Museum of Modern Art.

Norman Foster *1935

Foster studied town planning and architecture at the University of Manchester. On graduating in 1961 he won a scholarship to the University of Yale, where he gained his M.Arch. degree. Returning to England he founded Team 4, an architectural office with his wife Wendy and Su and Richard Rogers. They took on a few commissions such as the Mews Houses in London (1965), and the Reliance Controls Factory in Wiltshire (1964–1966). At this stage Foster was already experimenting with modular building parts and movable interior walls in order to allow in the planning for future changes of use. In 1967 he expanded his office with further partners. Foster Associates then built the Fred Olsen Passenger Terminal at London Docks (1970–1971) and the Headquarters of the firm Willis Faber & Dumas in Ipswich (1974–1975) with its undulating façade of frameless glazing. For the Sainsbury Centre for Visual Arts in Norwich (1978), the main supports of the hall were

housed together with the mechanical facilities in a two-layered outer covering. In 1981 Foster Associates built the Renault UK Parts Distribution Centre, a construction of hollow masts and bent metal supports emphasised by bright yellow paint. The high-rise building of the Hong Kong and Shanghai Bank in Hong Kong was a masterpiece of precision and technology built in only five years (1981–1986). By 1986, the year of its completion, Foster Associates numbered about 160 employees.

Richard Buckminster Fuller 1895–1983

Fuller was a student at Harvard University from 1913 to 1915. As a soldier in the navy in 1917, he was commended for his design of a mast fitted with derricks for the recovery of seaplanes. In 1922, with his father-in-law J.M. Hewlett, he founded the firm Stockade Building System, which, however, only lasted a few years. In 1927 he designed a house on a hexagonal plan with six triangular rooms suspended from a central well with integrated mechanical facilities. The total weight of the house, including furniture, was a mere 2,227 kg with a diameter of 15 m and a height of 12 m; it was tranportable and easy to assemble and disassemble. Known later as the 4D (fourth dimension) house, it embodied Fuller's basic principle, the greatest performance with the least investment of energy and materials, using all possible scientific and technical means. From 1932 to 1935, Fuller was founder, director and chief engineer of the Dymaxion Corporation in Bridgeport, Connecticut. During this period he patented his "Dymaxion car", a streamlined but sadly unroadworthy three-wheeler. In the war years he developed the prototype of his 1929 Dymaxion House further. Its outer appearance was characterised by a round plan, portholes and a flat, domed roof. Later Fuller became increasingly interested in systematically probing the nature of efficiency in structural form with structures quickly and cheaply erected that covered a maximum of space with the smallest surface area of material. The outcome was the geodesic dome, based on regular multi-faceted surface units. Working with his students, he tried out numerous experimental domes. In 1953 he built a round building of glassfibre-polyester for the Ford Motor Company. A year later he designed a dome made of wood and covered with transparent foil for a restaurant in Woods Hole. For the Union Tank Car Company in Baton Rouge, Louisiana, he covered 117 metres with a dome 36.5 m high made of 321 hexagonal steel plates (1958). A geodesic dome by Fuller was also to be seen at the American Exhibition in Moscow in 1959. His most famous building was the sphere for the US pavilion at "Expo 67" in Montreal. In 1976 its plastic covering caught fire during repair work. This put paid to his plans to cover whole areas of cities with such domes. In 1962

Fuller patented his Tensile Integrity Structures and improved them in 1973 by his design of an asymmetrical structural form, which even today exists only as a model.

Antoni Gaudí 1852–1926

Antoni Gaudí i Cornet studied from 1874 to 1878 in Barcelona. At this time he was already working in various architectural offices, including the office of Francisco de Paula de Villar, whose successor he was to become in 1883 on the building of the Sagrada Familia cathedral From 1878 he had his own practice in Barcelona, where he carried out most of his life's work. In 1879 work began on his first project, the Casa Vicens in Barcelona (1883–1885). Gaudí's love of quarry stones and coloured ceramic tiles is apparent here right from the start. Gaudí found a good friend and patron in the textile manufacturer Eusebi Güell, for whom he designed among other buildings a town palace, the Palacio Güell (1885–1889). From 1883 to 1889 Gaudí took over the building of the Colegio Teresiano. On both these projects he made the first-ever use of his paraboloid vaults. According to his calculations, the entire weight of the vaulting could be borne by appropriately angled pillars. To calculate the distribution of weight for the church Colonia Güell, begun near Barcelona in 1898, he devised for the purpose a hanging catenary cord model with pellet weights that simulated the weight distribution "upside down". He subsequently introduced these design aids for the Sagrada Familia. From 1900 to 1914 he constructed parts of a park designed for Güell, the Parque Güell. The parts actually completed were two residences, the entrance area, the terracing and a network of paths. Here, as elsewhere, Gaudí used his cha-

acteristic variety of soft, naturalistic forms, irregular plans and slanting masonry supports. Gaudí's most important apartment buildings include the Casa Batlló (1904–1906) and the Casa Milá (1906–1910) with their moulded façades. Gaudí devised a wave form for the roof and walls of the Sagrada Familia school-house, completed in 1909. Despite this wave form, only straight roof beams were necessary. Similar forms were not employed again until the use of concrete became popular. From 1914, Gaudí concentrated wholly on the completion of the Sagrada Familia, a project which occupied him for the rest of his life and still remains unfinished.

Frank O. Gehry *1929

Gehry was educated at the University of Southern California in Los Angeles which he attended until 1954. Then he studied town planning at the Harvard Graduate School of Design. Thereafter he worked in the offices of Welton Becket & Associates (1957–1958) and Victor Gruen (1958–1961) in Los Angeles, and André Remondet in Paris (1961). In 1962 he opened his own office in Los Angeles, which he runs today as the firm of Frank O. Gehry Associates. At the end of the seventies he built a series of residences with unusual use of space and industrial materials such as the Spiller Residence in Venice, California (1979–1980) and his own house in Santa Monica (1978); here he has covered the existing building with an envelope of pink asbestos panels, corrugated metal sheets and wire caging, all of which gives the impression of something unfinished, unstable, and do-it-yourself. Of his larger work the most noteworthy examples are in Los Angeles, such as the Loyola Law School (1981–1984), the California Aerospace Museum (1983–1984) and the Francis Howard Goldwyn Regional Branch Library (1986). The Fishdance Restaurant in Kobe, Japan (1987) and the recently completed museum for the Vitra Furniture Company in Weil am Rhein are evidence of Gehry's increasing activity abroad, while at home in California he is building detached houses in which each room is treated as a separate building structure.

Irving John Gill 1870–1936

Gill, son of a building engineer, joined the office of Dankmar Adler and Louis Sullivan in Chicago in 1890, worked as a draftsman on projects such as the Transportation Building for the Columbian Exposition of 1893, and met Frank Lloyd Wright. In 1896 he opened his own office in San Diego. In the following years he designed numerous buildings in California, mostly cubic, whitewashed concrete houses like Klauber House in San Diego (1907–1910) and the Wilson Acton Hotel in La Jolla (1908), whose completely featureless façade is sub-

Richard Buckminster Fuller

Frank O. Gehry

divided only by the gridded arrangement of the square window openings. On two buildings, however, he placed round arches and pillars onto the plain white surfaces, drawing here on the traditional forms of the Spanish missions. These are the Pacific Electric Railroad Building in Torrance (1912) and the Christian Science Church in San Diego (1904). Among his most important projects are Dodge House in Los Angeles (1914–1916), since demolished, and the loosely grouped buildings of the Lewis Courts development in Sierra Madre (1910), a plan that recurs in the later Horatio West Court in Santa Monica (1919–1921), this time supplemented by strip windows with the green frames that became characteristic of Gill's work.

Michael Graves *1934

Graves studied at the University of Cincinnati, Ohio, a course which included practical experience with Carl A. Strauss and Associates. He completed his studies at Harvard in 1959 and took a job with the designer and architect George Nelson. On a scholarship from the American Academy he spent two years in Rome. After his return he taught at Princeton University, New Jersey, where he has been professor of architecture since 1972. In 1964 Graves established his own practice and in 1967 built Hanselmann House in Fort Wayne, Indiana. He first became famous through a collaborative exhibition at the Museum of Modern Art in New York in 1969 with Peter Eisenman, Charles Gwathmey, John Hejduk and Richard Meier, and also through the publication "Five Architects". Graves soon distanced himself from the strict neo-modernism of this group and began to design houses with much greater use of colour, emphatic gables and walls and ab-

stract pillar motifs. To this phase can be assigned Kalko House in Green Brook, New Jersey (1978), the Sunar Company presentation rooms (1979–1987) and the Public Services Building in Portland, Oregon (1980–1982), a symmetrical, cube-shaped high-rise building on a square, colonnaded base. Also worthy of mention are the San Juan Capistrano Library in Southern California (1983), and the Humana Corporation Headquarters in Louisville, Kentucky (1982–1986).

Vittorio Gregotti *1927

Gregotti gained his Dip.Arch. at the Polytechnic of Milan in 1952, then worked as co-editor of "Casabella-continuità" and founded the office Architetti Associati in Milan with Lodovico Meneghetti and Giotto Stoppino. An example of the work of this group is the residence in Cameri (1956–1957), reminiscent of the classical villa. In 1968 they built the Bossi textile factory in Cameri with its stereometric, inter-penetrating buildings, and in 1973 the new University of Calabria in Arvacata. After Pier Luigi Cerri and Hiromichi Matusi had joined them the office became the firm Gregotti Associati. Together they worked on a residence for the International Exhibition in Berlin (1982–1986) which, like the university buildings in Calabria, was designed as a series of bridges over side streets. Besides his duties as director of the office, Gregotti is an active journalist and has run the journal "Rassegna" since 1980 and "Casabella-continuità" since 1982.

Walter Gropius 1883–1969

Gropius studied architecture from 1903 to 1907 at the Technische Hochschule of Berlin and Munich. On graduation he took the then customary trips abroad to various European countries. He acquired practical experience in the office of Peter Behrens. In 1910 he established his own practice with Adolf Meyer. The two collaborated on a design for the Fagus shoe factory in Alfeld an der Leine (1910–1914). The main building consists of a rectangular supporting skeleton without corner pillars and a gridded façade of glass sheets set in metal frames, one of the earliest examples of a curtain wall. In 1914 they built a model factory for the "Werkbund" Exhibition in Cologne. After the war, on the recommendation of Henry van de Velde, Gropius was appointed director of the Großherzogliche Kunstgewerbeschule Weimar (Grand Ducal School of Applied Arts in Weimar) and the Großherzogliche Hochschule für bildende Kunst (Grand Ducal Academy of Arts). In 1919 Gropius merged the two schools into one, the State Bauhaus. When the institute was forced to move, Gropius planned a new Bauhaus complex in Dessau (1925–1926). The basic idea was that the different forms of the building

Michael Graves

shaped PAN AM Building in New York (1958–1963), which was conceived in collaboration with TAC, Pietro Belluschi and Emery Roth and Sons, the Rosenthal China Factory in Selb (1965–1967) and the Thomas Glassworks in Amberg (1967–1969). Gropius has expounded his architectural theories in numerous publications such as "Internationale Architektur" (1925), "Bauhausbauten Dessau" (1930), and "The New Architecture and the Bauhaus" (1935).

Hector Guimard 1867–1942

Guimard attended the Ecole des Arts Décoratifs in Paris from 1882 to 1885 and then the Ecole des Beaux Arts. His first commission was a cafe on the Quai d'Auteil in 1886. He received greater acclaim with the Castel Béranger in Paris (1894–1898), an apartment house with 36 units. Guimard provided the complicated, still traditional building with a surprising, asymmetrical gate and railings at the main entrance. On a trip to Belgium in 1895 he met the Art Nouveau architect Victor Horta. Thereafter he designed the Canivet House in Paris, the Castel Henriette in Sèvres, the Maison Coilliot in Lille and the entrances to the Paris metro stations with their arches and railings decorated with organic plant forms and pre-fabricated ornamental masks. For the auditorium of the 1902 Humbert de Romans Building in Paris, Guimard designed a structure with branching, tree-like pillars on stone sockets supporting the central dome. He commissioned Henri Sauvage to design tube-like elements of asbestos cement for use in a country house, which was a significant innovation after the war. He spent the latter years of his life in New York.

Robert van't Hoff 1887–1979

Van't Hoff attended the School of Art in Birmingham, England, from 1906 to 1911 and then the Architectural Association School in London (1911–1914). During a one-year stay in the USA (1913–1914) he met Frank Lloyd Wright and worked for him on an inventory of his buildings. Back in Holland he designed the Verloop summer residence in Huis ter Heide near Utrecht (1914–1915) and the Henny Villa (1915–1919), one of the earliest reinforced concrete constructions in Europe. This building is characterised by its clear arrangement of rectangular surfaces and building parts. At the same time he became involved in the De Stijl movement and even built himself a house-boat of the same name. With Pieter J.C. Klaarhammer he developed a plan for a district development project in 1918 and 1919, but he left the De Stijl group after differences of opinion with Theo van Doesburg. After this, little was heard of him. He spent the years from 1922 to 1937 in England, America and Switzerland, and after 1937 he lived in England.

units, corresponding to the main functions of the school, should be interconnected. The complex included houses for the master-craftsmen and the director (1925–1926). From 1926 to 1928 he produced his first large scale project, the Törten estate near Dessau which partly used pre-fabricated reinforced concrete elements. Also in Dessau he built the Konsumverein (Cooperative Society) in 1927 and the City Employment Office (1927–1929). Further buildings followed for the Dammerstock Housing Development in Karlsruhe (1928–1929), a project which Gropius coordinated. At the same time, working for Erwin Piscator, he developed his concept of the "total theatre" with its revolving stage which could be transformed into a proscenium or stages of varying depths (1927). In 1928 he gave up the directorship of the Bauhaus in favour of Hannes Meyer and moved to Berlin, where he became supervising architect of the Siemensstadt estate (1929–1930) and himself designed two blocks, slender high-rise houses with pergolas. After the Nazi takeover he emigrated to England in 1934 and until 1937 worked with the architect Maxwell Fry on projects such as the Ben Levy House in London (1935) and the Impington Village College in Cambridgeshire (1936–1940). When he was offered the post of professor of architecture at Harvard, Gropius moved to the USA. There he collaborated closely with Marcel Breuer on such schemes as the workers' housing development in New Kensington (1941). Later he worked with Konrad Wachsmann on mass-produced houses (1943–1945). In 1946 Gropius founded with young artists the group TAC, The Architects Collaborative. One remarkable result of this collaborative effort was the Graduate Centre and dormitories at Harvard University with seven halls of residence and a community centre (1949–1950). The most important works of his later career include the 59-storey, prism-

Josef Hoffmann 1870–1956

After attending the Staatsgewerbeschule in Brno, Bohemia, Hoffmann worked for the Militärbauamt in Würzburg, Germany. In 1892 he moved to Vienna and studied under Carl von Hasenauer and Otto Wagner at the Academy of Arts. He won the Rome Prize, which gave him a scholarship for a protracted stay in Italy. On his return to Vienna he joined the office of Otto Wagner, where he met Joseph Maria Olbrich. Together with other artists they formed the "Siebener Club" (Club 7) in 1895 and the Vienna Sezession in 1897, which Hoffmann however left with the Klimt group in 1905. From 1899 Hoffmann taught at the Vienna Kunstgewerbeschule and in 1900 created an interior for the World's Fair in Paris. Shortly afterwards he was commissioned by the banker Fritz Wärndorfer to design a dining room. Hoffmann fi-

nally changed from the mere planning of interiors to real architectonic work when he designed and built several houses on the Hohe Warte, including the duplex for Koloman Moser and Carl Moll and Spitzer House. In 1903 he founded the "Wiener Werkstätte" (Vienna Workshop) with Koloman Moser, for which he designed a great deal of furniture and utility articles. His first large-scale commission was the sanatorium in Purkersdorf (1904–1906), a long horizontal, severely plain building, skillfully proportioned with symmetrically arranged window openings and, what was surprising for the time, a flat roof. A little later came the Palais Stoclet in Brussels (1905–1911), in which Hoffmann created an apotheosis of Art Nouveau with its costly interiors and with fine mosaics by Gustav Klimt. The outside of the villa also reveals its riches: gilded metal bands edge a white marble façade. In 1912 Hoffmann was involved in the foundation of the Austrian Werkbund. His later style became more severe, as clearly seen in the columns and façade of the Primavesi House in Vienna (1915). For the Werkbund Exhibition in Vienna in 1932 he built four terrace houses in which tall turret staircases were interspersed with cube-shaped building structures. It was a short excursion into the International Style, for at the Biennale in Venice in 1934, Hoffmann conceived a strictly neo-classical building more in keeping with the prevailing trends.

Hans Hollein *1934

Hollein studied first at the Kunstgewerbeschule in Vienna and at the Academy of Arts under Clemens Holzmeister, and thereafter at the Illinois Institute of Technology in Chicago. He completed his architectural studies at the University of California in Berkeley in 1960. In the following years he designed a series of visionary colour collages in which rock formations and oversize construction machines on stilts tower above the city skylines of Vienna or New York. His drawings in collaboration with Walter Pichler also contain the beginnings of a new, autonomous architecture. Hollein's first practical projects were conversions and alterations such as the Retti Candle Shop in Vienna (1964–1965). The frequently small-scale façades stand in spectacular contrast to their surroundings. What catches the eye, for instance, on the Richard Feigen Gallery in New York (1967–1969) are the twin, chrome-plated pillars at the asymmetrically arranged entrance set against the smooth white façade of the building. From 1967 to 1976 Hollein taught at the Staatliche Kunstakademie in Düsseldorf. From 1970 to 1972 he designed the interiors of the Siemens Company Administration in Munich. In 1974 the Schullin Jeweller's Shop was finished in Vienna with its optical sensation: a rip in the outer fabric of the building that continued as far as the main entry. For the Städtisches Museum am Abteiberg in Mönchengladbach (1972–1982), Hollein had

Walter Gropius

several structural compartments sunk into the hillside and linked together to form the museum complex. In 1976 Hollein became professor at the Hochschule für angewandte Kunst in Vienna. In the same year, he started work on the headquarters of the Vienna Tourist Office (1976–1978), where he placed travel slogans like golden palms and antique columns in a glass-domed pavilion to create a humorous and ironic effect. However, the interior has since been removed, as has that of the New York branch of the Munich fashion house Ludwig Beck in Trump Tower (1981–1983). For the Museum Moderner Kunst in Frankfurt (1982–1990), Hollein filled a triangular site with a huge piece of cake with symbolically arranged window openings. Hollein is active not only in the areas of architecture, art, and design but also in that of exhibitions. Examples of his work are the paper exhibition at the Vienna Design Centre (1971–1972), "Man Transforms" at the Cooper Hewitt Museum in New York (1974–1976), and "Die Türken vor Wien" (1983) and "Traum und Wirklichkeit" (1985) at the Vienna Künstlerhaus.

Victor Horta 1861–1947

Horta first studied at the Acacémies des Beaux-Arts in Ghent and Brussels. In 1880, he joined the office of the architect Alphonse Balat. After several smaller projects he designed and built the Hôtel Tassel in Brussels from 1892 to 1893. Here iron was used for the first time in a private house, both as a structural and stylistic element. Instead of the usual hallway there was a octagonal room and the other floors were reached by an iron staircase. Similar projects followed, such as the Maison Autrique (1893) and the Maison Winssinger (1895–1896). At the turn of the century Horta built the Hôtel Solvay (1895–1900), for which he also designed all the interiors, and the town house for Baron van Eetvelde (1897–1900). He was also commissioned for new and larger projects: from 1896 to 1899 he built the administrative headquarters and conference rooms of the Belgian Socialist Party, the "Maison du Peuple", and in 1901 the department store "A L'Innovation". All these buildings were in Brussels. From 1897 Horta taught at the Free University there; in 1912 he became professor at the Académie des Beaux-Arts and in 1927 its director. In later years, his style became stricter, as the reinforced concrete building of the Brussels Palais des Beaux-Arts testifies (1922–1928); he also became involved on various architectural committees and carried out research into contemporary building materials.

Helmut Jahn *1940

Born near Nuremberg, Jahn graduated at the Technische Hochschule in Munich, and then worked for Peter C. Seidlein until 1966, supplementing his education at the Illinois Institute of Technology in Chicago in 1965 and 1966. In 1967 he joined the office of C.F. Murphy Associates as assistant to Gene Summers. When Summers left in 1973 Jahn took over his position and became director in charge of planning and design. In 1981 he became a partner in the firm, now called Murphy/Jahn, and in 1982 its Chief Executive Officer, before taking over the firm completely in 1983. In a very short period in 1975, and at very low cost, Jahn built the Crosby Kemper Memorial Arena for 1,800 spectators in Kansas City, Missouri. Its ceiling was supported by three girders of round tubing on the outside and the façades were covered with metal panelling. For the sports' hall of St. Mary's College in South Bend, Indiana (1977), a friendly atmosphere is created by the light falling into the room from the side and shining on the red pillars and the blue and yellow piping. From 1979 to 1984 Jahn built the 17-storey complex of the State of Illinois Centre in Chicago, a building in the shape of a quarter-circle with a usable area of 103,500 square metres. The glass envelope is penetrated by a sloping glass cylinder that forms an open public courtyard in the centre of the building. Since 1981, Jahn has been professor of architecture at Harvard University. At the beginning of the eighties Jahn designed an extension to the Chicago Stock Exchange (1979–1982), the skyscraper One South Wacker Drive (1980–1982), and the North Western Atrium Centre. One of the many recent projects of note is the tower block for the Frankfurt Fair, which at 254 metres towers high above any other building in the city.

Philip Cortelyou Johnson *1906

Johnson studied classics at Harvard University. From 1930 to 1936 he was director of the department of architecture at the Museum of Modern Art in New York, and in 1932 with Henry Russell Hitchcock he published "The International Style: Architecture since 1922", an influential publication that accompanied the exhibition of the same name. In 1940 he began a three-year period of study under Walter Gropius and Marcel Breuer at Harvard and worked there from 1942 as a freelance architect. In 1946 he resumed his position as director of the department of architecture at the New York Museum of Modern Art and in 1947 ran an exhibition on Mies van der Rohe, with whom he had maintained close contacts since his trip to Germany in 1930. The influence of Mies van der Rohe was only too obvious in the design of his own house, the "Glass House" in New Canaan, Connecticut, that derives from Mies van der Rohe's Farnsworth House. In New Canaan he

Helmut Jahn

also built the Hodgson House (1951) and the
Wiley House (1953). In 1953 he produced the
successful design of the Sculpture Garden at
the Museum of Modern Art in New York. While
still working with Mies van der Rohe on the Seagram Building, he abandoned earnest functionalism and switched to a mannerist, playful use
of forms. In the main room of the synagogue in
Port Chester (1954–1956) he included an arched
ceiling of plaster and coloured window-
slits, and for the Sheldon Memorial Art Gallery
of the University of Nebraska (1963), symmetrical rows of round arches. Closed, weightier
structures characterise his work in the sixties, as
in the Kunsthalle in Bielefeld (1968). There followed a series of glass skyscrapers such as the
IDS Center in Minneapolis (1973), Pennzoil
Place in Houston (1970–1976), the acclaimed
American Telephone and Telegraph Building in
New York (1978–1982) with its rounded portal
and broken pediment, and the neo-Gothic-like
Pittsburgh Plate Glass Building, which manipu-
late the façade with architectural allusions whilst
retaining a standard administrative building
within. For public buildings like the Municipal Library in Miami, Johnson borrowed ideas from
Roman architecture such as the atrium in order
to give the functional building a greater sense
of identity.

Albert Kahn 1869–1942

Kahn was born in Germany and emigrated with
his parents to Detroit in 1880. There he worked
in various architectural offices, first with John
Scott and later with Mason and Rice, where he
eventually became draftsman in 1885. Kahn
gained his theoretical knowledge of architecture
at the firm from the exceptionally well equipped
library. In 1891 he received a travel scholarship
from the journal "American Architect" and, with
his colleague the architect Henry Bacon, he
visited many European cities. In 1896 he established his own firm with George W. Nettleton
and Alexander Trowbridge. Among their first
commissions was the children's hospital in De-

troit (1896). After Trowbridge's departure and
Nettleton's death he teamed up for a time with
George D. Mason, his earlier employer. The
two collaborated on the Palms Apartment
House in Detroit (1901–1902). In 1903 he appointed his brother Louis Kahn as chief engineer; with him he developed the concrete building for the University of Michigan in Detroit.
Albert Kahn became famous above all for his
numerous factory buildings. For Henry B. Joy he
designed the Packard Motor Car Company
Plant in Detroit. The most innovative structure in
this complex was building No.10 made of steel
and concrete with a plain glass gridded façade. At the same time various production
shops and storage buildings were built for the
Ford Motor Company. Kahn also built the new
Ford Works at Dearborn, Michigan, with the
enormous hall for the glass factory (1924). In
1928 Kahn built the Plymouth Factory in Detroit
for the Chrysler Corporation. After a Soviet
delegation had visited the factory buildings in
Detroit, Kahn was commissioned to build a trac-
tor plant in Stalingrad, which was completed in
1930. As a result, Kahn was entrusted with all
industrial building projects in the Soviet Union.
With the help of his brother Moritz Kahn, numerous Russian workers were trained and within a
period of two years, Kahn designed 521 factories. Even after his return to the USA, Kahn
continued to concentrate on industrial projects.
One particularly noteworthy achievement was
the Roll and Heavy Machine Shop of the Ohio
Steel Foundry Company in Lima (1938). At the
end of the thirties, Kahn's share in all the industrial construction projects in the USA amounted
to approximately nineteen percent. During the
Second World War the major priority was the
building of construction halls for the aircraft industry, such as the bomber plant built for the
Glenn L. Martin Company in Omaha in 1943.
After Albert Kahn's death, his brother Louis
took over as director of the firm Albert Kahn Associates.

Louis Isidore Kahn 1901–1974

Kahn attended the University of Pennsylvania in
Philadelphia from 1920 to 1924 and worked
there for Paul P. Cret (1929–1930) and for Zant-
zinger, Boire and Medary (1930–1932). Afterwards he travelled to Europe before estab-
lishing his own practice in Philadelphia in 1937
and entering into partnership with George
Howe and Oscar Stonorov at the beginning of
the forties. One example of their collaborative
work was the remarkable residential development Carver Court Housing in Coatesville,
Pennsylvania (1941–1944). In 1947 he accepted
a teaching post at Yale University, where he
supervised with Douglas Orr the building of the
annex to the Art Gallery (1951–1953). This first
modern building in New Haven was characterised by an obvious frame construction with a
roof made up of tetrahedrons. From 1953 to

1957 he worked with Ann Tyng, an admirer of Buckminster Fuller, on various models for the construction of serial structural elements, which were then employed in various projects such as the plan for the Center of Philadelphia (1956–1962). The Bath House for the Jewish Community Centre in Trenton, New Jersey, was a strict, regular cross-shaped structure consisting of centralised elements with four pyramid roofs (1954–1959). Other important works are the Alfred Newton Richards Medical Research Building of the University of Pennsylvaria (1957–1961) and the laboratory building of the Jonas Salk Institute in La Jolla, California (1959–1965) in which the integrated mechanical utilities are housed in intermediate storeys under the floor, allowing more efficient use of the work areas. From 1967 to 1972, in association with Preston Gerne and Associates, Kahn built the Kimbell Art Museum in Fort Worth. As early as 1962 Kahn had started designing the National Assembly of Bangladesh in Dacca. The plans for this had included extensive development projects for the city, which were eventually completed between 1973 and 1976. Kahn also built the Institute of Management in Ahmedabad (1962–1967), which he conceived as a massive, enclosed fortress. Here one of Kahn's favourite motifs, that of the "house in the house" is seen particularly clearly.

Le Corbusier 1887–1965

Charles-Edouard Jeanneret-Gris trained as a metal engraver under Charles L'Eplattenier at the School of Applied Arts in his native town of La Chaux-de-Fonds in Switzerland. As early as 1905 he built his first house, the Vallet Villa, for a member of the school. After this he visited Italy, Budapest, Vienna, and Paris, where under Auguste Perret he gained insights into the potential uses of reinforced steel constructions

(1908–1909). From 1910 to 1911 he acquired further experience in the office of Peter Behrens in Berlin. Among his early work is the idea of Dom-ino-houses, a system of industrial serial production in reinforced concrete, developed in 1914–1915. In 1916 he built the Schwob Villa in La Chaux-de-Fonds, a reinforced concrete building in a classical form. In 1917 Jeanneret settled in Paris and changed his name to Le Corbusier. There he met the painter Amédée Ozenfant, with whom he published the manifesto "Après le cubisme" in 1918 and from 1920 edited the journal "L'Esprit Nouveau". From 1920 to 1922 he developed the Citrohan Houses, box-like building units with load-bearing walls on the long sides, which in a second version are raised on supports. In 1922 he went into partnership with his cousin Pierre Jeanneret, worked on the Ozenfant Villa in Paris, and developed a design for a contemporary city with three million inhabitants. In 1923 Le Corbusier published his collected articles from "L'Esprit Nouveau" under the title "Vers une Architecture". In the following years he built, among others, the La Roche-Jeanneret duplex house in Auteuil (1923), a housing development in Pessac (1925), the Cook House in Boulogne-sur-Seine (1926) and the Stein Villa in Garches (1927). His "Pavillon de l'Esprit Nouveau" at the Paris Exhibition of 1925 became a model building block for a large apartment building. High-rise buildings became, in fact, the basis of his "Plan Voisin" for a new Paris (1925). In 1927 he entered the competition for the Palace of the League of Nations; he also designed two apartment houses for the Werkbund Exhibition in Stuttgart-Weißenhof. For both projects he attempted to implement his five-point programme for a new, contemporary architecture: the pilotis (posts), the roof garden, the free plan, horizontal strip windows, and the free façade. A year later Le Corbusier became a founder member of the Congrès Internationaux d'Architecture Moderne (CIAM). From 1929 to 1931 he built the Savoye Villa in Poissy, a white prism supported on slender posts with ramps and surprising perspectives inside. This was followed by the Cité de Refuge for the Salvation Army in Paris (1929–1932) and the Swiss Students' Hostel for the Cité Universitaire in Paris (1930–1932). For the Palace of Soviets in Moscow (1931) he contrived a hall that hung from a long parabolic curve. In 1935 he travelled to the the USA for the first time and also published a further plan for a city development entitled "La Ville radieuse". His plans for a government ministry in Rio de Jainero and the UN Headquarters in New York were eventually taken up by Costa, Niemeyer and Reidy on the one hand and Harrison and Abromowitz on the other. In 1942 he began preliminary work on the Modulor, a measuring system developed by Le Corbusier on the principle of the Golden Section, based on the proportions of the human body. In 1944 the set of reflections and demands that had been compiled by the CIAM in

Hans Hollein

1933 and further developed by Le Corbusier in 1941 were published as the Charta of Athens, which called for a contemporary, functional city. An important experiment in the building of mass apartment blocks was the Unité d'Habitation in Marseille (1945–1952), a high-rise complex on huge pilotis with 337 living units, a shopping street, and leisure and communication facilities. Further Unités followed, notably in Nantes-Rezé (1952–1957), Berlin (1956–1957) and Meaux (1957–1959). Le Corbusier's later work consisted of expressively formed, sculptural buildings which, unlike his pre-war buildings, no longer needed to fulfill the requirements of a prototype. Examples are the church of Notre-Dame-du-Haut in Ronchamp (1950–1954), the Dominican monastery of Sainte-Marie-de-la-Tourette in Evreux-sur-l'Arbresle (1957–1960), and the Palace of Justice at Chandigarh in the Punjab (1950–1956). Between 1950 and 1951 he had already worked with Maxwell Fry and Jane Drew on a plan for the whole of this In-

dian city. His only building in America was the Visual Arts Centre in Cambridge, Massachusetts, which was completed in 1964. Le Corbusier is not only one of the most important architects of the twentieth century but also an important theorist and painter.

Adolf Loos 1870–1933

Loos attended the Staatsgewerbeschule in Reichenberg before starting his studies at the Technische Hochschule in Dresden in 1890. He subsequently spent three years in the United States, visiting the World's Fair in Chicago and working his way round with occasional work as builder and draftsman. In 1896 he returned to Europe and settled in Vienna. He first became influential through his writing. From 1897 onwards he published articles, mainly in the Vienna "Neue Freie Presse". These articles were later collected and published as "Ins Leere Gesprochen" (1921) and "Trotzdem" (1931). Again and again he attacked superficial, decorative ornament which he felt was superfluous and no longer modern. His radical defence of these views and the polemical article "Die Potemkinsche Stadt" (The Potemkin City) eventually led to his breaking with the leading architects of the Vienna Sezession, Josef Hoffmann and Joseph Maria Olbrich. In 1903 he edited the journal "Das andere – ein blatt zur einführung abendländischer kultur in österreich", of which, however, only two editions were printed. Loos first received acclaim for his rebuilding of the "Café Museum" in Vienna, which because of its austere unembellished interior acquired the nickname "Café Nihilismus", and for his disciplined but elegant interior to the Knize Atelier. In 1907 he was commissioned to do the "Kärntner Bar" (Carinthia Bar), a tiny bar in which the skilful use of mirrors created the illusion of space; its spectacular façade sported the sign "American Bar" and four marble pilasters supported a sloping roof with a Stars and Stripes banner of coloured glass. In 1908 he published his famous "Ornament und Verbrechen" (Ornament and Crime), a passionate plea for beautiful, purposeful form. With the house on the Michaelerplatz (1909–1911) Loos demonstrated what he meant by that: the business on the ground floor was faced with green Cipollino marble while the façade of the apartment in the upper part of the building was done in simple whitewash. The windows were completely frameless, as though stamped into the building. The project was greeted with great hostility and the city authorities kept calling a halt to the construction work. At the same time Loos worked on the Steiner House in Vienna, where the size of the building was obscured at the front by the barrel roof which extended down to the street. In 1912 he founded a School of Architecture without official permission and taught his students, among them Richard Neutra and Rudolf M. Schindler, free of

Adolf Loos

Le Corbusier

charge. In 1920 Loos became chief architect of the Vienna Siedlungsamt but gave up this position after only two years and moved to Paris. He gave lectures at the Sorbonne and built the residence and artist's studio for the Dadaist Tristan Tzara (1925–1926). In 1928 he designed a corner house for Josephine Baker with a facing of black and white marble; the project was never carried out. Some of the most important buildings of his later work include the Moller House in Vienna (1927–1928) and the Müller House in Prague (1930), where again Loos achieves his effects by creating a tension between the costly material and the strict form.

Hans and Wassili Luckhardt 1890–1954/ 1889–1972

Hans Luckhardt studied at the Technische Hochschule in Karlsruhe, Wassili in Berlin-Charlottenburg. The brothers became involved in the "Arbeitsrat für Kunst", the "Novembergruppe" and the architects' association "Der Ring". From 1921 they worked closely together and in the first few years after the war produced various design projects such as the Hygieremuseum in Dresden (1921) and the competition entry for a high-rise building in the Friedrichstraße in Berlin (1922), which was still strongly Expressionist in influence. From 1924 the Luckhardt brothers also worked with Alfons Anker. In the following years they built numerous buildings, mostly in Berlin: the terrace houses constructed between 1925 and 1929 in three building sections in the Schorlemer Allee, the Hirsch business premises (1926–1927), the Telschow business on the Potsdamer Platz (1928), and the villas on Rupenhorn (1928). There were also projects for new buildings on the Alexanderplatz in Berlin (1929) and for the Medizinische Hochschule in Pressburg (1933). The Luckhardts designed the Berlin Pavilion for the Constructa Exhibition in Han-

nover in 1951. In 1952 Hans Luckhardt became professor at the Academy of Arts in Berlin. After his death in 1954 his brother Wassili continued to direct the office on his own and built a group of residences at the Kottbusser Tor (1955–1956), his own house (1957) and at the same time a residential complex in the Hansa district for the Interbau. Wassili's later work includes the Institute of Plant Physiology at the Freie Universität in Berlin-Dahlem.

Charles Rennie Mackintosh 1868–1928

Mackintosh was sixteen years old when he left the Alan Glen High School in 1884 to work for the architect John Hutchison. From 1885 he improved his qualifications by attending evening classes at the Glasgow School of Art. In 1889 he became a draftsman for the firm Honeyman & Keppie. It was here that he met the architect Herbert Mac Nair, who was later to be his brother-in-law. Among the prizes and awards that Mackintosh won at that time was a travel scholarship which enabled him to travel to Italy, France and Belgium. In 1897 he won the first prize in the competition for the new building of the Glasgow School of Art. Built in two phases from 1897 to 1899 and from 1907 to 1909, the building is a simple, block structure in brick with an asymmetrical façade and great studio windows. Filigree ornament of iron bars serves to lighten the effect of the heavy, square-shaped building. At about the same time Mackintosh was busy working on the interiors of teashops in Buchanan Street (1896) and Argyle Street (1897–1898) on commissions from Catherine Cranston. After this he worked on the country house Windy Hill in Kilmacolm (1899–1901) and on the extensive complex of Hill House in Helensburgh (1902–1903). However, the international acclaim which Mackintosh received at the turn of the century is due not to this work but rather to his furniture and interior designs. Fritz Wärndorfer invited him to Vienna to furnish a music salon. Mackintosh accepted and conceived a large frieze of white decorative panels with furniture to match. In 1902 he was given the opportunity to display the panels he had designed for the Cranston tea house in Glasgow at the Turin International Exhibition of Decorative Art; he also designed the Scottish Pavilion there. Mackintosh's last building project was the superb library wing addition that he built for the School of Art in Glasgow (1907–1909). In 1913 he moved to London and thereafter designed only furniture and textiles. From 1923 he lived in Port Vendres, France, where he devoted himself entirely to his water colour painting.

Wassili Luckhardt

Ernst May 1886–1970

May began his studies at University College, London in 1908, continued them at the Technische Hochschule in Darmstadt and finally studied under Friedrich von Thiersch and Theodor Fischer at the Technische Hochschule in Munich. He graduated in 1912. While still a student he gained his initial experience in town planning at the London office of Raymond Unwin (1910–1912). From 1913 he worked as a freelance architect in Frankfurt. In the post-war years he worked from 1919 to 1925 as director of the Silesian Landesgesellschaft in Breslau and from 1921 as technical director of the Gemeinnützige Siedlungsgesellschaft "Schlesisches Heim". In 1925 he became director of town planning in Frankfurt am Main and remained there until 1930. In these five years, with Martin Elsässer and a large team of assistants, May designed and built a series of housing estates for the "New Frankfurt". Despite simple construction techniques, May achieved new variety by his flexible arrangements of the individual buildings within the overall design; thus he used a right-angle arrangement for the Praunheim district development (1927–1929), a curved form for the Römerstadt development (1927–1928), or what became known as the "zig-zag houses" of the Bruchfeldstraße (1926–1927). Innovations were seen in the pre-fabricated elements and even in the "Frankfurter Küche" (Grete Schütte Lihotzky's rationally designed kitchens). From 1930 to 1934 May worked in the Soviet Union and then emigrated to Africa in 1934, where he lived in Tanzania as a farmer and architect until 1953. Back in Germany, he worked until 1961 for the welfare town planning organisation "Neue Heimat" in Hamburg and later as town planner in Wiesbaden. Besides this work he was also, from 1957, professor at the Technische Hochschule in Darmstadt.

Richard Alan Meier *1934

Meier graduated in 1957 at Cornell University and worked for various offices, including Skidmore, Owings & Merrill, and Marcel Breuer. On a visit to Europe he also got to know Le Corbusier. In 1963 he opened his own office in New York. At first, Meier built mainly detached houses reminiscent of the graceful elegance of the "white villas" of the twenties and thirties. Important examples are the Smith House in Darien, Connecticut (1965–1967), Saltzman House in East Hampton, New York (1967–1969), Weinstein House in Old Westbury, New York (1969–1971) and the Douglas House on steep, wooded land in Harbor Springs, Michigan (1971–1973). He became known at the beginning of the seventies for the collaborative exhibition "Five Architects" at the Museum of Modern Art in 1969 and the accompanying publication, which displayed the work of Meier, Peter Eisenman, Michael Graves, Charles Gwathmey and John Hejduk. With the Twin Parks Northeast Housing (1969–1974) and the Bronx Developmental Center (1970–1977), Meier had the opportunity to design large scale developments. One of Meier's most successful projects is the Atheneum built between 1975 and 1979 in New Harmony, Indiana. In recent years he has specialised in museum buildings like the High Museum of Art in Atlanta, Georgia (1980–1983) and the Museum für Kunsthandwerk in Frankfurt am Main (1979–1984). In 1984 he was commissioned to build the Paul Getty Center in Los Angeles, which is planned to be completed in 1993. Since 1983 he has been professor of the American Academy and the Institute of Arts and Letters.

Konstantin Stepanovich Melnikov 1890–1974

Melnikov studied at the Institute of Art, Sculpture and Architecture in Moscow, where he graduated in 1917. After the Revolution he worked in the architectural workshop of the Moscow Soviet and the architecture department of the People's Commissariat for Education. In 1921 he became Professor at the "Higher Artistic Technical Workshops" (VCHUTEMAS). At the beginning of the twenties Melnikov made some remarkable designs for a Moscow Workers' Quarter (1922) and the offices of the newspaper "Leningradskaya Pravda" (1923). In 1924 his designs were used for the Sukharevskii Market in Moscow. For the "Exposition Internationale des Arts Décoratifs et Industriels Modernes" in Paris in 1925 Melnikov designed the Soviet Pavilion, and in the same year his designs for a multi-storey car park in Paris were not executed. His own house in Moscow was an unusual building which consisted of two inter-penetrating cylinders, one with a huge glass wall, the other with strange hexagonal windows. At the same time he began work on five workers' club-houses in Moscow, which

Richard Meier

were completed by 1929. He also designed a Trade Union Theatre and the People's Commissariat of the Moscow Heavy Industry (1934). With the exception of a few interior designs Melnikov received no further commissions after this date.

Erich Mendelsohn 1887–1953

From 1908 to 1910 Mendelsohn studied at the Technische Hochschule in Berlin-Charlottenburg and then under Theodor Fischer at the Technische Universität in Munich until 1912. His first designs were drawings of fantastic architectural visions in steel and glass as well as costume and poster designs. His friends included Expressionist artists of the group "Der Blaue Reiter": Paul Klee, Wassily Kandinsky, and Franz Marc, and the poet Hugo Ball. After his military service on the Russian and Western fronts he opened his own office in Berlin in 1918 and became a founder member of the "Novembergruppe" and a member of the "Arbeitsrat für Kunst". His first building to gain attention was the Einstein Tower, an observatory and astrophysical institute in Potsdam (1920–1921). He received further commissions from open-minded clients such as the industrialist Gustav Hermann, the publisher Rudolf Lachmann-Mosse and the department-store owner Salman Schocken. In 1921 he worked on the new building for the hat-maker Friedrich Steinberg, Hermann & Co. in Luckenwalde and collaborated with Richard Neutra and the sculptor Rudolf Henning on the alterations to the publishing house Rudolf Mosse (1921–1923). Subsequent projects were the "double villa" in Berlin-Charlottenburg (1922), the Weichmann office block in Gleiwitz (1923) and the alteration to the Meyer-Kauffmann textile works in Wüstegiersdorf (1923). In 1924, Mendelsohn was co-founder of the association of architects "Der

Ring". On a trip to the United States financed by Mosse, Mendelsohn met Frank Lloyd Wright; he also went on visits to the Soviet Union. Characteristic of his language of forms were dynamically composed, stream-lined volumes, horizontal wall and window bands, and rounded corners. Examples are seen above all in the buildings for Schocken such as the department store in Stuttgart built 1926–1928 and demolished in 1960, or the building in Chemnitz (1928–1930). From 1927 to 1931 he designed and executed a community project on the Kurfürstendamm in Berlin for the "Wohnhausgrundstücksverwertungs-AG" with cafe, restaurant, shopping street, theatre, hotel, apartment block and the cinema Universum, which became a model for numerous cinemas. Also worthy of note are the Rudolf Mosse pavilion for the "Pressa" Exhibition in Cologne in 1928, Mendelsohn's own house "Am Rupenhorn" in Berlin (1928–1930), and the Columbus House in Berlin (1931–1932). In 1933 he emigrated via Holland to England and worked there with Serge Chermayeff on projects like the sanatorium De La Warr in Bexhill-on-Sea (1934–1935). During the same period he managed an office in Palestine, which built the hospital in Haifa from 1937 to 1938 and from 1937 to 1939 the building for the Hebrew University in Jerusalem. In 1941 he emigrated to the USA. He spent his last years in San Francisco, where his main work was building synagogues for the Jewish community.

Ludwig Mies van der Rohe 1886–1969

After attending the Aachen Domschule and the Aachen Gewerbeschule (1899–1901), young Mies designed stucco ornament for a firm of interior decorators. In 1905 he moved to Berlin, where he worked first for Bruno Paul and then for Peter Behrens (1908–1911). At that time Walter Gropius and Le Corbusier were also working for Behrens. In 1911 he took over the project for the German Embassy in Petersburg. In the same year he moved to The Hague, designed a country house for the Kröller-Müllers which was, however, never built, and got to know Hendrik Berlage. In 1913 he moved back to Berlin, opened his own office and during the war ended up in Rumania. For the "Turmhaus" competition in Berlin in 1921 he entered a programmatic design for a high-rise building in glass which, on the plan, placed three almost triangular wings round a circular utilities well; the building had a steel skeleton structure and external walls made entirely of glass without horizontal structuring. This was followed immediately by the design of a thirty-storey glass building with an irregular curved plan and sketches for an office building of reinforced concrete with long narrow strips of glass. In 1922 he became a member of the "Novembergruppe" and started to call himself Mies van der Rohe. With van Doesburg, Lissitzky and Richter he brought out the journal G (for "Gestaltung") in 1923

Erich Mendelsohn

ard worked on the designs for two country houses in brick whose far-reaching walls and open plans revolutionized the typology of building. In 1926 he became vice-president of the "Werkbund", and in 1927 became director of the exhibition at Stuttgart-Weißenhof for which he designed a block of flats with a steel skeleton structure. For the silk manufacturer Hermann Lange he built a villa in Krefeld from 1927 to 1930 and at the same time built the German Pavilion for the International Exhibition in Barcelona in 1929, an open-plan building of cool materials such as marble, travertine, glass and steel. In 1930 he completed the Tugendhat Villa in Brno, Bohemia, with the same free use of space as in the Barcelona pavilion but now applied for the first time to a town house. As at the exhibitions in Stuttgart and Barcelona, Mies used his own designs of tubular steel furniture to complement the building. From 1930 he directed the Dessau Bauhaus until its closure in October 1932. Attempts to continue the Bauhaus in Berlin failed and in 1938 he emigrated to the USA and became director of the department of architecture at what later became the Illinois Institute of Technology in Chicago. Here he designed a completely new campus for the Institute; the project was ready by 1940 and featured individual buildings for teaching and research in a strict, right-angled arrangement. They were built successively until the end of the fifties: the Metal Research Building in 1943, the Chemistry Building and the Alumni Memorial hall in 1945 and the Crown Hall, the centre and high point of the campus, in 1956. For Edith Farnsworth's weekend house in Plano, Illinois (1946–1951), he designed an envelope made completely of glass; the terraces, floors and ceiling seem to "hover" over the ground on white-painted pillars. Further designs for glass houses are the Caine House (1950) and the square

"50 by 50 House" (1950–1951). At the same time he also built skyscrapers of glass and steel, such as the famous apartment houses on Lake Shore Drive in Chicago with their curtain façades, followed by the Commonwealth Promenade Apartment House and the 900 Esplanade Apartments. Among Mies van der Rohe's most significant achievements are the Seagram Building which he built with Philip Johnson in New York (1954–1958) and the Neue Nationalgalerie in Berlin (1962–1967).

Charles Willard Moore *1925

After studying architecture at the University of Michigan in Ann Arbor, Moore took a doctorate in philosophy at Princeton University in 1957. From 1959 to 1962 he was professor of architecture at the University of Berkeley. Thereafter he established his own practice in Berkeley with Donlyn Lyndon, William Turnbull and Richard Whitaker, which from 1965 to 1970 became a partnership between Moore and Turnbull. In 1970 he founded the firm Charles W. Moore Associates in Essex. One of the most impressive of Moore's early works is the house he built for himself in Orinda, California, in 1962 with its pyramid shaped roof. Inside, two small aediculae on old wooden pillars accentuate the living area and bathroom. The holiday complex of wooden houses (1963–1965) and a sports club (1966) on the Sea Ranch in Sonoma County, California, are outstanding examples of buildings that blend with their natural surroundings. Moore also built low-budget housing for the Church Street development in New Haven, Connecticut (1966–1969) and the Maplewood Terrace estate in Middletown, Connecticut (1970–1971). During the same period he joined the Faculty of Architecture at Yale, where he taught from 1970 to 1975 before changing to the University of California in Los Angeles. For the Californian University in Santa Cruz he built Kresge College (1966–1974) in a woodland setting, a succession of theatrical backdrops which raises banal street furniture to the level of stars. From 1974 to 1978, Moore and the Urban Innovations Group designed the Italian opera back-drop on the Piazza d'Italia in New Orleans. Another remarkable project was for a leisure and residential complex at the harbour in Berlin-Tegel (1980). Recent commissions include the University of Oregon Science Building in Eugene (1985), the San Antonio Arts Institute in Texas, and the design worked out with Skidmore, Owings & Merrill for the 1992 World's Fair in Chicago. Since 1985 Moore has taught at the University of Texas.

Ludwig Mies van der Rohe

Pier Luigi Nervi 1891–1979

In 1913 Nervi graduated as a construction engineer at the University of Bologna and subsequently worked in the technical department of the Society for Concrete Construction in Bologna and Florence. In 1920 he founded his own firm, the Società Ing. Nervi e Nebbiosi. His first project to gain international acclaim was the City Stadium in Florence with 35,000 places, a low-cost structure clearly made of concrete with sweeping spiral staircases. From 1932 Giovanni Bartoli was co-director of the firm. In 1935 Nervi won the competition for the aircraft hangars in Orvieto, which he conceived as geodesic structures and tested as celluloid models before building them in the period up to 1938. For aircraft hangars in Orbetello and Torre del Lago (1940–1943) he further developed these lightweight structures, partly using pre-fabricated concrete elements. From 1946 to 1961 he was professor at the faculty of architecture in Rome, specialising in construction technology and materials. From 1948 to 1949 he planned and constructed an exhibition hall in Turin. The hall consists of two parts linked together, a rectangular building covered by a rippling roof supported on a concrete vault. The room itself is without supporting pillars. Here for the first time Nervi used his mobile metal-tube scaffolding, which he patented. Apart from this, his most significant achievements include the festival hall in Chianciano Terme with net-like vaulted roof (1950–1952), the UNESCO Headquarters in Paris, designed in collaboration with Marcel Breuer and Bernard Zehrfuss (1953–1958), and the Pirelli high-rise building in Milan (1955–1958), for which he collaborated with Gio Ponti. In addition, with Annibale Vitellozzi, he designed and built the two remarkable sports stadiums for the Rome Olympics in 1960.

Nervi also published numerous theoretical writings such as "The Art and Science of Construction" (1945), "The Architectonic Language" (1950), and "New Constructions" (1963).

Richard Josef Neutra 1892–1970

Neutra attended the Technische Hochschule in Vienna from 1911 to 1917 and, at the same time, the Architectural School of Alfred Loos. During the first few years after the war he worked as a landscape gardener in Zurich. From 1921 he worked at the Municipal Construction Office in Luckenwalde, where he met Erich Mendelsohn. He moved to Berlin with Mendelsohn and became his assistant in his office there. The two collaborated on a competition entry for a business centre in Haifa, for which they won first prize. In 1923 Neutra went to the USA where he worked first with William Holabird and Martin Roche in Chicago, and later with Frank Lloyd Wright in Taliesin. In Los Angeles he worked with Rudolf Schindler on such projects as the competition for the Palace of Nations in Geneva (1927). In 1926 he established his own practice and began with the Jardinette Apartment House in Los Angeles (1926–1927), a reinforced concrete construction with window bands. He also designed pre-fabricated houses, which he called "One plus two", and worked on a project for a future city "Rush City Reformed". In 1927 he published his book "Wie baut Amerika" and was given the commission for the Lovell House in Los Angeles (1927–1929). The steel skeleton which he designed for it could be erected in the short space of just forty hours. 1928 and 1929 Neutra founded the Academy of Modern Art in Los Angeles and became lecturer in architecture there. From 1931 to 1933 he built his own house, the "Van der Leeuw Research House", the cost of which was borne by the fund of the same name. In the thirties he experimented with new materials and constructions. Thus in 1936 he built a plywood model house, and also Josef von Sternberg's house in the San Fernando Valley in California with its outer surfaces of metal and a pool of water surrounding it. It has since been destroyed. Water was to remain an important design element in Neutra's buildings. He followed this project in 1938 with the Strathmore and Landfair apartment buildings in Los Angeles. During the Second World War when no modern materials were available, Neutra built the Nesbitt House in Los Angeles and the Channel Heights Estate in San Pedro (1942) using redwood, bricks and glass. Significant achievements by Neutra in the forties are the Kaufmann House (desert house) in Palm Springs (1946–1947), the Tremaine House in Santa Barbara (1947–1948), and the Holiday House Motel in Malibu (1948). From 1949 to 1959 he collaborated with Robert E. Alexander on larger public projects like churches, schools and shops: the elementary school on Kester Av-

Richard Neutra
and the photographer Julius Shulman

Joseph Maria Olbrich 1867–1908

Olbrich trained under Camillo Sitte and Julius Deininger at the Staatsgewerbeschule in Vienna. On finishing in 1886 he worked as an architect and engineer for the construction company August Bartel in his native town of Troppau until 1890, when he began his architectural studies under Carl von Hasenauer at the Academy of Fine Arts in Vienna that culminated in his winning the Rome Prize in 1893. After his return from Italy and North Africa, he worked until 1898 in Otto Wagner's office on projects like the planning of the Viennese Stadtbahn (metropolitan railway) and took part in the founding of the Vienna Sezession in 1897. He also designed their exhibition hall (1897–1898), a simple structure above which rises a central dome of gilded iron laurel leaves. In 1900 he took part in the Paris World's Fair with a "Vienna Interior". When invited by Grand Duke Ernst Ludwig to join the Artists' Colony in Darmstadt, Germany, Olbrich moved there in 1899 and for eight years was construction manager on the Mathildenhöhe. In the period up to 1901 seven houses were built, including his own house, the small and the large Glückert houses, and the building for exhibiting temporary presentation buildings. In 1908 the "Wedding Tower" and adjoining exhibition hall were completed as a present for Grand Duke Ernst Ludwig. Retaining

enue in Los Angeles (1953), the Miramar Chapel in La Jolla (1957), and the building for the Ferro Chemical Company in Cleveland, Ohio (1957), with cantilevered roof and what became characteristic for Neutra, the thin supports. His ideas for an architecture with a human face were set forth in his book "Survival through Design" (1954).

his Darmstadt office, Olbrich moved in the same year to Düsseldorf. Here, with his plan for the Tietz Department Store, Olbrich changed to a moderated but monumental neo-classicism. Olbrich died of leukaemia shortly before its completion.

Frei Otto *1925

In 1947 Otto began his studies at the Technische Hochschule in Berlin. In 1950 he went to the USA on a scholarship from the University of Virginia in Charlottesville. After receiving his Dip. Arch. he lived in Berlin from 1952 as a freelance architect and researched into lightweight construction, publishing his dissertation in 1954 on the topic "Das hängende Dach" (The Suspended Roof, 1955). At the Bundesgartenschau (garden exhibitions) in 1955 and 1957 he tried out his new architectonic forms on tent structures. He was particularly praised for the "Tanzbrunnen" in Cologne (1957), which consisted of an open-air dance floor in concrete with ornamental ponds and covered by a star-shaped textile pavilion. In 1957 Otto founded the "Entwicklungsstätte für den Leichtbau" in Berlin. In 1961 he met the biologist and anthropologist J.G. Helmcke. Together they founded the research group Biology and Nature, to examine the many and varied biomorphous constructions of algae, which became an important inspiration for Otto's own structures and constructions. In 1961 and 1962 he worked as an assistant at the Technische Universität in Berlin. Visiting professorships followed, above all in America. From 1964 he taught at the Technische Hochschule in Stuttgart and founded the "Institut für leichte Flächentragwerke". The Institute building in Stuttgart-Vaihingen, built 1967–1968, was a reconstruction of the model displayed at Expo 67 in Montreal. For swimming pools and open-air theatres Otto developed the retractable roof. This cable net structure with pre-stressed textiles supported by hollow masts could be opened or closed according to the weather. One of many examples of this is the open-air theatre in Bad Hersfeld (1968). The motif for Otto's further development became the design of acceptable living and working quarters for extreme climactic conditions. He designed such projects as a pneumatic enclosure for the "Stadt in der Arktis" (City in the Arctic, 1970–1971) and "Schatten in der Wüste" (Shadows in the Desert, 1972). Working with other architectural offices various large-scale projects were completed. With Günter Behnisch and Partner he built the roofs of the main stadium and arenas at the Olympic Park in Munich (1968–1972).

Jacobus Johannes Pieter Oud 1890–1963

From 1904 to 1907 Oud attended the Quellinus School of Applied Arts in Amsterdam and then joined the office of Petrus J.H. Cuypers there. Later he completed his education at the State School of Design in Amsterdam and subsequently at the Technical University in Delft. Encouraged by Hendrik Petrus Berlage, he worked with Theodor Fischer in Munich, before settling in 1912 as a freelance architect in Purmerend and later in Leiden. With his friend, the artist and architect Theo van Doesburg, he designed the Geus House in 1916 and founded the association "De Sphinx". In 1917 the two became co-founders, with Piet Mondrian, Vilmos Huszar, and Antony Kok, of the famous group of artists and the journal "De Stijl", which Oud however left in 1920 after differences of opinion with van Doesburg. Attempts to put the "De Stijl" theory into practice were, for example, the terrace house development for Scheveningen (1917) and the cafe, since demolished, "De Unie", in Rotterdam (1924–1925), where the surface of the façade was treated as a graphic design painted in bright, primary colours of red, yellow and blue, as well as black and white. In 1918 Oud became City Planner for Rotterdam and built large district developments such as the Oud-Mathenesse project with 343 apartment units on the plan of an isoceles triangle, and the De Kiefhoek development, and the apartment complex in Hoek van Holland (1924–1927). His terrace houses in the Weißenhof district in Stuttgart (1927) were frequently praised by experts for their solid construction. Thereafter Oud did very little. He turned down a chair at Harvard which was later accepted by Walter Gropius. After a long period without any commissions, Oud built the Shell Company Building in The Hague (1938–1942), but the clarity of his earlier designs was gone. Oud's later work includes the Children's

Convalescence home at Arnheim (1952–1960). In 1954 Oud was given an honorary doctorate at the Technical University of Delft.

Gustav Peichl *1928

Peichl attended the Staatsgewerbeschule in Mödling, Vienna and the Bundesgewerbeschule in Linz and thereafter studied architecture until 1953 under Clemens Holzmeister at the Vienna Academy of Fine Arts. He worked for Roland Rainer before opening his own office in 1956. Peichl's early work includes the Atriumschule Krim in Vienna (1962–1963), a concrete construction with extended, horizontal window bands, and the similarly built Dominican Convent in Hacking (1963–1965). The Rehabilitation Centre for victims of brain damage in Meidling (1965–1967) was designed by Peichl on a star-shaped plan with overhanging rectangular terraces. Peichl again used bare, visible concrete here as his main construction material. From 1969 to 1978 in the Diesterweggasse, Vienna, he built a school complex of serialised, pre-fabricated parts. Also in 1969, he won the competition for the studios of the Austrian Radio (ORF), which brought him international acclaim. In the period up to 1982 he built six complexes, all deriving from one basic type, in Linz, Salzburg, Innsbruck, Dornbirn, Graz, and Eisenstadt; the form was wholly dependent on production procedures. As it is made up almost entirely of prefabricated elements, additions can be made very easily to the building. The ground signal station in Aflenz (1976–1980) was for the greater part sunk into the earth and circular openings in the ground provide daylight to the work-rooms. For the International Exhibition of Architecture in Berlin, Peichl designed the Phosphate Elimination Plant in Berlin-Tegel (1979–1985). His current project is the Bundeskunsthalle (Federal Art Gallery) in Bonn. Since 1973 Peichl has taught at the Academy of Fine Arts in Vienna.

Auguste Perret 1874–1954

Perret attended the Ecole des Beaux-Arts in Paris and then founded the construction firm Perrets Frères Entrepreneurs in 1905 with his brothers Gustave and Claude. His first important project was the residence in the Rue Franklin in Paris (1903), a skeleton construction of reinforced concrete with a decorative pattern of glazed floral tiles. He also used a skeleton construction and large areas of glass for his next project, the garage in the Rue Ponthieu (1905). Here the whole façade is severely structured, linear surface ornament is confined to the entry and the middle window. Another project worthy of mention is the Théâtre des Champs-Elysées in Paris, originally conceived by Henry van de Velde (1911–1913), and the Esders Clothing Workshop with its twenty metre wide arch

Gustav Peichl

(1919). For the church Notre-Dame du Raincy in Paris (1922–1923), Perret designed the outside walls as pre-fabricated concrete elements with filigree bars on the windows. After this he took part in the competition for the design of the Palace of Nations in Geneva (1927) and the Palace of Soviets in Moscow (1931), built the Musée des Travaux Publics (1937) with a rounded, free-standing staircase. In the postwar years he was occupied above all with the reconstruction of Le Havre from 1945 to 1954. Perret's final project, the centrally constructed Church of St. Joseph, is also situated in Le Havre.

Renzo Piano *1937

After studying architecture in Florence and Milan, Piano worked as a lecturer at the Polytechnic of Milan from 1965 to 1968. In his father's construction company in Genoa he had the opportunity to experiment with structures and materials such as plastic envelopes which he then used at the Italian industrial pavilion at Expo 1970 in Osaka. Other remarkable experiments by Piano are the "adaptable" buildings such as the residence in Garrone near Alessandria (1969), which was assembled and modified by the client himself. Through his teaching at the Polytechnic and the Architectural Association School in London, Piano got to know Richard Rogers. At first their work together remained at the level of designs until in 1971 they won the competition for the Centre National d'Art et de Culture Georges Pompidou in Paris (1971–1977). In the same year they opened their office together in Paris and remained partners until 1977. A predecessor to the Pompidou Centre is the B & B Italia Office Building in Novedrate near Como (1973), a box hung with-

in the supporting structure, with colourfully painted service pipes on the outside. In 1977 Piano opened an office in Genoa with the engineer Peter Rice. Their collaborative projects include the "laboratory" for city development in Otranto (1979), a residential area in Corciano near Perugia (1978–1982) and the Menil Collection Museum in Houston, Texas (1981–1986). Piano's recent work includes a sports hall in Ravenna (1986), a stadium in Bari (1987–1990) and the Synchroton in Grenoble (1987).

Hans Poelzig 1869–1936

While still a student at the Technische Hochschule in Berlin-Charlottenburg, Poelzig worked in the office of Hugo Hartung. After his examination in 1899 he took a job in the Preußisches Staatsbauamt. A year later he became a professor at the Kunst- und Gewerbeschule in Breslau, where from 1903 to 1916 he was principal. In 1911 he executed here a remarkably clearly structured department store. The street corner of the building at the cross-roads is rounded and the window bands are uninterrupted; in short, it was an exemplary solution to the problem of the large inner-city building. In the same year he reconstructed a water tower for Posen with a market hall on sixteen-sided ground plan. For the Century Exhibition in Breslau in 1913 he designed large exhibition structures characterized by the use of low domes. In 1916 Poelzig became professor and "Stadtbaurat" (Municipal Architect) in Dresden. One of his most successful projects is the transformation of the Schuhmann Circus Building in Old Berlin into the Großes Schauspielhaus of the theatre director Max Reinhardt. Using the steel structure of the original market hall as he found it, he executed a theatre hall in which rows of stalactites hung dramatically from the roof. From 1920 Poelzig lectured at the Prussian Academy of Arts and from 1924 also at the Technische Hochschule in Berlin-Charlottenburg. At the beginning of the nineteen twenties Poelzig designed several stage-sets and film scenarios such as "Der Golem". In 1924 he executed the Capitol Cinema Building in Berlin and at the end of the twenties collaborated with Martin Wagner on the Berlin Trade Fair and nearby Broadcasting House (1930). At about the same time the huge adminstrative building for IG Farben was erected in Frankfurt. In the middle of the thirties Poelzig undertook a few projects in Turkey. He died before his planned emigration to Istanbul where he had accepted a professorship.

Gerrit Thomas Rietveld 1888–1964

Rietveld began his career learning cabinet making in his father's shop in Utrecht then found work at a jeweller's shop as a draftsman. He developed his skills at evening classes led by P. J. C. Klaarhammer, one of the circle of archi-

Gerrit Rietveld

John Dinkeloo
Kevin Roche

tects associated with Berlage. In 1917 he set up in private practice as a cabinet maker and experimented with new forms for furniture. Through Robert van't Hoff he joined the De Stijl movement and remained a member until it was dissolved in 1931. His "Red-Blue" Chair of 1918 was celebrated by the group as a manifesto. With the Schröder House in Utrecht (1924), his first commission as an architect which he designed with the client, the interior designer Mrs. Truus Schröder-Schräder, Rietveld produced the only successful application of De Stijl architectural principles. Between 1927 and 1928 Rietveld built the cubic Garage and Chauffeur's Quarters in Utrecht using pre-fabricated concrete slabs integrated within a framework of coloured steel mountings. In 1928 he was a founder member of the CIAM. In the following years he executed a few buildings, again in collaboration with Truus Schröder-Schräder, and in 1932 designed a four-family terrace house for the Werkbund Exhibition in Vienna. Another important building is the Vreeburg Cinema in Utrecht, built in 1936. His later work includes the Stoop House in Velp (1951) and the Dutch Pavilion for the Biennale in Venice in 1954, a union of several rectangular structures on a square plan. Other projects were the Sculpture Pavilion in Sonsbeek Park in Arnheim (1954), which was rebuilt in Otterlo in 1965, and a school in Badhoevedorp (1958–1965). Rietveld's last large project was the Van Gogh Museum in Amsterdam (1963–1972), which was completed by his colleague J. van Tricht.

Kevin Eamonn Roche *1922

Roche studied until 1945 in the faculty of architecture at the National University of Ireland in Du-

blin. He gained practical experience with Michael Scott and Partners in Dublin and in the London offices of Maxwell Fry and Jane Drew. In 1948 he moved to the USA and worked at the Illinois Institute of Technology (1948–1949) and in the United Nations Planning Office (1949). From 1950 to 1954 Roche worked in the planning department of Eero Saarinen and Associates in Bloomfield Hills, Michigan, and from 1954 to 1961 he was principal associate. After Saarinen's death in 1961 he moved the office to Hamden, Connecticut, with John Dinkeloo and occupied himself with the successful completion of Saarinen's major projects. In 1966 they changed the name of the firm to Kevin Roche John Dinkeloo and Associates. From 1961 to 1968, they built the Oakland Museum in California, a concrete building sunk partly into the hillside with terraces on many levels. Plants thrive in the twelve-storey glass courtyard of the Ford Foundation Headquarters in New York (1963–1968). Two further buildings are worthy of note. The Fine Arts Center of the University of Massachusetts in Amherst (1964–1974) is a combination of stereometric, partly bridge-like concrete compartments, which are reflected in the lake. The "Knights of Columbus" Headquarters in New Haven, Connecticut (1965–1969), has four massive round masonry pillars which bear the weight of the storeys suspended between them. From 1966 to 1972 Kevin Roche John Dinkeloo and Associates built the Aetna Life and Casualty Computer Building in Hartford, Connecticut, and at the same time the pyramid-shaped glass and concrete structures for the headquarters of the College Life Insurance Company of America in Indianapolis, Indiana (1967–1971), and the extensions to the Metropolitan Museum of Modern Art in New York (1967–1985). The white, twin-winged building of the General Foods Corporation in Rye, New York (1977–1982), is reflected in the waters of a garden pool, while the sky is reflected in the numerous mirror-walls of the building itself; here lush vegetation also serves to emphasise the separation between interior and exterior. After Dinkeloo's death in 1981, Roche continued with the practice on his own.

Richard Rogers *1933

Rogers studied at the Architectural Association School in London and at Yale University in New Haven, Connecticut, under Serge Chermayeff. In 1963, with his wife Su and Norman and Wendy Foster, he founded Team 4, whose most important industrial building was the Reliance Control Factory in Swindon, Wiltshire (1967). In the same year he represented British architects for the second time at the Paris Biennale. At the same time Rogers also taught in Cambridge at the Architectural Association School and the Polytechnic in London. At the end of the sixties he and his wife conceived a lightweight, flexible house made of plastic ring elements which he further developed in 1971 as the project "Zip-

Aldo Rossi

up". At the same time he built his own house in Wimbledon (1968–1969) with its synthetic material supported by a painted steel frame. From 1969 Rogers not only lectured at Yale University, Massachusetts Institute of Technology and Princeton University but also worked with Renzo Piano on various projects, which however were never executed. In 1971 the two won the competition for the Centre National d'Arts et de Culture Georges Pompidou in Paris (1971–1977). Characteristic of this six-storey complex is visible technology in the form of construction grids, utility elements in bright colours and transparent pipes. After the break with Piano in 1977 Rogers moved his office to London, where he designed an enormous complex for Lloyd's Bank (1979–1986). During the same period he built the Inmos Microprocessor Factory in Newport Swent, South Wales, the PA Technology Laboratories Building and Corporate Facility in Princeton, New Jersey, the PA Technology Cambridge Laboratory Building, built in three phases from 1975 to 1983.

Aldo Rossi *1931

Rossi graduated in 1959 at the Polytechnic in Milan and worked for the magazines "Casabella-continuità" and "Il Contemporaneo". At the beginning of the sixties he completed his designs for the redevelopment of the Via Sarini district of Milan and a shopping centre in Turin (1962). Already in these early drawings we can see Rossi's typical architectural language reducing everything to basic forms. In 1963 he was assistant to Lodovico Queroni at the Scuola Urbanistica in Arezzo and assistant to Carlo Aymonino at the University of Venice. In collaboration with Luca Meda he took over the planning in 1964 for the 13th Triennale in Milan and built an access bridge in two parts with a triangular cross-section. He used a similar motif for the

Memorial Fountain on the Town Hall Square in Segrate (1965). Here, as elsewhere, light and shadow play a dominant role in Rossi's creations. He put forward his ideas on architecture in the book "L'Architettura della Città" published in 1966. In 1969 he became Professor at the Polytechnic in Milan and began by designing a four-storey apartment block in the Gallarate district, which was completed in 1973. Running colonnades and grid pattern window openings are reminiscent of Georgio de Chirico's style of painting. In 1971 Rossi and Gianni Braghieri won the national competition for the cemetery of San Cataldo in Modena, which was begun in 1980. In 1972 he became professor at the Eidgenössische Technische Hochschule in Zurich, where he taught for three years. In the same year he became director of the international department of architecture at the Triennale in Milan. For the Biennale in Venice in 1980 he built a tower-like, floating "Teatro del Mondo" made of iron piping with wooden planking. For the International Exhibition of Architecture in Berlin in 1984 Rossi designed an apartment block in the southern Friedrichstadt and also won the competition for the proposed Deutsches Historisches Museum (German Historical Museum) in Berlin.

Paul Marvin Rudolph *1918

Rudolph studied first at the Alabama Polytechnic Institute in Auburn and then under Walter Gropius and Marcel Breuer at Harvard University, Cambridge, before becoming an associate with Ralph Twitchell in Sarasota, Florida. Soon after he had established his own practice in 1952 he abandoned the strict Bauhaus direction for one more expressive, seen for instance as early as 1955–1958 in the Mary Cooper Jewett Center at Wellesley College in Wellesley, Massachusetts. Great controversy arose over the Sarasota High School in Sarasota (1958–1959) and the horizontal and vertical box-like structures of the Art and Architecture Building at Yale University in New Haven, Connecticut (1958–1964). The ambivalence of this architecture is seen in the open generous-seeming effects of the Milam House in Jacksonville, Florida, with a frame protruding from the façade (1960–1962), and the parking garage planned at the same time in Temple Street, New Haven, with its huge, threatening aspect. From 1958 Rudolph was the Chairman of the School of Architecture at Yale University in New Haven, Connecticut, and in 1965 he moved to New York. For the State Service Centre in Boston he surrounded the inner public courtyard with a complex of terraces (1967–1972). Subsequently his work concentrated on town planning projects and the development of modular systems.

Eero Saarinen 1910–1961

Born in Finland, Saarinen moved with his family to America in 1923. From 1929 to 1930 he studied sculpture at the Académie de la Grande Chaumière in Paris and from 1930 to 1934 he studied architecture at Yale University, New Haven, Conneticut. Thereafter he worked at his father Eliel Saarinen's practice in Ann Arbor and in 1941 became a partner with J. Robert Swanson. In 1950 he opened his own office in Birmingham under the name Eero Saarinen and Associates. He first achieved acclaim for his winning entry in the competition for the Jefferson National Expansion Memorial in St. Louis (1948), a project in which his father also participated. This 192 metre concrete building with its parabolic arch design was not built until 1963, two years after Saarinen's death. In this period Saarinen began to develop more expressive designs based on rectilinear, steel and glass cubic forms as in the General Motors Technical Center in Warren, Michigan (1949–1956). For the Kresge Auditorium at the Institute of Technology in Cambridge, Massachusetts (1953–1955), he designed a concrete roof in the form of a spherical, domed triangle and, for the Institute Chapel, a cylinder of brickwork. Among the most important of the projects executed by Saarinen's office are the David S. Ingalls Ice Hockey Hall at Yale University (1953–1959), the Trans World Airlines Terminal at the John F. Kennedy Airport in New York (1956–1962), the hovering pavilion roof at the Dulles International Airport in Washington DC (1958–1962), and the John Deere and Company Administration Center in Moline, Illinois (1957–1963). After Saarinen's death his colleagues John Dinkeloo and Kevin Roche ensured his unfinished projects were completed and continued to keep the Hamden Connecticut Office in his name until 1966.

Eero Saarinen und Charles Eames

Carlo Scarpa 1906–1978

Scarpa studied at the Academy of Fine Arts in Venice and worked at the same time in the office of Vincenzo Rinaldo until 1926, when he became full-time assistant to Guido Cirilli at the newly founded Istituto Universitario di Architettura. His early work includes interiors of the glassware shop for Maestri Vetrai Muranesi Cappellin & Co. in Florence (1928). Over a period of more than thirty years Scarpa worked again and again as design consultant for the Biennale in Venice. Among the projects he did there, two of note are the design of the Paul Klee Exhibition in 1948 and the Art Publications Pavilion in 1950. From 1955 to 1961 he executed the Veritti House in Udine. He won greater acclaim for his alterations to the Museo Correr (1953–1960) and to the La Foscari Palace (1954–1956), both in Venice. At the same time, with Ignazio Gardella and Giovanni Michelucci, he built the first six rooms of the Galeria degli Uffizi in Florence (1954–1956) and planned the extension to the Gipsoteca Canova in Possagno (1955–1957). In order to display the sculptures here in the most effective way possible, Scarpa worked ingeniously with daylight through unusual lightsources, windows and openings. For his next project he designed the Olivetti Showrooms in his home town of Venice (1957–1958). In 1962 he was made Associate Professor for Interior Design. Two years later he completed the alterations to the Castelvecchio Museum in Verona. After trips to the USA and Japan he was commissioned by Rino Brion to design a cemetery and family tomb near Treviso. In 1972 he became the director of the Istituto Universitario di Architettura in Venice, where he taught until 1977. His last large project, the Banca Popolare di Verona was begun in collaboration with Arrigo Rudi, who completed it in 1980. All his life, however, Scarpa failed to gain recognition as an architect.

Hans Scharoun 1893–1972

Scharoun studied from 1912 to 1914 at the Technische Hochschule in Berlin. Here he met Paul Kruchen, who as well as being an assistant lecturer also had his own office in which Scharoun could work. He worked as an architect from 1915 to 1918 on Kruchen's instigation for the "Militärbaukommando" on the East Prussia Reconstruction Programme and thereafter became acting director of town-planning in Insterburg. Eventually he became an independent architect from 1919 to 1925 in Kruchen's office there and directed several housing and rebuilding projects and the Kamswyken district development (1920) known as "Die Bunte Reihe" (the Colourful Row). He also designed numerous competition entries such as the high-rise building for the Friedrichstraße in Berlin (1922). Scharoun was also a member of the group founded by Bruno Taut, the "Gläserne Kette"

(Glass Chain) and, like Taut, made fantasy sketches of architectural Utopias. From 1925 to 1932 he taught at the State Academy in Breslau and in 1926 became a member of the association of architects "Der Ring". He took part in the Weißenhof District Development in Stuttgart in 1927 with a detached house and in 1929 designed an apartment building for the Werkbund Exhibition in Breslau. In Berlin he worked on a series of apartment blocks and was also director of the Siemensstadt housing development (1929–1930). His own contribution to this large-scale project were the apartment buildings on the Jungfernheideweg and the Mäckeritzstraße. From 1932 he had his own office in Berlin. Among his most successful buildings were the elegant villas he built in the thirties: the Schminke House in Löbau (1933), the Mattern House in Bornim (1934), the Dr. Baensch House in Berlin-Spardau (1935), and the Moll House in Berlin (1937). After the War, Scharoun became director of the Bau- und Wohnungswesen (Building and Housing Department) in Berlin and with a group of architects designed a reconstruction program known as the Collective Plan (1946). In the same year he became senior professor of town planning at the Technische Universität in Berlin, a post he held until 1958. In addition, from 1947 to 1950 he was director of the Institut für Bauwesen der Deutschen Akademie der Wissenschaften in East Berlin. His idea of arranging a school building according to the grade or form was put into practice at the Geschwister-Scholl-Gymnasium in Lünen (1956–1962). In the same period he also built the famous Berlin Philharmonic Hall in Berlin (1956–1963). To achieve the best possible acoustics for all seats, he grouped them dynamically, like terraces, in ascending levels around the orchestral stage. The corridors of the connecting rooms surprise the visitor with their vistas through the building and unusual details. Views of the building from the outside are granted variety by the sweep of the roof. Further remarkable projects appeared in the seventies such as the German Embassy in Brasilia (1970), the City Theatre in Wolfsburg (1965–1973) and the Staatsbibliothek Preußischer Kulturbesitz (State Library) in Berlin (1964–1978), which was completed by his partner Edgar Wisniewski.

Rudolf Michael Schindler 1887–1953

Schindler began his architectural studies in 1906 at the Technische Hochschule in Vienna, where he recieved his Diploma in Construction Engineering in 1911. He continued his education under Otto Wagner at the Academy of Fine Arts in Vienna. In 1913 he was a member of the School of Architecture run by Adolf Loos. At the same time he worked from 1911 to 1914 in the office of Hans Mayr and Theodor Mayer. He then moved to Chicago where he was employed as a draftsman in the firm of Henry A. Ottenheimer, Stern and Reichert. From 1917 he worked for Frank Loyd Wright, mainly on the project for the Imperial Hotel, Tokyo. At Wright's instigation, Schindler moved to Los Angeles in 1920, where he directed the building of the Barnsdall House and in 1921 opened his own practice. His first commissions include the house for C.P. Lowes at Eagle Rock in Los Angeles (1923), the house for John Packard in South Pasadena (1924) and the Pueblo Ribera Court Holiday Community in La Jolla, a smoothly formed concrete structure, which was built from 1923 to 1925. Together with Richard Neutra, who he had known since 1912, he founded the Architectural Group for Industry and Commerce (AGIC) in 1926. One of his most important houses from this period was Philip M. Lovell Beach House at Newport (1925–1926), a steel frame concrete structure with expansive areas of glass. In 1933 he designed the "Schindler Shelter", a scheme for pre-fabricated houses of reinforced concrete. In the following years he built numerous private houses especially in Los Angeles: the Oliver and Buck Houses (1934), the hillside house for Ralph C. Walker (1935–1936), the Viktoria McAlmon House (1935), and a three-storey residence for Henwar Rodakiewicz. These were all made with wood framing and a stucco skin, a "plaster skin design" that was cheaper than concrete and drew on the American tradition of building in wood. Later Schindler also designed apartment buildings such as the house for A. Bubeshko (1938) and the Falk Apartments (1939–1940). In addition, Schindler participated in many exhibitions such as the project "Contemporary Creative Architecture of California" in Los Angeles in 1930. Schindler also wrote many articles expounding his views on architecture. His pioneering article "Space Architecture" was published in "Dune Forum" in 1934 and in the "Los Angeles Times" in 1935.

Carlo Scarpa

Hans Scharoun

Vladimir Grigorevich Schuchov 1853–1939

Schuchov studied engineering at the Polytechnic of Moscow from 1871 to 1876. Thereafter he travelled to the United States, where he visited the World's Fair in Philadelphia and met his later employer Alexander V. Bari. After his return Schuchov worked in St. Petersburg on the planning of locomotive sheds and from 1878 he was commissioned by Bari to work for two years on pipelines in Baku. In 1880 he became chief engineer of Bari's Moscow office and in 1886 developed a new water supply system for Moscow. For the enlargement of the Russian railway network Schuchov built from 1892 onwards particularly light bridge constructions partly with pre-fabricated elements, thus saving on the cost of materials. At about the same time he began to explore the possibilities of new types of roof, as in the Petrovskij Arcade in Moscow, with its barrel roof of glass, or the arcade for the department store GUM. In 1895 he patented his net roof and exhibited it for the first time in 1896 at the All-Russian Exhibition in Nishny-Novgorod, now Gorky. He provided four of the exhibition halls with barrel-shaped lattice roofs and four with suspended roofs which were conceived as surface structures. A new type of structure he built for the water supply system was a 25 metre tower with a hyperbolic network of criss-cross iron bars. In 1897 he built a workshop for the blast furnace works in Vyksa with a net roof of curved metal bars. In the same year he published his book "The Roofing Bond". One of his most important towers was the 68 metre high lighthouse at Cherson on the Black Sea (1911), since demolished in the War. In 1912 he built a glass roof for the Central Post Office in Moscow. From 1912 to 1917, on the basis of Rerberg's design, he built the Kiev Railway Station in Moscow, a building

230 metres long, 30 metres high and 48 metres wide. After Bari's death and after the years of the Revolution, Schuchov, now director of the nationalised company, was commissioned to build the transmitting tower for the Comintern Radio Station Shabolovka in Moscow (1919–1922). Due to lack of steel the filigree tower made of six hyperboloids placed on top of each other had to be built at the reduced height of 150 metres instead of the originally planned 350 metres. The construction methods developed here were employed by Schuchov for numerous electric pylons, which are still standing to this day.

SITE / James Wines *1932

Wines studied at Syracuse University in Chicago and worked from 1955 to 1968 as a sculptor. In 1970, with Alison Sky, he founded the multi-disciplinary organisation SITE (Sculpture in the Environment) in New York and was joined by Michelle Stone and Emilio Sousa. The aim of their collaborative work was to make art and architecture a unity, for which Wines has coined the term "de-architecture". Since 1975 he has been professor at the New Jersey School of Architecture in New York. For the Best Products Company the group were able to implement many unusual architectural ideas and through this work became known internationally. Certain alienating details have a shock effect and are intended to force the observer to perceive them in a new light, as with the "Peeling Project" Building in Richmond, Virginia (1972), where a brick façade appears to peel away, or the "Indeterminate Façade" of the Houston Showrooms (1974), which looks like a broken, crumbling ruin after a bomb explosion. Clients had difficulty in accepting more extreme dissolutions of the building structure, such as the "Parking Lot Showroom". In this, a curved layer of asphalt covering the building interprets the showroom as a victim of the parking lot. The basic idea, however, appears again with the "Ghost Parking Lot" in Hamden, Connecticut (1978), where a row of about twenty cars are covered with a layer of asphalt, which makes these everyday objects appear as strange archaeological finds of our era. "Highrise of Homes" (1981) is a theoretical project in which family houses, including gardens, would be placed within the skeletal framework of a highrise building, in order to save space. For the Expo 86 in Vancouver, Canada, in 1986, the team accompanied the exhibition theme "Transport and Communication" with a 217 metre long, four-lane, undulating road entitled "Highway '86". This road, dotted with vehicles painted completely in white, plunges at one end into the sea while at the other it towers abruptly into the sky.

James Stirling

in Chicago (1982). For the National Commercial Bank in Jidda, Saudi Arabia, Skidmore, Owings & Merrill developed a skyscraper especially suited to extreme climatic conditions (1982). The smooth façade is interrupted by two square openings revealing a view onto lush vegetation. In 1982 an enormous pavilion roof was built for the Haj Terminal of the King Abdul Aziz International Airport. More recent work by Skidmore, Owings & Merrill such as the AT&T Building in Chicago look back to the ornamental style of the Chrysler Building or the Empire State Building.

James Stirling *1926

Stirling studied architecture at the University of Liverpool from 1945 to 1950. Thereafter he attended the School of Town Planning and Regional Research in London until 1952. From 1953 to 1956 he was assistant at the firm of Lyons, Israel and Ellis, where he also met James Gowan, with whom he opened an office in 1956 and planned the engineering department building of the University of Leicester (1959–1963). At the beginnig of the sixties he was visiting professor at Yale University. After 1963 he continued to run the office on his own. Important projects of the following years were: the History Building for the University of Cambridge (1964–1967), the Residence Hall at St Andrews University (1964–1968), the project for the Dorman Long Headquarters in Middlesborough (1965), the Queen's College Building around a hexagonal courtyard in Oxford (1966–1971), the fairly uninviting housing at Runcorn New Town (1967–1976), and the Olivetti Training Centre at Haslemere (1969–1972), a pastel-coloured complex made of synthetic materials strengthened with glass-fibre and consisting of two buildings joined by a glass connecting structure. In 1971 Michael Wilford joined Stirling as a partner in his office. Together they designed and built the Olivetti Headquarters in Milton Keynes. For the low-cost housing in Southgate (1972–1977), Stirling juxtaposed brightly coloured living units faced with synthetic material and with porthole windows; the district heating pipes, supported by metal framework, were for reasons of economy placed at roof height. From 1977 to 1984, Stirling built one of the most daring buildings of culture in Germany: the extension to the Stuttgart Staatsgalerie (State Gallery) and, added to it, the Kammertheater of the Württembergisches Staatstheater (State Theatre). However, the new building of the Fogg Art Museum in Cambridge, Massachusetts (1979–1985) did not share the same success. After a ten-year break in which like many of his British colleagues he worked exclusively abroad, he was commissioned to build the extension to the Tate Gallery in London (1980–1985).

Skidmore, Owings & Merrill

Louis Skidmore (1897–1962) and Nathaniel Owings (*1903) established their architectural practice in Chicago in 1936 and almost immediately opened a branch office in New York in 1937. In 1939 John Merrill (1896–1975) became an associate of the firm, which at the time was building numerous pavilions for the World's Fair in New York. Their 21-storey office building Lever House in New York (1951–1952), a thin, high-rise block built on a low, flat building as a base, became a new prototype for the inner-city commercial building. The Connecticut General Life Insurance Company in Bloomfield (1957), on the other hand, was a flat, transparent, cubic building set in park-like surroundings. This structural form was also used for team projects like the Upjohn Company Building in Kalamazoo, Michigan (1961). A considerable further development of the skeleton structure was the building for the Business Men's Assurance Co. of America in Kansas City, Missouri (1963), with a gridded steel construction located outside the set-back glass curtain wall. In addition to this, the office of Skidmore, Owings & Merrill also developed new construction methods, for example that of Fazlur Khan known as the "tube construction". The weight-bearing parts of a skyscraper were strutted diagonally on the outside to enable much taller buildings to be built for the same cost, as for example the 340 metre John Hancock Center in Chicago (1970). The 450 metres of the Chicago Sears Tower (1974) were achieved using a "cluster" of nine tubes of varying heights. The team built a series of remarkable buildings with atriums whose roofs also served as gardens: the Fourth Financial Center in Wichita, Kansas (1974), the First Wisconsin Plaza Building in Madison, Wisconsin (also 1974), and the 33 West Monroe Building

Louis Henry Sullivan 1856–1924

After a year of study at the Massachusetts Institute of Technology in Cambridge, Sullivan was employed in 1873 at the office of the architect William Le Baron Jenney in Chicago. From 1874 to 1876 he continued his studies at the Ecole des Beaux-Arts and at Vaudremer's atelier in Paris. Back in the USA, he joined the firm of the engineer Dankmar Adler in 1879 and became joint director of the office, now called Adler & Sullivan, in 1881. Together they executed the Auditorium Building in Chicago (1886–1893), a building with hotel, offices, and a theatre for 4,000 spectators. At this early stage we can already see Sullivan's predilection for uniting several storeys through rows of pilasters ending in arches; the feature also occurs in the more simply and sturdily built Walker Warehouse in Chicago (1888–1889). Other notable structures are the Wainwright Building in St. Louis (1890–1891) with its tall, narrow metal columns faced with masonry and capped by an ornamental frieze of sprouting plant forms, the Guaranty Building in Buffalo (1894–1896), the Bayard Building in New York (1897–1898) and the Gage Building in Chicago (1898–1899). In an article "The Tall Office Building Artistically Considered", which he published in 1896, Sullivan propounded his model for a high-rise building in which "form follows function". Its basis was the separation of base, grid-patterned tower and roof moulding and it marks the start of a deliberate move away from the traditional façade. With the Schlesinger & Mayer Store in Chicago (1899–1904), now Carson Pirie Scott & Co., a twelve-storey skeletal construction only decorated with ornament on its two lower floors, Sullivan made a significant contribution to the development of the 20th century office building. Of his later work, the most important projects are the Farmers' National Bank in Owatonna, Minnesota (1907–1908), and the building for the Van Allen Store in Clinton, Iowa (1913–1915). It was in Sullivan's office that Frank Lloyd Wright first gained his practical experience.

Kenzo Tange *1913

Tange studied from 1935 at the University of Tokyo and, on gaining his diploma in 1938, won the the Tatsuno Prize. His practical experience was acquired in the office of Kunio Mayekawa, a former colleague of Le Corbusier. After the war he became a free-lance architect and from 1946 also taught at the University of Tokyo, successfully combining the two activities in a fruitful alliance. In 1949 he won the competition for the Peace Centre in Hiroshima. The long, low hall of the memorial museum rests on set-back concrete pillars; the glass façade is made up of vertical concrete beams and horizontal slats. In 1951 Tange was invited to exhibit this project at the CIAM Congress "The Urban Centre". Numerous public buildings followed: the library on a rectangular plan for the Tsuda College in Tokyo (1953–1954), the three-storey town hall in Shimizu (also 1953–1954), the town halls in Kurayoshi (1956) and Tokyo (1957), the Kagawa Prefectural Office in Takamatsu (1956–1958), composed of two buildings. A typical feature of Tange's buildings is the dominance of vertical and horizontal structural parts, but Tange also built numerous buildings in which the form was much freer such as the two stadiums for the Olympic Games in Tokyo in 1964. In the composition of both buildings tall columns tower up bearing the weight of the roofs, in one case a spiral roof, in the other a polygon; and both roofs fall in a soft curve down to the edge of the arena. Tange's research was mainly in the area of town planning. His 1959 dissertation topic had dealt with the further planning of the city of Tokyo and in 1960 he developed a plan for the structural reorganisation of the city over the surface of the bay. The model consisted of cell-like structures connected by branching utility passages and was also envisaged for the design of the Press and Radio Centre in Kofu (1964–1966). This model with its buildings suspended between cylindrical concrete towers could be expanded easily and came to be seen as a flexible implementation of "Metabolist" ideas. Later his buildings lost their Japanese character and gradually moved closer to international architectural practice.

Bruno Taut 1880–1938

Taut attended the Baugewerksschule (school for master builders) in Königsberg until 1901 and then worked in various architects' offices: in 1902 with Fabry in Wiesbaden, a year later with Bruno Möhring in Berlin and from 1904 to 1908 with Theodor Fischer in Stuttgart. In 1908 he received his first commission, a turbine-house in Wetter an der Ruhr. In the following year he established his own practice with Franz Hoffmann and they were joined later by his brother Max Taut. In 1909 they built a convalescent home in Bad Harzburg for the Siemens Company. As architectural adviser to the "Deutsche Gartenstadtgesellschaft" (German Garden City Promotion Society), Taut was commissioned to build two garden suburbs: "Reform" in Magdeburg (1913–1921) and "Am Falkenberg" in Berlin-Grünau (1913–1914), which however were only partly completed. Taut became known through two exhibition projects. For the Building Trade Exhibition in Leipzig in 1913, he designed the pavilion of the "Deutscher Stahlwerkverband" (Federation of German Steel Manufacturers) and the "Verband Deutscher Brücken- und Eisenbahnfabriken" (Federation of German Bridge and Railway Manufacturers). Known as the "Monument to Steel", it was a steel skeleton structure on an octagonal plan with four levels diminishing in size like a telescope. For the "Werkbund" Exhibition n Cologne in 1914, Taut designed the glass industry pavilion with a dome covered in rhomboids of coloured glass. After the War he published books on Expressionist architectural utopias: "Alpine Architektur" (1918) and "Die Stadtkrone" (1919); he also wrote articles for the journal "Frühlicht" and later became a co-editor. In 1918 he became co-founder and director of the "Arbeitsrat für Kunst" (Council for Art) and also in 1919 of the "Gläserne Kette" (Glass Chain), a group of artists and architects whose members communicated with each other by so-called "chain letters". From 1921 to 1923 Taut was City Architect in Magdeburg and provoked lively discussion with his colourful façades. As adviser to the Gemeinnützige Heimstätten-, Spar- und Bau-Aktiengesellschaft in Berlin, Taut became involved from 1924 to 1932 with problems of large-scale housing. His most important work from this period includes the horseshoe-shaped Britz housing estate in Berlin,

which was executed in collaboration with Martin Wagner from 1925 to 1930 and the forest district development "Onkel Toms Hütte" (Uncle Tom's Cabin) in Berlin-Zehlendorf (1926–1931). In 1926 he became a member of the group of architects known as "Der Ring". In 1927 he took part in the "Werkbund" Exhibition in Stuttgart and from 1930 to 1932 he taught as a professor at the University of Berlin-Charlottenburg. In 1933 he moved to Moscow and finally emigrated to Japan, where he worked at the Crafts Research Institute in Sendai. In 1936 he became the successor to Hans Poelzig who had died before taking up his position as professor at the Academy of Art in Istanbul.

Giuseppe Terragni 1904–1943

After finishing at the Technical School in Como, Terragni studied at the Milan Polytechnic and in 1927 he opened his own office with his brother Attilio in Como. Along with Luigi Figini, Gino Pollini, Sebastiano Larco, Ubaldo Castagnoli, Guido Frette and Carlo Enrico Rava he was a co-founder of the "Gruppo 7", which called for a contemporary, rational approach to Italian architecture. In the same year at the Biennale in Monza, Terragni exhibited his highly acclaimed design for a gasworks. Despite the academicism and hefty resistance of opponents like Marcello Piacentini, Terragni managed to get his Novocomum Apartments built in Como (1927–1928), a strict rectilinear building of which the middle storeys had rounded corners decorated with glass segments. In 1928 he joined the MIAR movement (Movimento Italiano per l'Architettura Razionale). Terragni's best known work is usually considered to be the Fascist Party Building in Como, the Casa del Fascio (1932–1936): a prism of white marble with dramatic effects of light and shade in the geometrical façade. For the first Milan Triennale, in collaboration with other architects he built the Lakeside Artist's Studio in 1933. In 1936 he built the kindergarten Antonio Sant'Elia in Como and in 1936 and 1937 the Bianca House in Seveso; at the same time he worked with Pietro Lingeri on the project for the Danteum in Rome. A further Fascist Party House was designed with Antonio Carminati in 1938 for the city of Lissone. The Frigerio House in Como (1939–1940) is considered to be Terragni's last important piece of work.

Bernard Tschumi *1944

Tschumi studied until 1969 at the Eidgenössische Technische Hochschule in Zurich. From 1970 to 1979 he taught at the Architectural Association in London, and from 1976 also at the Institute for Architecture and Urban Studies in New York and at Princeton University. From 1980 to 1983 he was visiting professor at the Cooper Union School of Architecture in New

Henry van de Velde

Robert Venturi

York. In 1975 he organized the exhibition "A Space, a Thousand Words" in New York. From 1977 to 1981, after his move from London to New York, Tschumi produced the "Manhattan Transcripts", designs and collages in which he tackles new forms of "architectonic notation", including such ideas as "form follows fiction". Although his œuvre is still limited in size, he has already won prizes for several of his projects, such as his entry for "La Defense" in Paris (1983), his design for the opera-house in Tokyo (1986), which won second prize, and the Parc de la Villette in Paris (1982), which is still being constructed.

Henry-Clément van de Velde 1863–1957

Van de Velde studied painting from 1880 to 1883 at the Académie des Beaux-Arts in Antwerp and from 1884 to 1885 under Carolus Duran in Paris. He soon became involved in various associations of artists. In 1887 he participated in the founding of "L'Art indépendant" and in 1889 he became a member of the Brussels avantgarde group "Les XX". Van de Velde's first project was the Bloemenwerf House, which he built for himself in Uccle near Brussels (1895) The art collector Samuel Bing commissioned van de Velde to design four rooms for his Paris gallery "L'Art Nouveau", which were exhibited on the occasion of the Dresden "Kunstgewerbe" Exhibition in 1897. Van de Velde's furniture designs with their powerful curves also made one of the most important contributions to the development of Art Nouveau. In 1898 he founded the company "Henry van de Velde" for the production of furniture and other objects and in 1899 opened a branch in Berlin; but in 1900 he sold it to Wilhelm Hirschwald, the owner of the Hohenzol-

lern-Kunstgewerbe House. Projects completed in Berlin include the tobacco shop for the Habana Company (1899) and the Haby hairdressing salon (1901). On a commission from Karl Ernst Osthaus he designed the interior decoration of the Folkwang Museum in Hagen (1900–1902). In 1901 he was appointed art counsellor to the court of Grand Duke Wilhelm Ernst in Weimar and in 1904 was commissioned to build the "Kunstgewerbeschule", of which he was director until 1914. For the "Werkbund" Exhibition in Cologne in 1914 van de Velde built a theatre with an innovative auditorium shaped like an amphitheatre. For the outside van de Velde employed heavy masonry and a curved roof. He had also made a design for the Théâtre des Champs-Elysées in Paris from 1910 to 1911, but in the end Auguste Perret was entrusted with the project. From 1917 van de Velde lived in Switzerland. In 1921 he moved to Holland, where he advised the Kröller-Müllers as the successor to Hendrik P. Berlage and started on the first designs for what today is known as the Rijksmuseum in Otterlo, which was built in a simplified form between 1937 and 1954. Back in Brussels he became director until 1935 of the "Institut Supérieure d'Architecture et des Arts Décoratifs". At the same time he taught as professor at the University of Ghent (1925–1936). In 1939 he collaborated with Victor Bourgeois and Léon Stijnen on the design of the Belgian Pavilion for the World's Fair in New York. In 1947 he moved back to Switzerland.

Robert Venturi *1925

After studying architecture at Princeton University, Venturi lived in Rome from 1954 to 1956 on a scholarship from the American Academy. Thereafter he worked until 1958 in the offices of Eero Saarinen and Louis I. Kahn. He also taught as professor at the Universities of Princeton and Yale. Important early projects include the old people's home Guild House in Philadelphia, which he built with the architects Cope and Lippincott (1960–1963), and the house for his mother in Chestnut Hill, Philadelphia (1962–1964). From 1964 he went into partnership with John Rauch and was later joined by Denise Scott Brown, Steven Izenour and David Vaugham. The name of the firm became Venturi, Rauch and Scott Brown. Numerous projects were completed such as the Humanities Building for the New York State University in Purchase (1968–1973), the Dixwell Fire Station in New Haven, Connecticut (1967–1974), the Brant House in Greenwich, Connecticut (1970–1973), Franklin Court in Philadelphia (1972–1976), the additions to the Allen Memorial Museum in Oberlin, Ohio (1973–1976), the Institute for Scientific Information in Philadelphia (1970–1978) with a façade of coloured mosaic-like strips of masonry, and the Gordon Wu Hall at Princeton University (1980–1983). In contrast to the highly symbolic façades of his town houses, which follow his principle of "decorated sheds", Venturi's vacation houses which he built on Nantucket Island, Block Island or in Vail, Colorado, are faced with wooden tiles or shingles in keeping with the natural setting; their unusually placed window openings create surprising interior spaces. In his publications "Complexity and Contradiction in Architecture" (1966), "Learning from Las Vegas", which he wrote in conjunction with Denise Scott Brown and Steven Izenour (1972), and "A View from the Campidoglio" with Denise Scott Brown (1985), Venturi reinforced his point that the life of modern architecture depends on its historical links but, at the same time, architecture must also recognize a very real competitor in the chaotic everyday architecture of comic strips and popular art.

Frank Lloyd Wright

Otto Koloman Wagner 1841–1918

From 1857 Wagner studied at the Vienna Polytechnic and from 1860 to 1861 at the Royal Building Academy in Berlin; he completed his studies at the Vienna Academy of Fine Arts. His practical experience was acquired in the office of Ludwig von Förster. Among Wagner's early work is a house "am Schottenring" in Vienna (1877) with an unusual facing, on the upper storey, of flat triangular shapes in two colours. He also built his own house in Vienna (1886–1888) with a symmetrical arrangement, pillars and staircase reminiscent of the buildings of Palladio. In 1890 he was commissioned to redevelop the city of Vienna. From 1894 he was City Planner ("Oberbaurat"), his main duties being the construction of the Stadtbahn (Municipal Railway System) and the re-routing of the Danube. In the period up to the completion of the Stadtbahn in 1901, 34 stations and numerous bridges and viaducts were built. Other architects such as Carl von Hasenauer were entrusted with the tall apartment buildings on the Ringstraße. On Hasenauer's death in 1894 Wagner took the chair of architecture at the Academy of Fine Arts. A year later he published his inaugural lecture "Moderne Architektur". Wagner's teaching duties played a large part in his professional life and many important architects studied under him, such as Josef Hoffmann, Joseph Maria Olbrich, Richard Neutra, and Rudolf M. Schindler. In 1899 he joined the Vienna Sezession group of artists. In the same year he also completed the Linke Wienzeile apartment buildings. For the telegraph office of the "Die Zeit" newspaper in 1902, Wagner designed an uncompromising, modern building whose aluminium façade reveals how daring he could be in his use of new construction materials. The Post Office Savings Bank in Vienna built between 1904 and 1912 is usually considered to be the peak of his career. The main buildings of his later period are the church am Steinhof with its impressive dome covered in what originally were gilded copper plates (1902–1907), the apartment buildings on the Neustiftgasse (1910) and the Döblergasse (1912), the simple, enclosed complex on a T-shaped plan of the Lupus Sanatorium (1910–1913), and the second Wagner House (1912–1913). Wagner left a huge œuvre of unexecuted projects, sketches and competition designs.

Frank Lloyd Wright 1867–1959

Wright studied engineering from 1885 to 1887 at the University of Wisconsin, Madison. At the same time he worked for D. Conover and Joseph L. Silsbee until 1888 when he joined the office of Dankmar Adler and Louis Sullivan, where he worked principally on residences and soon went independent. In 1889 he moved into his own studio in the Chicago suburb of Oak

Otto Wagner

Park. In 1893 he went into temporary partnership with Cecil Corwin until he finally opened
his own office in 1896. With the Winslow House
in River Forest, Illinois, in 1894, he began the
series of "prairie houses" which he described
fully in the article "A Home in a Prairie Town"
in the magazine "Ladies' Home Journal" in
1900. The typical characteristics of these free-
standing houses which blend well with their surroundings are a broad-overhanging roof, horizontal window bands and a free plan around a
central chimney; examples are the Willitts
House in Highland Park, Illinois (1901–1902),
and the Martin House in Buffalo (1904). It was
in Buffalo that he also built the fully air-conditioned offices of the Larkin Building (1904–
1905) with open gallery floors around a central
hall. This was followed by the reinforced concrete structure Unity Temple in Oak Park, Illinois
(1904). His most successful prairie houses include the Robie House in Chicago (1906–1910)
with an extended roof of thin slabs and the
Coonley House in Riverside, Illinois (1907–
1908). In 1909 Wright left his family for a trip to
Europe, where, through the exhibition of his
work in Berlin (1910) and the publication "Ausgeführte Arbeiten und Entwürfe von Frank Lloyd
Wright" (The Wasmuth Portfolio) he became an
important influence on European architecture.
On his return to America in 1911 he founded
the association of Spring Green in Wisconsin
and built his house "Taliesin" there, which over
the years burnt down three times and was rebuilt by Wright on each occasion. Between
1915 and 1922 he designed a new construction
technique with Antonin Raymond to secure
buildings against earthquakes and employed it
to build the Imperial Hotel in Tokyo. From 1917
to 1920 Wright built the sturdy, enclosed Barnsdall House in Los Angeles with its ornamental
motifs derived from the Maya culture. The "textile blocks", the pre-fabricated concrete parts
developed by Wright, were then used for the

Millard House in Pasadena (1921–1923). During a period when commissions were scarce,
Wright gathered his ideas on town planning
under the title "Broadacre City" (1932), the
model for a dispersed community of car-driving
inhabitants. One of his most ingenious projects
is the house "Fallingwater" in Pennsylvania
(1935–1939), which was built on a cliffside directly over a waterfall. During the years of the
Great Depression, Wright developed a new
type of residence known as the Usonian House,
a low, economical, detached house which was
executed in numerous variations. Usonia was
Wright's own personal synonym for America.
Between 1936 and 1950 he designed and built
the headquarters for the chemical firm S.C.
Johnson & Son in Racine, Wisconsin. With its
perimeter closed to the outside, the building
had tapered mushroom columns on the inside
and a laboratory tower with glass envelope
walls (1944–1950). Shortly afterwards he built
his only high-rise house, the Price Tower in Bart-
lesville, Oklahoma (1953–1956). Wright also
used unusual forms: a spiral for the Solomon R.
Guggenheim Museum in New York (1956–
1959) and the tent-like structure of steel, glass
and synthetic materials for the Beth Sholom Synagogue in Philadelphia (1958–1959). Altogether, Wright has about 800 building designs to his credit, and numerous articles and
books that expound his ideas of an organic
architecture in democratic America such as "In
the Cause of America" in the journal "Architectural Record" and the books "When Democracy Builds" (1945), "The Future of Architecture" (1953), and "The Living City" (1958).

Bibliography

We would like to thank all the architects who kindly placed descriptions of their buildings at our disposal. Particular use was made of the periodicals Bauen + Wohnen (after 1982 Werk, Bauen + Wohnen), Baukunst und Werkform, Bauwelt, Dekorative Kunst, Der Baumeister, Der Industriebau, Global Architecture Document, Innen-Dekoration, and Wasmuths Monatshefte für Baukunst.

General Works

Leonardo Benevolo, History of Modern Architecture. 2 vols., London, 1971.

David Dunster, Key Buildings of the Twentieth Century, vol. 1, Houses 1900–1944. London, 1985.

Kenneth Frampton, Modern Architecture 1851–1919. Global Architecture Document Special Issue 2, Tokyo, 1981.

Kenneth Frampton, Modern Architecture 1920–1945. Global Architecture Document Special Issue 3, Tokyo, 1983.

Sigfried Giedion, Space, Time and Architecture. Harvard and Oxford, 1941.

Henry-Russell Hitchcock, Architecture. Nineteenth and Twentieth Centuries. Harmondsworth and Baltimore, 1958.

Werner Hofmann and Udo Kultermann, Baukunst unserer Zeit. Die Entwicklung seit 1850. Essen, 1969.

Falk Jaeger, Bauen in Deutschland. Ein Führer durch die Architektur des 20. Jahrhunderts in der Bundesrepublik und in West-Berlin. Stuttgart, 1985.

Charles Jencks, Architecture Today, London, 1988.

Vittorio Magnago Lampugnani (ed.), The Thames and Hudson Encyclopedia of Twentieth Century Architecture. London, 1986.

Wolfgang Pehnt, Das Ende der Zuversicht. Architektur in diesem Jahrhundert. Ideen – Bauten – Dokumente. Berlin, 1983.

Julius Posener, Vorlesungen zur Geschichte der neuen Architektur (1750–1933), in: Arch+ 48/1979, 53/1980, 59/1981, 69/70/1983.

Vincent Scully, American Architecture and Urbanism. New York, 1969.

Prologue

Ecole nationale supérieure des Beaux-Arts (ed.), Les Architectes de la Liberté 1789–1799. Paris, 1990.

Walter Benjamin, Das Passagen-Werk. Frankfurt am Main, 1982.

Eric Forssmann, Karl Friedrich Schinkel. Bauwerke und Baugedanken. Zurich, 1981.

Sigfried Giedion, Bauen in Frankreich. Leipzig and Berlin, 1928.

Claude Mignot, Architecture of the Nineteenth Century in Europe. New York, 1984

M. Viollet-Le-Duc, Entretiens sur l'Architecture. Paris, 1864.

Adolf Max Vogt, Boullées Newton-Denkmal. Sakralbau und Kugelidee. Basle and Stuttgart, 1969.

Of Iron Giants and Glass Virgins

Lothar Bucher, Kulturhistorische Skizzen aus der Industrie-Ausstellung aller Völker. London, 1851.

Festschrift zur XXXV. Hauptversammlung des Vereins Deutscher Ingenieure. Berlin, 1894.

Great Exhibition 1851. Official, Descriptive and Illustrated Catalogue. London, 1851.

Volker Hütsch, Der Münchner Glaspalast 1854–1931, Berlin, 1985

Robert Mallet, The Record of the International Exhibition 1862. London, 1862.

Alfred Gotthold Meyer, Eisenbauten. Ihre Geschichte und Ästhetik. Esslingen, 1907

Tom F. Peters, Time is Money. Die Entwicklung des modernen Bauwesens. Stuttgart, 1981.

M.E. Schleich, Pimplhuber in der Industrieausstellung. Munich, 1854.

E. Schneider, Die Bauten der Weltausstellung 1889 in Paris, in: Stahlbau 12/1989.

Vladimir G. Schuchov 1853–1939, Die Kunst der sparsamen Konstruktion. Ed. Rainer Graefe, Murat Gappoev, Ottmar Pertschi. Stuttgart, 1990.

The Chicago School

Albert Bush-Brown, Louis Sullivan. New York, 1960.

John Zukowsky (ed.), Chicago Architecture 1872–1922. Birth of a Metropolis. Munich, 1987.

Gottfried Semper, Wissenschaft, Industrie und Kunst. Mainz and Berlin, 1966.

O.F. Semsch, A History of the Singer Building Construction. New York, 1908.

Louis H. Sullivan, The Tall Office Building Artistically Considered, in: Metropolitan Review, Exhibition Edition, 7/8/1988.

L'Entrée du Siècle

William Buchanan (ed.), Mackintosh's Masterwork. The Glasgow School of Art. Glasgow, 1989.

Heinz Geretsegger and Max Peintner, Otto Wagner 1841–1918. London, 1970.

Marco Pozzetto, Max Fabiani. Gorizia, 1966.

Frank Russell, Art Nouveau Architecture. London, 1979.

Klaus-Jürgen Sembach, Henry van de Velde. Stuttgart, 1989.

Rainer Zerbst, Antoni Gaudi, A life devoted to architecture. Cologne, 1990.

In the Far Landscape

Hendrik Petrus Berlage, Neuere amerikanische Architektur, in: Schweizerische Bauzeitung, 1912.

William H. Jordy, American Buildings and Their Architects. Progressive and Academic Ideals at the Turn of the 20th Century. Garden City, New York, 1976.

Yukio Futagawa (ed.), Frank Loyd Wright. Monography Vol. 1–3. Tokyo, 1986.

Frederick Gutheim (ed.), Frank Lloyd Wright on Architecture. Selected Writings 1894–1940. New York, 1941.

Circle and Square

Fritz Hoeber, Peter Behrens. Munich, 1913.

Maßsystem und Raumkunst. Das Werk des Architekten J. L. M. Lauweriks. Krefeld, Hagen and Rotterdam, 1987.

Burkhard Rukschio and Roland Schachel, Adolf Loos. Leben und Werk. Salzburg and Vienna, 1982.

Otto Wagner, Einige Skizzen, Projekte und ausgeführte Bauwerke, vol. IV, Vienna, 1922.

The Modern Factory

The Detroit Institute of Arts (ed.), The Legacy of Albert Kahn. Detroit, 1970.

Tilmann Buddensieg, Industriekultur. Peter Behrens und die AEG 1907–1914. Berlin, 1979.

Karl-Heinz Hüter, Architektur in Berlin 1900–1933. Dresden, 1988.

Jahrbuch des Deutschen Werkbunds. 1913.

Julius Posener, Berlin auf dem Wege zu einer neuen Architektur. Das Zeitalter Wilhelm II. Munich, 1979.

Karin Wilhelm, Walter Gropius. Industriearchitekt. Brunswick and Wiesbaden, 1983.

Creative in Concrete

Max Berg, Die Jahrhunderthalle und das neue Ausstellungsgebäude der Stadt Breslau, in: Deutsche Bauzeitung 51/1913.

Festschrift aus Anlaß des fünfzigjährigen Bestehens der Wayss & Freytag AG. Stuttgart, 1925.

Günter Günschel, Große Konstrukteure I. Freyssinet, Maillart, Dischinger, Finsterwalder. Frankfurt am Main and Vienna, 1966.

Helmuth Hanle and Judith Strempler, Der selbstgemachte Stein, in: NGBK (ed.), Absolut modern sein. Zwischen Fahrrad und Fließband – culture technique in Frankreich 1889–1937. Berlin, 1986.

Gert v. Klaas, Weit spannt sich der Bogen. 1865–1965. Die Geschichte der Bauunternehmung Dyckerhoff & Widmannn. 1965.

The Return of Art

Claes Caldenby and Olof Hultin, Asplund. Stockholm, 1985.

Erich Mendelsohn 1887–1953. Ideen, Bauten, Projekte. Edited by Sigrid Achenbach. Berlin, 1987.

J.G. Wattjes, Nieuw-Nederlandsche Bouwkunst. Amsterdam, 1924.

Wim de Wit, Expressionismus in Holland. Die Architektur der Amsterdamer Schule. Stuttgart, 1986.

Volumetric Experiments

S.O. Chan-Magomedow, Pioniere der sowjetischen Architektur. Dresden, 1983.

Mildred Friedman (ed.), De Stijl: 1917–1931. Visions of Utopia. Oxford, 1986.

Walter Gropius, Die neue Architektur und das Bauhaus. Grundzüge und Entwicklung einer Konzeption. Mainz, 1965.

Walter Müller-Wulckow, Architektur der Zwanziger Jahre in Deutschland. New edition of the four Blue Books: Bauten der Arbeit und des Verkehrs, 1929, Wohnbauten und Siedlungen, 1929, Bauten der Gemeinschaft, 1929, and Die deutsche Wohnung, 1932. Königstein im Taunus, 1975.

Winfried Nerdinger, Walter Gropius. Berlin, 1985.

Günther Stamm, J. J. P. Oud, Bauten und Projekte 1906 bis 1963. Mainz, 1984.

Housing Estates

Akademie der Künste Berlin (ed.), Bruno Taut 1880–1938. Berlin, 1980.

Karin Kirsch, Die Weißenhofsiedlung. Werkbundausstellung «Die Wohnung» Stuttgart 1927. Stuttgart, 1987.

Christoph Mohr and Michael Müller, Funktionalität und Moderne. Das neue Frankfurt und seine Bauten 1925–1933. Frankfurt am Main, 1984.

Internationale Kongresse für Neues Bauen (ed.), Rationelle Bebauungsweisen. Ergebnisse des 3. Internationalen Kongresses für Neues Bauen. Stuttgart, 1931.

Reichsforschungsgesellschaft für Wirtschaftlichkeit im Bau- und Wohnungswesen e. V. Sonderheft 7. Bericht über die Versuchssiedlung in Dessau. 1929.

Siedlungen der zwanziger Jahre – heute. Vier Berliner Großsiedlungen 1924–1984. Berlin, 1987.

Machines for Living In

Deutscher Werkbund (ed.), Bau und Wohnung. Die Bauten der Weißenhofsiedlung in Stuttgart errichtet 1927 nach Vorschlägen des Deutschen Werkbundes im Auftrag der Stadt Stuttgart und im Rahmen der Werkbundausstellung «Die Wohnung». Stuttgart, 1927.

Timothy J. Benton, Les Villes de Le Corbusier et Pierre Jeanneret 1920–1930. Paris, 1984.

W. Boesinger and O. Stonorov, Le Corbusier et Pierre Jeanneret. Œuvre complète, vol. 1, 1910–1929. Zurich, 1964.

Le Corbusier, Vers une Architecture, Paris, 1922.

The International Style

Annitrenta. Arte e Cultura in Italia. Milan, 1982.

Architectural Design Profiles 24. Britain in the Thirties. London.

Die Brünner Funktionalisten. Moderne Architektur in Brünn. 1985.

David Dean, Architecture of the 1930s. Recalling the English Scene. New York, 1983.

Richard Döcker, Terrassentyp. Stuttgart, 1929.

Arthur Drexler, Ludwig Mies van der Rohe. London, 1961.

Henry-Russell Hitchcock and Philip Johnson The International Style. New York, 1932.

Hans and Wassili Luckhardt, Zur neuen Wohnform. Berlin, 1930.

August Sarnitz, R. M. Schindler. Architect. 1878–1953. Vienna, 1986.

Alberto Sartoris, Gli Elementi dell'Architettura funzionale. Milan, 1942.

Klaus-Jürgen Sembach, Style 1930. New York, 1986.

Martin Steinmann (ed.), CIAM. Dokumente 1928–1939. Basle and Stuttgart, 1979.

The New Deal

Alastair Duncan, American Art Déco. New York, 1986.

Martin Greif, Depression Modern. The Thirties Style in America. New York, 1975.

Robert A. M. Stern, Gregory Gilmartin and Thomas Mellins, New York 1930. Architecture and Urbanism between the two World Wars. New York, 1987.

Richard Guy Wilson, Dianne H. Pilgrim and Dickran Tashjian, The Machine Age in America 1918–1941. New York, 1987.

Martin Tschechne, Baudenkmal zwischen Kunst und Kommerz. Bernard Hoetgers Haus «Atlantis . . . », in: art 11/1988.

Case Studies

Sam Hall Kaplan, LA Lost & Found. An Architectural History of Los Angeles. New York, 1987.

Esther McCoy, Case Study Houses 1945–1962. Los Angeles, 1977.

Esther McCoy, Richard Neutra. New York, 1960.

Less is More

Henry-Russell Hitchcock and Arthur Drexler (ed.), Built in USA. Post-war Architecture. New York, 1952.

William H. Jordy, American Buildings and Their Architects. The Impact of European Modernism in the Midtwentieth Century. Garden City, New York, 1976.

Franz Schulze, Mies van der Rohe. A Critical Biography. Chicago and London, 1986.

Stonebound

Alvar Aalto. Band 1. 1922–1962. Zurich, 1963.

Tobias Faber, New Danish Architecture. London, 1968.

David G. De Long, Bruce Goff. Toward Absolute Architecture. New York, 1988.

Frank Lloyd Wright. A Testament. New York and London, 1957.

The Flying Roof

Alberto Galardi, Neue italienische Architektur. Stuttgart, 1987.

Jürgen Joedicke, Schalenbau. Konstruktion und Gestaltung. Stuttgart, 1962.

Udo Kultermann, «Une Architecture Autre». Ein neugeknüpfter Faden der architektonischen Entwicklung, in: Baukunst und Werkform, 1958.

Aline B. Saarinen (ed.), Eero Saarinen on his Work. New Haven and London, 1962.

Concrete Containers

Sigfried Giedion, Stadtform und die Gründung von Brasilia, in: Bauen + Wohnen 1960.

Romaldo Giurgola and Jaimini Mehta, Louis I. Kahn. Architect. Boulder, Colorado, 1975.

Paul Heyer, Architects on Architecture. New Directions in America. New York, 1966.

Udo Kultermann (ed.), Kenzo Tange 1946–1969. Architecture and Urban Design. Zurich and London, 1970.

Lewis Mumford, Der «Nonsens» von Marseille, in: Baukunst und Werkform 1958.

Learning from Las Vegas

Eugene J. Johnson (ed.), Charles Moore. Bauten und Projekte 1949–1986. Stuttgart, 1987.

Stanislaus von Moos, Venturi, Rauch & Scott Brown. Buildings and Projects 1960–1985. New York, 1986.

SITE. Architecture and Urbanism, extra edition, 1986/12. Tokyo, 1986.

Robert Venturi, Complexity and Contradiction in Architecture. New York, 1966.

Robert Venturi, Denise Scott Brown and Stephen Izenour, Learning from Las Vegas. Cambridge, Massachusetts, 1972.

Charles Jencks, The Language of Post-Modern Architecture. New York, 1984.

The Whites

Werner Haker, «Five Architects» – Zehn Jahre Danach, in: Werk, Bauen + Wohnen 1982.

Werner Haker, New Harmony und das Athenaeum von Richard Meier, in: Bauen + Wohnen 1980.

Institute for Architecture and Urban Studies (ed.), Five Houses. Gwathmey Siegel Architects. New York, 1978.

Heinrich Klotz (ed.), Revision der Moderne. Postmoderne Architektur 1960–1980. Munich, 1984.

Richard Meier. Architect. 1964/1984. New York, 1984.

Karen Vogel Wheeler, Peter Arnell and Ted Bickford, Michael Graves. Buildings and Projects 1966–1981. New York, 1982.

Work on Modernism

Peter Arnell, Ted Bickford and Colin Rowe, James Stirling. Buildings and Projects 1950–1980. New York, 1984.

Yukio Futagawa (ed.), Kevin Roche John Dinkeloo and Associates 1962–1975. Tokyo and Friburg, 1975.

Charles Jencks, Spätmoderne Architektur. Beiträge über die Transformation des Internationalen Stils. Stuttgart, 1981.

Wulf Schirmer (ed.), Egon Eiermann 1904–1970. Bauten und Projekte. Stuttgart, 1984.

The Rational South

Emilio Ambasz, The Architecture of Luis Barragán. New York, 1976.

Peter Arnell and Ted Bickford, Aldo Rossi. Buildings and Projects. New York, 1987.

Alberto Campo Baeza. Architect. Almeria, 1989.

Francesco Dal Co, Mario Botta. Architecture 1960–1985. New York, 1987.

Open Structures

Norman Foster, Buildings and Projects of Foster Associates. Vol. 2 1971–1978, vol.3 1978–1985. London and Berlin. 1989.

Joachim Andreas Joedicke, Helmut Jahn. Design einer neuen Architektur. Stuttgart and Zurich, 1986.

Gert Kähler, Zweck oder Selbstzweck? Kritische Anmerkungen zur High-Tech-Architektur, in: Werk, Bauen + Wohnen 1987.

Heinrich Klotz (ed.), Vision der Moderne. Das Prinzip Konstruktion. Munich, 1986.

Max Mengeringhausen, Komposition im Raum. Die Kunst individueller Baugestaltung mit Serienelementen. Würzburg, 1983.

Conrad Roland, Frei Otto – Tension Structures. New York, 1970.

The Post-Modern City

Marc M. Angélil and Sarah R. Graham, «Man kann nicht die Geschichte nicht kennen.» Philip Johnsons Architektur, eine Frage des Stils, in: Werk, Bauen + Wohnen 9/1987.

Paul Goldberger, Jetzt wird die Kiste dekoriert, in: art 8/1983.

Josef P. Kleihues and Heinrich Klotz (ed.), Internationale Bauausstellung Berlin 1987. Beispiele einer neuen Architektur. Stuttgart, 1986.

Heinrich Klotz, Moderne und Postmoderne. Architektur der Gegenwart 1960–1980. Brunswick and Wiesbaden, 1984.

Paulhans Peters, Wolkenkratzer und Stadt, in: Baumeister 2/1984.

Romantic Modernism, Arquitectonica. Process Architecture 65. Tokyo, 1986.

The Charlottesville Tapes. Transcript of the Conference at the University of Virginia School of Architecture, Charlottesville, Virginia, November 12 and 13, 1982. New York, 1985.

Bellevue

Yukio Futagawa (ed.), Tadao Ando. Global Architecture Architect 8. Tokyo, 1987.

Concrete Poems

Georg Büchi, Die Architektur von Ereignis, Raum und Bewegung. Über die Arbeiten von Bernard Tschumi, in: Werk, Bauen + Wohnen 1984.

Kurt Forster, Volumini in libertà. Frank Gehrys architektonische Improvisationen, in: Archithese 3/1988.

Peter Arnell and Ted Bickford (ed.), Frank Gehry. Buildings and Projects. New York, 1985.

Andreas Papadakis (ed.), Dekonstruktivismus. Eine Anthologie. Stuttgart, 1989.

Bernard Tschumi, Cinegram Folie. Le Parc de la Villette. Seyssel, 1987.

Jacques Derrida, Am Nullpunkt der Verrücktheit – Jetzt die Architektur, in: Wolfgang Welsch (ed.), Wege aus der Moderne. Schlüsseltexte der Postmoderne-Diskussion. Weinheim, 1988.

Architecture for the Arts

Jochen Bub, Die Neue Staatsgalerie Stuttgart, in: Bauwelt 20/1984.

Hans Hollein, Architecture and Urbanism 1985/2. Tokyo, 1985.

Josep M. Montaner and Jordi Oliveras, Die Museumsbauten der neuen Generation. Stuttgart and Zurich, 1987.

Index of names

Sources of Illustrations

The majority of the plans, prints, diagrams and sketches used were kindly placed at our disposal by the appropriate architectural offices. For older buildings, contemporary publications were referred to and many of the drawings were touched up or drawn afresh. Further material came from the following archives: Akademie der Künste, Berlin; library of the Landesgewerbeanstalt, Nuremberg; Fondation Le Corbusier, Paris; Frank Lloyd Wright Foundation, Scottsdale, Arizona; Institut für Baugeschichte der Universität Karlsruhe: Suomen Rakennustaiteen Museo, Helsinki.

For the illustrations to the biographical section we are grateful to the following sources: CIAM Archiv, Institut für Geschichte und Theorie der Architektur der Eidgenössischen Technischen Hochschule, Zurich (p.393); Suomen Rakennustaiteen Museo Helsinki, photograph Pertti Ingervo (p.394); Mario Botta, photograph Gitty Darugar (p.396); Hamburger Abendblatt newspaper, photograph Krüger (p.397); Foster Associates, photograph Andrew Ward (p.398); USIS, Bonn (p.399); Frank Gehry, photograph Wesley Harrison (p.400); Michael Graves, photograph William Taylor (p.401); Bauhaus-Archiv, Berlin (p. 402, 411); Murphy/Jahn Associates (p.404); Ingrid von Kruse (p.405); Loos-Archiv, Albertina, Vienna (p.406); Cassina, Meda/Milan (p.407, 414); Akademie der Künste, Sammlung Baukunst, Berlin (p.408, 419); Richard Meier & Partners, photograph Scott Frances/Esto (p.409); Bildarchiv Preußischer Kulturbesitz, Berlin (p.410); Julius Shulman (p.412); Gustav Peichl (p.413); Kevin Roche John Dinkeloo and Associates (p.415); Ullstein Bilderdienst, Berlin (p.416); Knoll International, Murr (p.417); Tobia Scarpa (p.418); James Stirling, Michael Wilford Associates (p.420); Archiv La Cambre (p.422); Venturi, Scott Brown & Associates, photograph John T. Miller (p.423); Pedro Guerrero (p. 424); Bildarchiv der Österreichischen Nationalbibliothek, Vienna (p.425).